Camper's Guide
MICHIGAN
Parks, Lakes, and Forests
Where to Go and How to Get There

Mickey Little

Gulf Publishing Company

Library of Congress Cataloging-in-Publication Data

Little, Mildred J.
    Camper's guide to Michigan parks, lakes, and forests: where to go and
how to get there/Mickey Little.
        p.   cm.
    Includes index.
    ISBN 0-87201-207-7
    1. Camping—Michigan—Guide-books. 2. Outdoor recreation— Michigan—
Guide-books. 3. Parks—Michigan—Guidebooks. 4. Michigan—Description and
travel—1981—Guidebooks.
    I. Title.
    GV191.42.M5L58   1992
    796.54′09774—dc20   91-24115
                                                                      CIP

10 9 8 7 6 5 4 3 2 1

This title and graphic design are a trademark of Gulf
Publishing Company.

All photos are by the Author unless otherwise noted.

Title page photo of Laughing Whitefish Falls courtesy of
Michigan Travel Bureau.

Also of Interest to Campers—

Camper's Guide to California Parks, Lakes, Forests, and Beaches
Volume 1: Northern California
Volume 2: Southern California
Camper's Guide to Colorado Parks, Lakes, and Forests
Camper's Guide to Florida Parks, Trails, Rivers, and Beaches
Camper's Guide to Minnesota Parks, Lakes, Forests, and Trails
Camper's Guide to Texas Parks, Lakes, and Forests/Third Edition

Contents

Introduction, 1

Region 1, 13

Region 2, 60

Region 3, 120

Appendix, 153

Index, 161

Courtesy Michigan Travel Bureau

Acknowledgments

Courtesy Michigan Travel Bureau

I am indebted to and wish to thank the following agencies and individuals for information—in the form of maps, brochures, photographs, telephone conversations, and personal interviews—without which this book would not have been possible:

Michigan Department of Natural Resources
    Forest Management Division
    Land and Water Management Division
    Parks Division
    Recreation Division
    Wildlife Division
Michigan Department of Transportation
Michigan Travel Bureau
National Park Service, U.S. Department of the
    Interior
North Country Trail Association
U.S. Forest Service
    Hiawatha National Forest and all Ranger
        Districts
    Huron-Manistee National Forests and all Ranger
        Districts
    Ottawa National Forest and all Ranger Districts
Upper Peninsula Tourism & Recreation Association

While every effort has been made to ensure the accuracy of the information in this guide, neither I nor the publisher assume liability arising from the use of this material. Park facilities and policies are subject to change, so verify the accuracy of important details before beginning a trip.

Mickey Little

I went to the woods because I wished to live deliberately, to front only the essential facts of life, and see if I could not learn what it had to teach, and not, when I came to die, discover that I had not lived.

—Henry David Thoreau

Introduction

Michigan is touched by four of the five Great Lakes. It is divided into an Upper and Lower Peninsula by the 4½-mile-wide Straits of Mackinac, which links Lakes Michigan and Huron and which is spanned by one of the world's longest suspension bridges. Michigan has the longest shoreline of any state this side of Alaska. No place in Michigan is more than 85 miles from one of these bodies of fresh water.

Michigan was initially part of the old Northwest Territory and later the Indiana Territory; it was made a separate territory in 1805. By 1835 the territory was ready for statehood, but a boundary dispute with Ohio delayed admission. Finally, Ohio was given a strip of land along its southern border in return for the entire Upper Peninsula, which had been a part of the Territory of Wisconsin. Michigan became the 26th state in 1837. The capital moved from Detroit to Lansing in 1847.

Because of the Great Lakes, you can enjoy two national lakeshores, Sleeping Bear Dunes and Pictured Rocks, and the only island national park in America, Isle Royale. Michigan's shoreline is defined not only by hundreds of beaches and numerous sand dune areas, but also by more than 100 lighthouses. (See Appendix for more information on sand dunes and lighthouses.) With some 11,000 inland lakes and 36,000 miles of rivers and streams, along with its forests, mountains, and waterfalls, the state is truly a sportsman's paradise.

The purpose of this *Camper's Guide* is to suggest places to go and to provide directions to get there. You will discover information about the popular, well-known campgrounds as well as the lesser used camping areas. The public campgrounds presented

Michigan Facts
Capital: Lansing
Nickname: The Wolverine State
Statehood: January 26, 1837 (26th state)
Area: 58,216 square miles; ranks 23rd
Population: 9,240,000; ranks 8th (1988)
State Motto: If you seek a pleasant peninsula, look about you
State Bird: Robin
State Flower: Apple Blossom
State Tree: White Pine
State Fish: Brook Trout
State Gem: Isle Royale Greenstone
State Stone: Petoskey
Time Zone: Eastern/Central (along Wisconsin border) (DST)

in this guide, provided and operated by state and federal agencies, afford varied options for outdoor recreation. You can fish, boat, canoe, backpack, swim, sail, picnic, bicycle, horseback ride, water ski, or walk along a nature trail. In season, you can also downhill ski, cross-country ski, snow shoe, ice skate, ice fish, or snowmobile. You can pursue your favorite hobby as a bird watcher, photographer, botanist, geologist, or naturalist. You may choose to rough it along a backpacking trail or enjoy all the comforts of home in a recreational vehicle. You can spend a day, a weekend, or an entire vacation doing what you like best, no matter how active, or inactive.

The state and federal agencies in Michigan offer more than 20,000 individual campsites at developed campgrounds. These are located at the 70 state parks that have camping facilities, the 75-plus campgrounds within the four national forests, the 160-plus campgrounds within the six state forests, and the five car-accessible campgrounds at the three national parks. Michigan's location gives it a moderate climate that is unique to the Midwest—a coastal climate in the heart of the continent. Because of the "lake effect," Michigan's summer is a little cooler, its winter a little milder, and its snow a little deeper and more consistent. The seasons are well-defined and the weather is pleasant for all outdoor activities, from camping in July to skiing in January.

The Lower Peninsula, shaped like a mitten, has an extreme width of approximately 200 miles and an extreme length of approximately 280 miles. The terrain is relatively low and gently rolling, with countless lakes and marshy areas. The flat plains in the southeast rise to a moderate plateau in the north. Along the western shore, sand dunes sometimes reach elevations of 600 feet. The Lake Huron shore is lined with beaches in the south but becomes cliffbound in the north. The Upper Peninsula is relatively level in the east, with swampy areas, while the western region is high and more rugged. The hills in the south are low, but those along the north coast create picturesque cliffs along Lake Superior. The Upper Peninsula, with an extreme length of approximately 330 miles, is laced with streams and numerous waterfalls. (See Appendix for more information on waterfalls.)

Lakes Huron, Michigan, and Superior are generally not for craft of less than 20 feet, but the smaller lakes and rivers offer good boating and excellent fishing. Michigan's clear lakes and streams, especially in the Upper Peninsula, yield trout, muskellunge, perch, pike, bass, bluegill, and coho salmon. Several lakes are noted for sturgeon. Deer, rabbit, partridge, and pheasant are the principal game on the more than 7 million acres of federal and state land open to public hunting.

Michigan has many excellent canoe streams; some classified as wilderness, some as wild-scenic, and others as country-scenic. From the early days of the Indians and later the fur-trading French Voyageurs, paddling the waterways in Michigan has been a tradition. The Land and Water Management Division of the Department of Natural Resources is responsible for the natural rivers program. To date,

Fishing ranks as the most popular outdoor pastime . . .

14 rivers have been designated as State Natural Rivers and 25 other rivers are proposed for designation. Of the 14 rivers, two are in Region 1 (Upper Peninsula)—the Fox River and the Two Hearted River; eight are in Region 2—Au Sable, Betsie, Boardman, Jordan, Pere Marquette, Pigeon, Rifle, and White; and four are in Region 3—Flat, Huron, Lower Kalamazoo, and Rogue. Two of these rivers have segments that are also Federally Designated Scenic Rivers; both are in Region 2. They are a 23-mile mainstream segment of the Au Sable River from Mio to Alcona Pond, and a 66-mile mainstream segment of the Pere Marquette River from the "Forks" to the US 31 bridge. These rivers alone offer almost 1,700 miles of canoeable waters.

Michiganders obviously like to travel when they "recreate," because in addition to the miles and miles of canoe trails, there are also thousands of miles of other trails: hiking, backpacking, bicycling, cross-country skiing, snowmobiling, horseback, and ORV (off-road-vehicle) trails. Information on all of these trail opportunities is available from various state agencies. Four of the major hiking trails are: the North Country National Scenic Trail, the Greenstone Ridge Trail, the Bay de Noc-Grand Island Trail, and the Michigan Shore-to-Shore Trail. When completed, the North Country Trail will extend 3,200 miles from the Appalachian Trail in Vermont to the Lewis and Clark Trail in North Dakota. The trail runs the entire length of the Lower Peninsula from south to north and the entire length of the Upper Peninsula from southeast to west. Portions of the trail pass through the Manistee, Hiawatha, and Ottawa national forests.

The Greenstone Ridge Trail is a 45-mile trail running the entire length of Isle Royale National Park from Windigo to Rock Harbor. Five or more days are recommended for this hike. The Bay de Noc-Grand Island Trail is a 40-mile trail on the Rapid River and Munising Ranger Districts of the Hiawatha National Forest. It follows the approximate location of an ancient Chippewa Indian portage route used to carry canoes and supplies between Lake Superior and Lake Michigan. The trail is designed for horseback riders, hikers, and cross-country skiers. The Michigan Shore-to-Shore Hiking and Riding Trail extends from Lake Huron to Lake Michigan. Eighty-five miles of the trail are on the Huron National Forest.

Bicyclists claim that there is no better bicycling country than Michigan. Although the motor traffic is too heavy on many state highways, county roads are suggested; more than 88,000 miles of county roads exist, and many of them make excellent bike routes. The Michigan Department of Transporta-

. . . along with winter sports. Michigan has as much as 200 inches of snow a year in some areas; when it snows, the land becomes a winter wonderland.

tion has maps available for each county, showing designated bike facilities, roads with paved shoulders, and roads with low traffic volumes.

The Kal-Haven Trail Sesquicentennial State Park is a 38-mile rails-to-trails park that extends from Kalamazoo to South Haven. This trail provides a unique experience for bicyclists, hikers, equestrians, snowmobilers, and cross-country skiers. Contact Van Buren State Park for information. The Hart-Montague Bicycle Trail State Park, another rails-to-trails park, parallels US 31 and extends 23 miles from Montague to Hart. Although the primary use of this park is as a bicycle route, the trail can also be used as a bridle path and foot trail in the summer, and as a cross-country ski and snowmobile trail in the winter. This park is presently under construction. Contact Silver Lake State Park for information.

Winter sports rank with fishing as the most popular outdoor pastime. Michigan has more than 40 downhill ski resorts, 4,200 miles of snowmobile trails, thousands of miles of cross-country ski trails, as much as 200 inches of snow a year in some areas, and snow-making equipment at virtually every downhill resort. The snow is different in Michigan! The lakes generate "lake-effect" snow, and lake-effect snow is denser, heavier, and actually more durable than its air-blown mountain cousin. Ten inches of mountain snow might pack down to a one-inch base, while 10 inches of Great Lakes snow will pack down to a five-inch base. Now you know why skiing remains possible well into the Michigan spring. For information on cross-country skiing, snowmobile trails, and downhill skiing areas, request a copy of the "Michigan Winter Travel Guide and Calendar of Events" from the Michigan Travel Bureau.

There are more than 1,600 miles of ORV (off-road-vehicle) trails in Michigan, including a marked trail of 750 consecutive miles in the Lower Peninsula. The Michigan Cross-Country Cycle Trail passes through state and national forests in 17 counties; it starts near Newaygo and winds its way up to Indian River and back down the east side of the Lower Peninsula above Midland. A free brochure, available from the Department of Natural Resources (DNR) Information Services Center, includes a map of these trails. The DNR Information Services Center also has detailed maps and information about the snowmobile trail system.

Michigan's 13 Welcome Centers are conveniently located and staffed with trained personnel who can answer any questions you may have on travel in Michigan. They can provide you with needed directions, maps, and travel-related literature. They have computerized information stations located in the Centers and also offer a toll-free reservation system. Welcome Centers are open 8 a.m. to 8 p.m., mid-June to Labor Day, and 9 a.m. to 5 p.m. the remainder of the year.

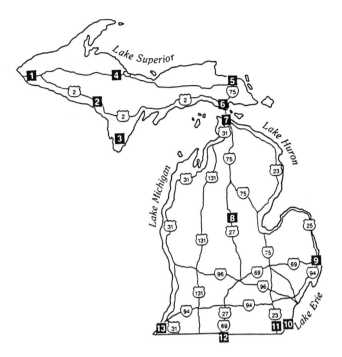

1—Ironwood (US 2, at state line)
2—Iron Mountain (US 2, 2 miles north of state line)
3—Menominee (US 41, at state line)
4—Marquette (2201 South US 41)
5—Sault Ste. Marie (I-75, south of the International Bridge)
6—St. Ignace (I-75, north of the Mackinac Bridge)
7—Mackinaw City (M-108, in Mackinaw City)
8—Clare (US 27, north of Clare)
9—Port Huron (I-94, 2260 Water Street)
10—Monroe (I-75, 10 miles north of state line)
11—Dundee (US 23, 6 miles north of state line)
12—Coldwater (I-69, 6 miles north of state line)
13—New Buffalo (I-94, at state line)

Prior to a trip, a map and other free vacation information such as the *Michigan Travel Planner* may be obtained from the Michigan Travel Bureau. They also have three travel guides, available in season: summer, fall, and winter. These guides include a calendar of events.

Michigan Travel Bureau
P.O. Box 30226
Lansing, MI 48909
1-800-5432-YES

The Information Services Center of the DNR can also supply you with information on state parks and various recreational opportunities. Please refer to Resources in the Appendix for a listing of the various DNR divisions and the specific responsibilities of each.

Department of Natural Resources
Information Services Center
P.O. Box 30028
Lansing, MI 48909
(517) 373-1220

There are rules and regulations encountered at all public campgrounds, whether administered by a state or national agency. Please remember that policies, fees, regulations, and available facilities change from time to time. It's easy for campers to stay informed; merely request updated information and, when you are camping, read the materials posted or distributed at the park. And speaking of becoming informed . . . don't quit reading now! The remaining pages of this introduction provide information that will enable you to have and enjoy great camping trips in Michigan for years to come.

HOW TO USE THE CAMPER'S GUIDE

In this *Camper's Guide*, Michigan is divided into three geographic regions, and the parks and forests within each region are arranged alphabetically and are cross-listed by name and city in the index. The first page of each region locates the park or forest on the map and gives the page number(s) where you can find more detailed information and maps of that specific area.

All the information in this *Camper's Guide* has been supplied by the respective operating agency, either through literature distributed by them, through verbal communication, or through secondary sources deemed reliable. The information presented is basic—it tells you how to get there, cites outstanding features of the area, and lists the facilities and the

recreational activities available. Mailing addresses and telephone numbers are given in case you want additional information prior to your trip. For some state forest or national forest campgrounds, it's a good idea to confirm weather and road conditions before heading out. Also keep in mind that during the off-season some camping areas may be closed or some facilities may be discontinued.

The maps showing the location of facilities within a park or campground should be of considerable help. These maps are usually available to you at the park headquarters, but they can also aid you in planning a trip to an unfamiliar park. Arriving at a park after dark can be tough if you don't know the layout of the campground. And those of you who have attempted to meet up with friends at a predetermined spot at a large campground can readily appreciate the value of having such a map. Most parks are easily found with the help of a good road map, but vicinity maps have been included in some instances. Signs along the way can also be relied upon after you reach the general vicinity of a park.

Because each ranger district within a national forest operates somewhat independently of the national forest as a whole, distributes its own materials, and in many ways has its own "personality" because of terrain, recreational opportunities, etc., information on each national forest is arranged by ranger districts. Visitors who wish to camp off the beaten path should consider purchasing either the official national forest map or the atlas of back road maps, because even the best road map often does not show the many back roads in the forest. However, maps that do show the back roads are often not in agreement with the posted road numbers. This problem has recently been compounded by the fact that many forest service roads and county roads have either been renumbered or assigned a name rather than a number. Perhaps it might be wise to carry a compass as you travel a back road!

The facilities at a campground are always changing, but a change in status usually means the addition of a service rather than a discontinuation. In other words, a camper often finds better and more facilities than those listed in the latest brochure. During the summer camping season, many parks offer interpretive programs, including nature walks, guided tours, and campfire talks, conducted by park personnel.

May this *Camper's Guide* serve you well in the years ahead, whether you are a beginner or a seasoned camper. Take time to camp, to canoe, to fish, to hike and backpack the trails, to become truly acquainted with nature . . . and with yourself, your family, and your friends! Don't put off until tomorrow what can be enjoyed today!

STATE PARKS

Michigan has more than 90 state parks; some are designated for day-use only, but 70 of them have family camping facilities. All are administered by the Michigan Department of Natural Resources (DNR). Actually, 55 of them are called "state parks," and 15 are called "recreation areas." Henceforth, all will be referred to simply as "state parks." In this *Camper's Guide*, the state parks that receive major emphasis are the 70 that have camping facilities.

State parks literally span the length and breadth of Michigan. In the Upper Peninsula, some 15 state parks stretch from the westerly Porcupine Mountains Wilderness State Park to Brimley State Park near Sault Ste. Marie to the east, and as far north as historic Fort Wilkins State Park at the tip of the Keweenaw Peninsula. In the Lower Peninsula, Wilderness State Park is near the Straits of Mackinac; the others are spread between Warren Dunes State Park in the southwest corner of the state and Sterling State Park to the far southeast.

The number of family campsites available at Michigan state parks, where you can pitch a tent or set up a travel trailer, totals more than 14,700. Most feature

Virtually every state park has a picnic area for day-use visitors; more than three-fourths of the parks have picnic shelters.

electrical hookups and modern toilets with showers. Six campgrounds offer rustic camping only while fewer than 20 campgrounds offer both modern and rustic campsites. Park size and the number of available campsites vary greatly. In the Upper Peninsula, Porcupine Mountains Wilderness State Park is the largest park, with some 63,000 acres; Baraga has just 56 acres. Straits State Park has 322 campsites, while Twin Lakes has 62. In the Lower Peninsula, Waterloo is the largest park with 19,750 acres, while 36-acre Wilson is the smallest. Ortonville has 32 campsites, while both South Higgins Lake and Interlochen have more than 500 sites each.

Michigan state parks provide the setting for a wide variety of recreational activities, but each park offers its own unique opportunities for fun and adventure. Consider the following facts:

 9 parks have interpretive centers
64 parks have swimming facilities
55 parks provide beach houses
35 parks have beach concessions
49 parks have boat launches
54 parks have picnic shelters; the majority can be rented
65 parks offer fishing opportunities
47 parks allow hunting, in season
65 parks have hiking trails
38 parks have areas suitable for cross-country skiing
28 parks have areas suitable for snowmobiling
11 parks have trails for horseback riding
 4 parks have horse rental stables
 6 parks have horseman's campsites

This *Camper's Guide* contains detailed information on facilities and activities available at each state park. Each year various parks may upgrade and/or add facilities and services. To keep abreast of these changes, obtain the latest copy of *Michigan State Parks*, the free brochure on the state parks published by the Department of Natural Resources. You may also want to obtain the individual park brochure on any that you plan to visit. These are available free through individual parks; addresses have been included in this *Camper's Guide*. The Parks Division of the DNR is the state office responsible for the state parks.

Permits/Fees/Season

A state park motor vehicle permit, available at each park entrance gate, is required for entry to all state parks. The annual permit ($25), affixed to a vehicle, will admit that vehicle to any park as often as desired. A special annual vehicle permit is available for Michigan resident vehicle owners who are 65 years or older; the cost is $3.75. Daily permits, for $3, admit each vehicle only on the date issued.

There is a separate fee for camping. Camping fees differ according to the type of campground: modern (electrical hookups, flush toilets, and showers); semi-modern (lack either electricity or modern restrooms); or rustic (no hookups and usually vault toilets and hand pumps for water). Fees range from $5 to $10 per night. Checkout time is 3:00 p.m. on the day the permit expires. Extensions may be made, if space is available, by contacting the park office the evening before the permit expires. A camper may not stay longer than 15 consecutive days in any one park.

Campgrounds are open all year long. However, prior to May 15 and after October 15, water systems at some units may not be in service. Sufficient facilities are in operation to make the visit enjoyable, however.

Reservations

You may make a camping, rent-a-tent/tipi, cabin, or shelter reservation either by mail, phone, or in person. Telephone and in-person reservations may be made at most park offices from 8:00 a.m. to noon, and 1:00 p.m. to 5:00 p.m. Reservation requests must be made directly with the park you plan to visit. A $4 reservation fee is charged. Free application forms for camping reservations are available from any state park, DNR region or district office, the DNR Information Services Center in Lansing, or the Michigan Travel Bureau in Lansing. You also may have these forms mailed to you by telephoning any of these offices. Camping reservations may be made for one night or more at all Upper Peninsula parks. All other parks require a minimum two-night reservation. Only half of the campsites in each park are available for reservations. This leaves half of the sites for those who wish to camp on a first-come, first-served basis. For more detailed information, request a copy of the *Campsite Reservation Application*.

Rustic Cabins/Rent-A-Tent or Tipi

Seventeen different parks have a total of 85 cabins available to rent. These rustic cabins can be a functional and enjoyable base camp for hunting, fishing, or hiking, cross-country skiing, ice fishing, or snowmobiling. Cabin capacity varies from 2 to 24, and prices range from $25 to $35 per night. The cabins have single-size beds or bunks with mattresses, a table, chairs, and a broom. Most cabins are heated by wood stoves. There are outside hand pumps for water and vault toilets. You must bring bedding, cookware, tableware, etc.; a portable stove is recommended for cooking. For more detailed information, request a copy of the *State Park Rustic Cabins in Michigan* brochure; the cabin application form is included in the brochure.

At 18 state park campgrounds you may rent a tent already set up within the campground and equipped with two cots plus two sleeping pads, a broom, and a picnic table. Authentic Indian replica tipis are available at 8 state parks and are equipped similarly to a tent. Lanterns, propane stoves, and ice chests are also available for rent when renting a tent or tipi. You must bring bedding, cookware, tableware, etc. Although the Rent-A-Tent/Tipi program is available to everyone, the program is designed for people with little or no camping experience and, evidently, little or no camping equipment. The rental fee is $15 per night. For more detailed information, request a copy of the *Rent-A-Tent, Rent-A-Tipi in Michigan State Parks* brochure; the tent-tipi application form is included in the brochure.

Outdoor Centers

These centers specialize in camping facilities for organized groups, both youth and adult. In general, each outdoor center has buildings for sleeping, a modern dining hall and kitchen, and a bathhouse serving groups of 30–120 campers. Outdoor centers are located at five parks: Proud Lake, Waterloo, Yankee Springs, Onaway, and Sleeper. A nominal overnight fee ($2.50 per person per night) is charged for each person. Further information may be obtained from these parks.

Regulations

To make your visit as pleasant, trouble-free, and fair to others as possible, these rules have been adopted for all state parks:

▲ Camping is permitted only in established camping areas.
▲ Fires are permitted only in stoves, grills, or designated fire circles.
▲ Pets must be kept under immediate control on a leash not exceeding six feet. They must not be left unattended. Pets are not allowed on bathing beaches or in buildings.
▲ Some parks do not allow alcohol and others do not allow guests in the campgrounds. Check with the park you plan to visit.

Complete park rules and regulations are posted conveniently at all state parks.

Indian replica tipis are quite a contrast to the large trailers and RVs seen at state park campgrounds.

STATE FORESTS

More than 160 state forest campgrounds, with over 3,100 individual campsites, are scattered across the northern two-thirds of Michigan. Forest campgrounds generally are small, ranging from 4 to 60 campsites. With plenty of space between campsites, they range from well-developed sites to sites that appeal to people who like to "get away from it all." Most are located on lakes or rivers; some are remote and can only be reached by a hike through the woods or a paddle down the river. Whether you wish to hike, swim, canoe, boat or fish, these campgrounds can meet your needs for rustic outdoor recreation.

Campsites are available on a first-come, first-served basis; no reservations are accepted. Camper user fees are collected through a volunteer, self-registration system; fees are nominal. Senior citizens camp for half price. You may stay up to 15 days;

longer with permission from the local manager. Dogs must be kept on a leash less than six feet in length.

Three state forests are located on the Upper Peninsula and three are on the northern part of the Lower Peninsula. For specific information on recreational opportunities, contact the state forest office administering the area. For your convenience, addresses and phone numbers for these six offices are included in this *Camper's Guide*. The Forest Management Division of the Department of Natural Resources is the state office responsible for the six state forests.

NATIONAL PARKS

There are three national park areas in Michigan: these include one national park and two national lakeshores. The word "park" is henceforth used as a general term to refer to all of the national areas. All three of these national parks offer camping: Isle Royale National Park and Pictured Rocks National Lakeshore are located in Region 1, and Sleeping Bear Dunes National Lakeshore is located in Region 2. Information that is basic to national parks in general is cited here; for more detailed information, refer to the individual park.

▲ All parks have a visitor/information center containing interpretive displays; Pictured Rocks and Sleeping Bear Dunes have museums. Most sell literature with in-depth explanations of history, geology, flora, and fauna. Usually an introductory film or slide show is offered.
▲ The visitor/information center should always be your first stop; brochures, maps, and a schedule of activities are readily available.

▲ Campsite users are charged recreation use fees at all car-accessible campgrounds during season. The season varies with the park, but fees are usually collected from April or May through October. After the camping season, when water may not be available, no fees are charged. Pictured Rocks and Sleeping Bear Dunes are open year round; Isle Royale is closed the end of October.
▲ The length of stay for the car-accessible campgrounds is 14 days; during the off-season it may be longer. The 36 backcountry campgrounds at Isle Royale have lengths of stay ranging from 1 to 5 days.
▲ Individual campsites are available on a first-come, first-served basis and cannot be reserved. An exception to this is that a limited number of backcountry sites for individuals can be reserved at Pictured Rocks.
▲ A group campground is available at Sleeping Bear Dunes on the mainland; reservations are re-

Beach dunes, common all along Michigan's western coast, form near lake level, as onshore winds carry beach sand inland.

quired. Backcountry campsites are available for groups at all 3 parks: reservations are available at Pictured Rocks; they are required on South Manitou Island at Sleeping Bear Dunes; they are not available at Isle Royale.

▲ Backcountry camping is permitted at designated sites in all 3 parks. Backcountry permits are free, but are required. Contact the specific park for information about backcountry restrictions.

▲ All parks have some facilities that are accessible to the handicapped; disabled visitors who have questions about their ability to use a particular facility should contact that park for more information.

▲ Interpretive programs, including nature walks, guided tours, and campfire talks are conducted by personnel at all parks during the summer.

▲ Pets are allowed in most areas at two of the parks if they are kept on a leash or under other physical restraint at all times; they are prohibited at Isle Royale. At Pictured Rocks and Sleeping Bear Dunes, they are not allowed in the backcountry.

▲ Every area of a park is a museum of natural or human history; removal or destruction of any feature is not allowed. The ideal visitor "takes nothing but memories, leaves nothing but footprints."

FEDERAL RECREATION PASSPORT PROGRAM

Some federal parks, refuges, and facilities can be entered and used free of charge. Other areas and facilities require payment of entrance fees, user fees, special recreation permit fees, or some combination. A 1987 brochure by the U.S. Department of the Interior entitled "Federal Recreation Passport Program" explains the five programs. Briefly stated, they are as follows:

Golden Eagle Passport

An annual entrance pass to those national parks, monuments, historic sites, recreation areas, and national wildlife refuges that charge entrance fees. It admits the permit holder and accompanying persons in a private, noncommercial vehicle. For those not traveling by private car, it admits the permit holder and family group. Cost: $25, good for one calendar year (January 1 through December 31); permits unlimited entries to all federal entrance-fee areas.

Golden Age Passport

A free lifetime entrance pass for citizens or permanent residents of the United States who are 62 years or older. Also provides 50% discount on federal use fees charged for facilities and services, except those provided by private concessionaires. Must be obtained in person, with proof of age.

Golden Access Passport

A free lifetime entrance pass for citizens or permanent residents of the United States who have been medically determined to be blind or permanently disabled and, as a result, are eligible to receive benefits under federal law. Offers same benefits as Golden Age Passport. Must be obtained in person, with proof of eligibility.

Locations where these three passes are obtainable include all National Park System areas where entrance fees are charged, all National Forest Service supervisor's offices, and most Forest Service ranger station offices.

Park Pass

An annual entrance permit to a specific park, monument, historic site, or recreation area in the National Park system that charges entrance fees. The park pass is valid for entrance fees only and does not cover use fees. Cost: $10 or $15, depending upon the area; good for one calendar year (January 1 through December 31); permits unlimited entries only to the park unit where it is purchased.

Federal Duck Stamp

Officially known as the Migratory Bird Hunting and Conservation Stamp and still required of waterfowl hunters, the Federal Duck Stamp now also serves as an annual entrance fee permit to national wildlife refuges that charge entrance fees. The Duck Stamp is valid for entrance fees only and does not cover use fees. Cost: $10, good from July 1 through June 30 of the following year; permits unlimited entries to all national wildlife refuges that charge entrance fees. Can be purchased at most post offices.

NATIONAL FORESTS

Michigan's four national forests, covering nearly 2.8 million acres, are managed by the Forest Service of the U.S. Department of Agriculture. The Forest Service is dedicated to multiple-use management for the sustained yield of renewable resources such as water, forage, wildlife, wood, and recreation. This multiple-use management is directed by a Forest Supervisor. In Michigan, there are four national forests but only three Forest Supervisors; the Huron and Manistee are administratively combined. Each national forest is divided into districts, with a District Ranger responsible for multiple-use administration for the district. The best source of specific and local information is the District Ranger's or Forest Supervisor's office administering the area. For your convenience, addresses and phone numbers for these offices are included in this *Camper's Guide* for each national forest.

Because each ranger district within a national forest operates somewhat independently of the national forest as a whole, distributes its own materials, and in many ways has its own "personality" because of terrain, recreational opportunities, etc., information on each national forest in this Camper's Guide is arranged by ranger districts. Visitors to a national forest are encouraged to visit either the office of the forest supervisor or the individual ranger district office. They will be able to supply you with numerous brochures on the various recreational activities available, as well as give information on such items as campground accommodations, location of primitive campsites, dispersed camping opportunities, and road conditions. Those who wish to camp off the beaten path should consider purchasing either the official national forest map or the at-

las of back road maps, because even the best Michigan road map often does not show the many back roads in the forest.

General information is given here. For specific information on campground locations and facilities, refer to the appropriate national forest.

▲ Michigan's four national forests consist of 18 ranger districts. More than 75 developed campgrounds are operated and maintained by these ranger districts, making available more than 1,800 individual campsites.

▲ Four-season outdoor recreation that can be enjoyed on these lands include: camping, fishing, hunting, boating, canoeing, hiking, backpacking, cross-country skiing, snowmobiling, and viewing wildlife and wildflowers.

▲ The managed season for most Forest Service campgrounds is from Memorial Day through Labor Day weekend. Some remain open later in the fall; however, water systems are usually turned off and visitors are asked to pack out their own trash (contact District Ranger for closures).

▲ A typical campground offers secluded sites for tent or RV, picnic tables, fire rings, and a central water supply. The majority of the campgrounds have pit or vault toilet facilities.

▲ The majority of campsites are available on a first-come, first-served basis. A few forest campgrounds are on the reservation system with MISTIX; reservations are taken for a limited number of units at these campgrounds, so noted in this guide for each ranger district. For an additional fee, a campsite can be reserved via check or credit card through MISTIX at 1-800-283-CAMP.

A typical national forest campground offers secluded sites, picnic tables, fire rings, and a central water supply.

▲ The maximum limit of stay is usually 14 days. Camper user fees are collected at most campground entrances through a volunteer, self-registration system; fees are nominal.

▲ Some campgrounds are operated by private concessionaires under a special-use permit issued by the Forest Service. Signs will be posted near the fee collection facility stating a particular site is under concessionaire management.

▲ Water from developed systems at recreation sites is safe to drink. Open water sources are easily contaminated by human or animal waste. Water from springs, lakes, ponds, and streams should be treated. A recommended method of treatment is to bring clear water to a rolling boil for five minutes.

▲ With a few exceptions, most lands in the national forests are open to dispersed camping, that is, "primitive" style outside developed campgrounds. Primitive campsites are also available on some ranger districts; these are designated campsites that have minimal facilities.

▲ Those who want to "rough it" can also backpack into one of Michigan's 10 federal Wilderness Areas, canoe camp along a stream or river, or winter camp close to cross-country ski or snowmobile trails.

▲ Backcountry rules are simple: pack out what you pack in, use campfires wisely, or better yet, use backpack stoves for fire safety.

▲ As a user of national forest lands, you have significant responsibility for your personal safety during any activity you might pursue. It is your responsibility to know the hazards involved in your activities and to use the proper safety procedures and equipment to minimize the inherent risks and hazards related to your activity.

Backcountry Ethics

Rules imposed by those who administer the various backcountry areas are commonsense rules meant to control actions that may damage natural resources. In recent years, the term "going light" has taken on new meaning. To a backpacker, "going light" is the skill of paring down the load and leaving at home every ounce that can be spared. But "going light" also means to spare the land and travel and camp by the rules of "low impact." The National Forest Service suggests the following "low-impact" rules. Although these suggestions were written for the hiker and backpacker, they are quite appropriate for anyone using the backcountry, whether they are traveling by foot, canoe, bicycle, or horse.

General Information
1. Don't short-cut trails. Trails are designed and maintained to prevent erosion.
2. Cutting across switchbanks and trampling meadows can create a confusing maze of unsightly trails.
3. Don't pick flowers, dig up plants, or cut branches from live trees. Leave them for others to see and enjoy.

Plan Your Trip
1. Keep your party small.
2. Take a gas stove to help conserve firewood.
3. Bring sacks to carry out your trash.
4. Take a light shovel or trowel to help with personal sanitation.
5. Carry a light basin or collapsible bucket for washing.
6. Check on weather conditions and water availability.
7. Before your hike, study maps of the area, get permits if necessary, and learn the terrain.

Setting Up Camp
1. Pick a campsite where you won't need to clear away vegetation or level a tent site.
2. Use an existing campsite, if available.
3. Camp 300 feet from streams or springs. Law prohibits camping within ¼ mile of an only available water source (for wildlife or livestock).
4. Do not cut trees, limbs, or brush to make camp improvements. Carry own tent poles.

Breaking Camp
1. Before leaving camp, naturalize the area. Replace rocks and wood used; scatter needles, leaves, and twigs on the campsite.
2. Scout the area to be sure you've left nothing behind. Everything you packed into your camp should be packed out. Try to make it appear as if no one had been there.

Campfires
1. Use gas stoves when possible to conserve dwindling supplies of firewood.
2. If you need to build a fire, use an existing campfire site. Keep it small. Before you leave, make sure it is out.

3. If you need to clear a new fire site, select a safe spot away from rock ledges that would be blackened by smoke; away from meadows where it would destroy grass and leave a scar; away from dense brush, trees and duff, where it would be a fire hazard.
4. Clear a circle of all burnable materials. Dig a shallow pit for the fires. Keep the sod intact.
5. Use only fallen timber for firewood. Even standing dead trees are part of the beauty of wilderness, and are important to wildlife.
6. Put your fire cold out before leaving, let the fire burn down to ashes, mix the ashes with dirt and water. Feel it with you hand. If it's cold out, cover the ashes in the pit with dirt, replace the sod, naturalize the disturbed area. Rockfire rings, if needed or used, should be scattered before leaving.

Pack It In—Pack It Out
1. Bring trash bags to carry out all trash that cannot be completely burned.
2. Aluminum foil and aluminum lined packages won't burn up in your fire. Compact it and put it in your trash bag.
3. Cigarette butts, pull-tags, and gum wrappers are litter, too. They can spoil a campsite and trail.
4. Don't bury trash! Animals dig it up.
5. Try to pack out trash left by others. Your good example may catch on!

Fourteen Michigan rivers have been designated as State Natural Rivers; these rivers alone offer almost 1,700 miles of canoeable waters.

L. Peterson

Porcupine Mountains Wilderness State Park, with more than 90 miles of hiking/backpacking trails, permits trailside camping; rules of "low-impact" camping should be observed.

Keep The Water Supply Clean
1. Wash yourself, your dishes, and your clothes in a container.
2. Pour wash water on the ground away from streams and springs.
3. Food scraps, toothpaste, even biodegradable soap will pollute streams and springs. Remember, it's your drinking water, too!
4. Boil water or treat water before drinking it.

Disposing of Human Waste
1. When nature calls, select a suitable spot at least 100 feet from open water, campsites, and trails. Dig a hole 4 to 6 inches deep. Try to keep the sod intact.
2. After use, fill in the hole completely burying waste. Then tramp in the sod.

Emergency Items
1. According to conditions, carry extra warm clothing such as windbreakers, wool jackets, hats, and gloves. Keep extra high-energy foods like hard candies, chocolate, dried fruits, or liquids accessible. Don't overload yourself, but be prepared for emergencies.
2. Travel with a first-aid kit, map, compass, and whistle. Know how to use them.
3. Always leave your trip plan with a member of your family or a close friend.
4. Mishaps are rare, but they do happen. Should one occur, remain calm. In case of an accident, someone should stay with the injured person. Notify the nearest state, local, or federal law enforcement office for aid.

See Appendix on page 153 for a hiking/backpacking checklist.

Region 1

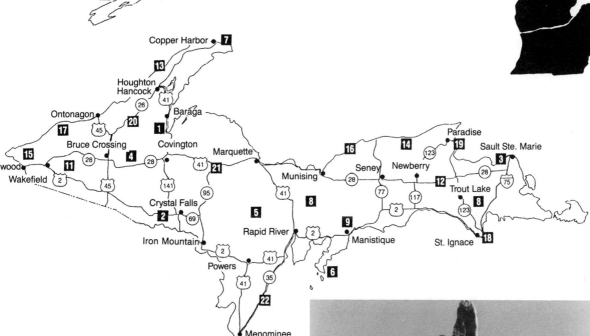

"Leading Man," the magnificent creation of Peter Wolf Toth, is located at Sunday Lake in Wakefield; Indianhead Mountain Winter Sports Area is just a few miles to the northwest.

Baraga State Park

For Information

Baraga State Park
Route 1, Box 566
Baraga, MI 49908
(906) 353-6558

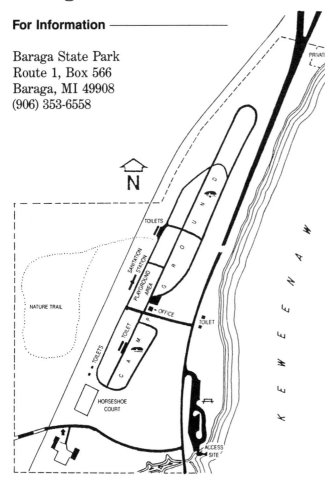

LEGEND

▬▬▬	PAVED ROAD
▭▭▭	GRAVEL ROAD
↑	HEADQUARTERS
⌂	PICNIC AREA
🐟	ACCESS SITE
	CAMPGROUND
— — —	AREA BOUNDARY
⋯⋯⋯	NATURE TRAIL

Location

Baraga State Park is located on Keweenaw Penin-sula 1 mile south of Baraga on US 41. The day-use area of this 56-acre park is on Keweenaw Bay across from L'Anse.

The Indian tipis, available for rent at several state parks, are quite roomy; each one is 21 feet in diameter.

Facilities & Activities

109 modern campsites
  electrical hookups
  flush toilets
  showers
  sanitation station
rent-a-tipi
picnic area
playground
swimming
beach house
fishing
boating
boat launch
nature trail

A ranger shares information with park visitors at an afternoon nature session.

Bewabic State Park

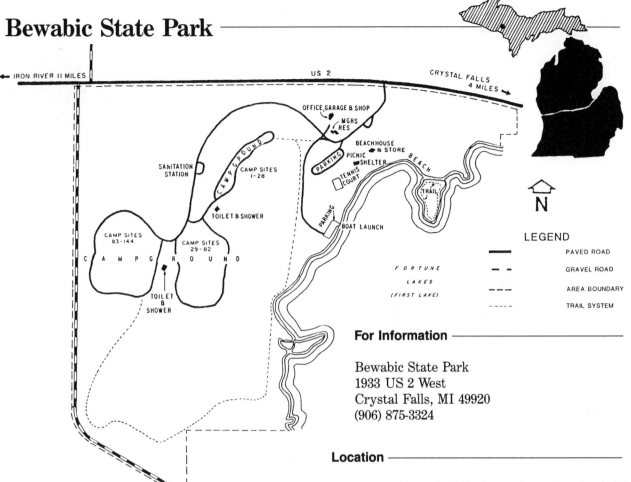

US 2

CRYSTAL FALLS
4 MILES →

OFFICE,GARAGE & SHOP

MGRS
RES

BEACHHOUSE
& STORE

PICNIC
SHELTER

BEACH

SANITATION
STATION

CAMP SITES
1-28

PARKING

TENNIS
COURT

TRAIL

CAMP SITES
83-144

CAMP SITES
29-82

PARKING

TOILET & SHOWER

BOAT LAUNCH

C A M P G R O U N D

FORTUNE
LAKES
(FIRST LAKE)

TOILET
&
SHOWER

N

LEGEND

———	PAVED ROAD
— —	GRAVEL ROAD
– – –	AREA BOUNDARY
- - - - -	TRAIL SYSTEM

For Information

Bewabic State Park
1933 US 2 West
Crystal Falls, MI 49920
(906) 875-3324

Location

Bewabic State Park is located 4 miles west of Crystal Falls on US 2. The 315-acre park is on First Lake, one of a chain of four small lakes that make up Fortune Lakes. The other lakes can be reached by heading south in a boat or canoe.

Facilities & Activities

144 modern campsites
  electrical hookups
  flush toilets
  showers
  sanitation station
rent-a-tent/tipi
picnic area
picnic shelter
playground
tennis court
swimming
beach house and concession
fishing
boating
boat launch
canoeing
hiking trails

Courtesy Michigan Travel Bureau

Canoeing is popular at Bewabic since the state park is situated on Fortune Lake, one of a chain of four lakes.

Brimley State Park

For Information

Brimley State Park
Route 1, Box 202
Brimley, MI 49715
(906) 248-3422

WHITEFISH BAY

BEACH

TOILET & SHOWER

TOILET & SHOWER

TOILET & SHOWER

BATHHOUSE & SHELTER

PLAY AREA

SANITATION STATION

CONTACT STATION

ORGANIZATION CAMPSITE

HEADQUARTERS

6 MILE ROAD — SAULT ST. MARIE 17 MILES

BRIMLEY 1 MILE

N

LEGEND

▬▬▬	PAVED ROAD
▭▭▭	GRAVEL ROAD
- - -	FOOT TRAIL
⬆	HEADQUARTERS
⊼	PICNIC AREA
🐟	ACCESS SITE
🐟	CAMPGROUND
– – –	AREA BOUNDARY

There is a lot of room to spread a blanket on this beach, as the park has almost a mile of shoreline.

Location

Brimley State Park is located 1 mile east of Brimley on Six Mile Road; Brimley is southwest of Sault Ste. Marie and is reached by traveling north on M-221 from M-28. The 151-acre park has almost a mile of shoreline along Whitefish Bay; the hills of Canada are visible across the St. Mary's River.

Facilities & Activities

270 modern campsites
   electrical hookups
   flush toilets
   showers
   sanitation station
rent-a-tent
organization campground
picnic area
picnic shelter
playground
swimming
beach house
fishing
boating
boat launch
hiking trail

Copper Country State Forest

For Information

Copper Country State Forest
US 41N
Baraga, MI 49908
(906) 353-6651

Campground Locations

1. *Emily Lake*—2½ miles south of Twin Lake State Park via M-26 and Pike Lake County Road.
2. *Big Eric's Bridge*—6 miles east of Skanee.
3. *Big Lake*—9 miles northwest of Covington via US 141 and Plains Road.

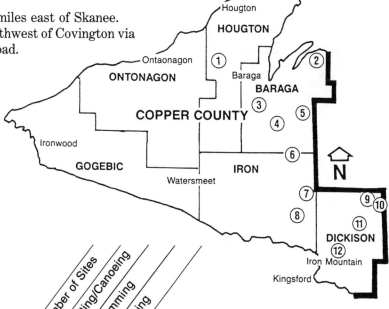

4. *King Lake*—15 miles east of Covington via M-28, US 41, and King Lake Road.
5. *Beaufort Lake*—1½ miles southeast of Three Lakes via US 41 and Beaufort Road.
6. *Deer Lake*—17 miles north of Crystal Falls via US 141 and Deer Lake Road.
7. *Lake Ellen*—4 miles west of Channing via Campground Road.
8. *Glidden Lake*—6 miles southeast of Crystal Falls via M-69 and Lake Mary Road.
9. *West Branch*—7 miles north of Ralph via County Road 581.
10. *Lower Dam*—11 miles northeast of Ralph via County Road 581.
11. *Gene's Pond*—6½ miles northwest of Theodore via County Road 581 (G-67), County Road 422, and Campground Road.
12. *Carney Lake*—16 miles northeast of Iron Mountain via M-95 and Merriman Truck Trail.

Campgrounds	Number of Sites	Boating/Canoeing	Swimming	Fishing
1. Emily Lake	9	B	2	C W
2. Big Eric's Bridge	20		2	C
3. Big Lake	15	B	1	W
4. King Lake	5	B	3	W
5. Beaufort Lake	10	B	1	W
6. Deer Lake	12	B	1	W
7. Lake Ellen	10	B	3	C W
8. Glidden Lake	23	B	1	W
9. West Branch	24	C	3	C
10. Lower Dam	5	C	3	C
11. Gene's Pond	14	B	3	W
12. Carney Lake	11	B	2	W

Swimming: 1—Sandy beach & bottom.
2—Gravel or rocky bottom with little or no beach.
3—Swimming is not recommended.

Fishing: C—Cold-water species.
W—Warm-water species.

Escanaba River State Forest

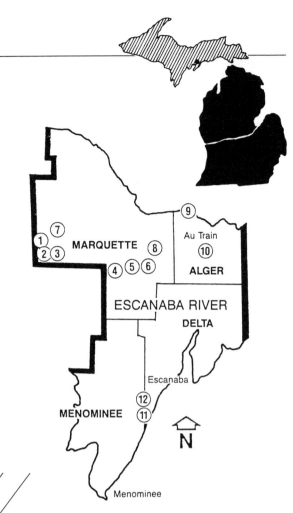

For Information

Escanaba River State Forest
Box 495
Escanaba, MI 49829
(906) 786-2351

Campground Locations

1. *Squaw Lake*—4 miles northwest of Witch Lake via Fence River Road and Squaw Lake Road.
2. *Horseshoe Lake (North Unit)*—1¼ miles west of Witch Lake via Fence River Road.
3. *Horseshoe Lake (South Unit)*—1 mile west of Witch Lake via Fence River Road.
4. *Bass Lake*—12 miles southwest of Gwinn.
5. *Pike Lake*—9 miles southwest of Gwinn.
6. *Anderson Lake West*—7 miles southwest of Gwinn via County Road 577.
7. *Witbeck Rapids*—2¼ miles north of Witch Lake via M-95 and Campground Road.
8. *Little Lake*—1 mile southeast of Little Lake via M-35.

9. *Laughing Whitefish*—12 miles west of Au Train via M-28, then 2 miles north on Campground Road.
10. *Forest Lake*—2½ miles southwest of Forest via M-94 and Campground Road.
11. *Cedar River*—5 miles northwest of Cedar River via M-35 and River Road.
12. *Cedar River North*—6 miles northwest of Cedar River via M-35 and River Road.

Campgrounds	Number of Sites	Boating/Canoeing	Swimming	Fishing
1. Squaw Lake	15	B	2	C W
2. Horseshoe Lake (North Unit)	11	B	1	W
3. Horseshoe Lake (South Unit)	13	B	1	W
4. Bass Lake	21	B	1	C W
5. Pike Lake	10	B	3	W
6. Anderson Lake West	19	B	1	W
7. Witbeck Rapids	19	C	3	C W
8. Little Lake	26	B	1	W
9. Laughing Whitefish	15		3	C
10. Forest Lake	23	B	2	W
11. Cedar River	8	C	2	C W
12. Cedar River North	15	C	2	C W

Swimming: 1—Sandy beach & bottom.
2—Gravel or rocky bottom with little or no beach.
3—Swimming is not recommended.
Fishing: C—Cold-water species.
W—Warm-water species.

Looks like some creative outdoor cooking is taking place here!

Fayette State Park

For Information

Fayette State Park
13700 13.25 Lane
Garden, MI 49835
(906) 644-2603

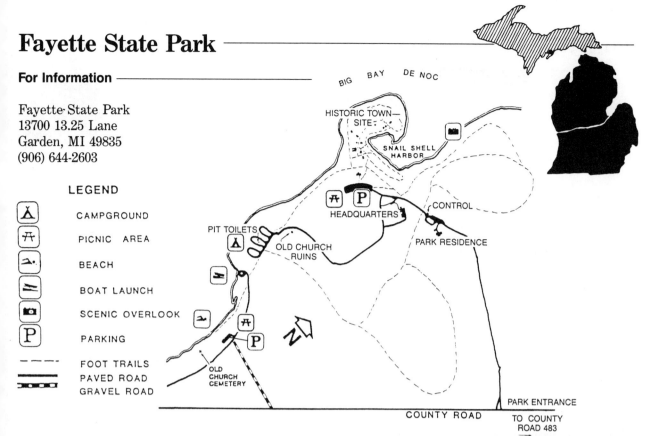

LEGEND

⚠	CAMPGROUND
⛱	PICNIC AREA
⛱	BEACH
⛵	BOAT LAUNCH
📷	SCENIC OVERLOOK
P	PARKING
– – – –	FOOT TRAILS
▬▬▬	PAVED ROAD
▬■▬■	GRAVEL ROAD

Location

Fayette State Park is located on Garden Peninsula overlooking Big Bay De Noc. The interpretive area of the 711-acre park contains the remains of one of the most complete iron-smelting towns in the Midwest. More than 20 original buildings are still standing; some are furnished as they may have looked in the 1800s; other buildings serve as museums. From US 2, near Garden Corner, the park is 17 miles south on M-183.

Facilities & Activities

80 semi-modern campsites
  electrical hookups
  pit toilets
Interpretive Center
picnic area
playground
swimming
beach house
hunting
fishing
boating
boat launch
7 miles of hiking trails
snowmobiling
11.3 km of cross-country ski trails

Courtesy Michigan Travel Bureau

Michigan's clear lakes and streams, especially in the Upper Peninsula, yield trout, muskellunge, perch, pike, bass, bluegill, and coho salmon.

Fort Wilkins State Park

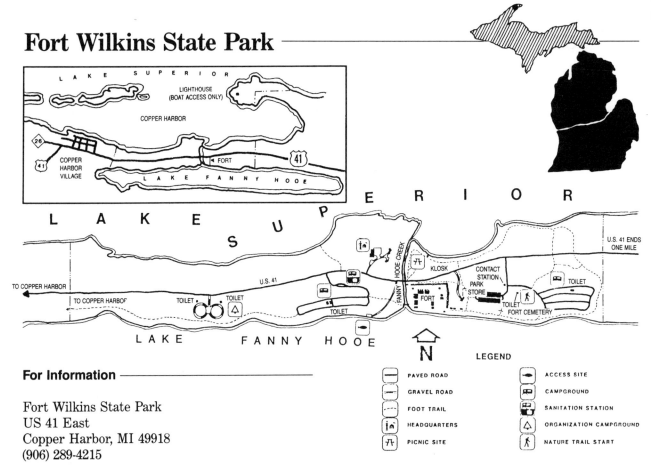

For Information

Fort Wilkins State Park
US 41 East
Copper Harbor, MI 49918
(906) 289-4215

There are two campgrounds at Fort Wilkins; both are in wooded areas with a row of sites near the shoreline of Lake Fanny Hooe.

Location

Fort Wilkins State Park is located 1 mile east of Copper Harbor on US 41. The 203-acre park is located on a narrow strip of land between Copper Harbor and Lake Fanny Hooe. Park visitors may tour the restored fort and the Copper Harbor Lighthouse. Access to the lighthouse is by boat; there is a fee for the boat tour.

Facilities & Activities

165 modern campsites
  electrical hookups
  flush toilets
  showers
  sanitation station
organization campground
Interpretive Center
picnic area

picnic shelter
playground
park store
fishing
boating
boat launch
hiking trails
cross-country skiing

Courtesy Michigan Travel Bureau

Fort Wilkins State Park is the site of one of the few surviving wooden forts east of the Mississippi River.

Hiawatha National Forest

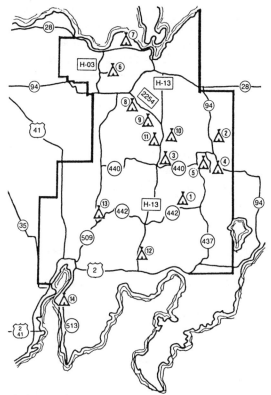

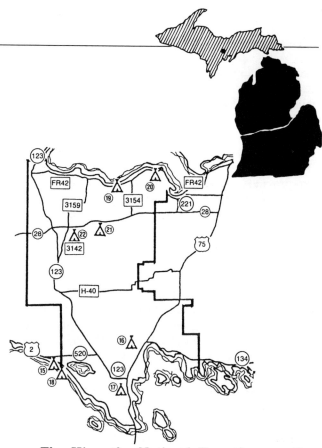

For Information

Forest Supervisor's Office
Hiawatha National Forest
2727 N. Lincoln Road
Escanaba, MI 49829
(906) 786-4062

Screened picnic shelters are appreciated the most
when the mosquitoes and blackflies are out in force.

The Hiawatha National Forest's more than
879,600 acres lie within the eastern and central Upper Peninsula of Michigan. Hiawatha's location on
three of the Great Lakes makes it unique among
the nation's forests. Within its boundaries, it offers
two Great Lakes islands (Round Island and Government Island) and numerous scenic inland lakes and
streams. The forest's expanses of Great Lakes
coastline have added three historic lighthouses to
its numerous cultural resources: the Point Iroquois
Lighthouse at Lake Superior's Whitefish Bay, the
Round Island Lighthouse near Mackinac Island in
the Straits of Mackinac, and the Point Peninsula
Lighthouse.

Materials are available from each of the District
Ranger offices, as well as from the office of the Forest Supervisor, describing recreational opportunities in the Hiawatha National Forest. Contact these
offices for maps and specific information on fishing,
hunting, trails, winter activities, river trips for canoeists, opening and closing dates for campgrounds
and wilderness areas, and so forth.

Camping

The twenty-two campgrounds of the Hiawatha
National Forest offer a wide variety of camping experiences. Most of the areas are located on a scenic
lake or river in a northwoods setting. All camp-

grounds include picnic tables, tent pads, fire grates, water supply, and toilet facilities. Most campsites will accommodate trailers up to the legal length of 55 feet. No electrical hookups or showers are provided.

A nightly fee is charged at most campgrounds for the summer recreation period when full services are provided; several are available free of charge. The seasons vary, but most campgrounds offer full services between Memorial Day and Labor Day. During the remainder of the year the sites may be open at a reduced charge and with reduced services.

All camping is on a first-come, first-served basis, except at the seven campgrounds so noted. For these, reservations can be made, for a small additional fee, via check or credit card through MISTIX at 1-800-283-CAMP. Reservations for the two group sites at Little Bay de Noc Recreation Area can be made by calling the Rapid River Ranger District at (906) 474-6442. Several of the campgrounds are operated by concessionaires.

The Manistique Ranger District also offers dispersed camping at some 20 primitive sites. These undeveloped campsites are all located on good fishing lakes. Camping permits are required and campsites may be reserved for up to seven days for a $5 administrative fee. Munising Ranger District has two primitive campsites available on this same basis; reservations can also be made for Ewing Point Campground, a walk-in site off Bruno's Run trail. St. Ignace Ranger District lists some 17 popular sites for dispersed camping, accessible by vehicle, by boat, or hike-in. There is no charge, nor can reservations be made.

Wilderness Areas

There are six areas managed as Wilderness under the National Wilderness Preservation System. Their use is regulated to the extent necessary for their protection and public safety. You will need proper equipment and outdoor skills to safely enjoy many of their unique opportunities. These areas do not include roads so you must travel on foot or by canoe; camping is permitted.

Rock River Canyon Wilderness is situated 25 miles east of Marquette, 15 miles west of Munising, and 4 miles northwest of M-94 at Chatham. Two canyons, Rock River and Silver Creek, lie within the area. Each canyon is about 150 feet deep. Elevations within the wilderness range between 680 and 1,000 feet above mean sea level. The canyons are considered points of interest because few such landscape features exist in the eastern Upper Peninsula of Michigan. Foot travel is difficult along the steep walls and through the densely vegetated and wet canyon floor. High ground around the canyons is covered by northern hardwoods and is easily traveled. Old roads provide trail access into the area, although no trail system has been marked. The wilderness is administered as a part of the Munising Ranger District.

Big Island Lake Wilderness lies about one-half mile northwest of the city of Manistique and about 18 miles southeast of the city of Munising. There are 23 small lakes within the area, ranging in size from 5 to 149 acres. These lakes are situated among low, rolling hills. The lakes are near enough to each other for canoe portaging, and are currently linked by marked portage trails. Although the area does not have rugged terrain, a degree of challenge is present for visitors. People must make their own way through the forest, for, other than the portage trails, there are no marked footpaths. Off the lakes and canoe trails, a visitor will need good orientation skills. The wilderness is administered as a part of the Munising Ranger District.

Mackinac Wilderness is approximately 12 miles northwest of St. Ignace. The southwest boundary lies along the Soo Line railroad and M-123. The northeast quarter of the area contains low ridges and is forested mostly with northern hardwoods; the south half has fairly large areas of wetland that lie between sand ridges. Mackinac's most notable feature is the Carp River. The north branch of the Carp River, Taylor Creek, and Spring Lake Creek all flow into the portion of the Carp River within the wilderness. The diverse nature of the area attracts a wide range of wildlife. The wetlands and dense forests of Mackinac present a challenge to visitors. There are no marked trails. Current recreation use of the area is primarily along the Carp River and includes canoeing, fishing, hunting, and trapping. The Mackinac Wilderness is administered as a part of the St. Ignace Ranger District.

Delirium Wilderness is 22 air miles southwest of Sault Ste. Marie. The village of Rudyard lies 3 miles to the southeast; 3 miles to the north is M-28 at Raco. The landscape, which was formed from old glacial lakes, is flat to rolling. The overall character of the land can be described as swampy. As the headwaters for the Pine and Waiska rivers, these wetlands serve to help recharge the aquifer, purify the headwaters, and provide habitat for waterfowl and furbearing wildlife species. The thickly forested swamps, surface water, and biting insects limit most forms of recreation. In wintertime, visitors may discover a greater ease of travel, freedom from insects, and quiet. There are no marked pathways. The Delirium Wilderness is administered as a part of the Sault Ste. Marie Ranger District.

Horseshoe Bay Wilderness is on the north shore of Lake Huron. The area lies four miles north of St. Ignace immediately to the east of I-75. The area contains seven miles of Great Lakes frontage on Horseshoe and St. Martins bays, in northern Lake Huron. A sandy beach is found along the southern third of the area. The northern two-thirds vary from marshy to rocky. The marshy portion of the shore is productive habitat for waterfowl and other water-oriented wildlife. The outstanding feature of the area is the Lake Huron shoreline. Access at present is via the 2½-mile Horseshoe Bay trail from the Foley Creek National Forest Campground along H-63. The Horseshoe Bay Wilderness is administered as a part of the St. Ignace Ranger District.

Round Island Wilderness is located in Lake Huron, in the Straits of Mackinac. It lies approximately four miles southeast of the town of St. Ignace and one mile south of Mackinac Island. The 378-acre island has a limestone cliff on the northeast side that rises 76 feet above the lake. A sandy beach on the east side extends for about two-thirds of a mile. No roads or developed trails exist. Access is by boat in the summer, or over ice in the winter. Several historic sites exist on the island. The Round Island Lighthouse is the only permanent improvement on the island; however, the lighthouse is not a part of the wilderness. The Round Island Wilderness is administered as part of the St. Ignace Ranger District.

Recreational Trails

The recreational trails on Hiawatha National Forest are popular with a wide variety of people. The *Bay de Noc-Grand Island Trail* follows the approximate location of an ancient Chippewa Indian portage route used to carry canoes and supplies between Lake Superior and Lake Michigan. The trail parallels the Whitefish River, staying from ½ to 2 miles east of the river. It begins from a point 2¼ miles east of the town of Rapid River and one mile north of US 2 and extends northward for approximately 40 miles, terminating at its intersection with M-94 at Ackerman Lake. There are 3 main trailheads to this scenic pathway, designed for horseback riders, hikers, and cross-country skiers. The trail lies on the Rapid River and Munising ranger districts.

The *North Country Trail* is a federally legislated National Scenic Trail. When completed, it will extend 3,200 miles from the Appalachian Trail in Vermont to the Lewis and Clark Trail in North Dakota. The trail is on the St. Ignace, Sault Ste. Marie, and Munising ranger districts. About 35 miles of the trail on the St. Ignace Ranger District is flat to rolling, passing through stands of northern white cedar, aspen, pine, and northern hardwoods. Blue diamonds painted on trees mark the pathway. The trail is for hikers only.

Courtesy Michigan Travel Bureau

Horseback riding is popular on National Forest lands; eleven state parks also have designated riding trails.

Canoeing

There are numerous opportunities for canoeists on the Hiawatha National Forest, whether it is at a lake setting or on a river. Popular rivers include the Indian, Sturgeon, Au Train, Carp, and Whitefish. The Sturgeon River canoe trail is 41 miles in length and has six access points. The trail starts 3 miles west of Forest Hwy 13 at County Road 440 near the Alger-Delta County line. The best time to canoe the Sturgeon River is when the water is high, between April 30 and the end of June, or after mid-September. Check with the Ranger District office for details of this canoe trail, as well as for details of other trails.

Manistique Ranger District

For Information

Manistique Ranger District
499 E. Lake Shore Drive
Manistique, MI 49854
(906) 341-5666

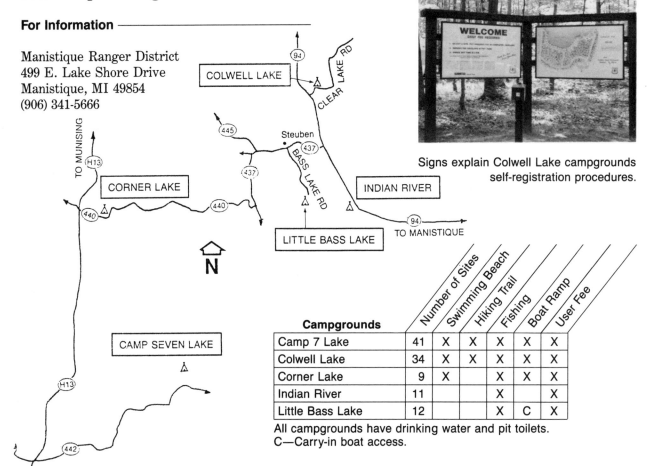

Signs explain Colwell Lake campgrounds
self-registration procedures.

Campgrounds	Number of Sites	Swimming Beach	Hiking Trail	Fishing	Boat Ramp	User Fee
Camp 7 Lake	41	X	X	X	X	X
Colwell Lake	34	X	X	X	X	X
Corner Lake	9	X		X	X	X
Indian River	11			X		X
Little Bass Lake	12			X	C	X

All campgrounds have drinking water and pit toilets.
C—Carry-in boat access.

Campground Locations

Camp 7 Lake is about 8 miles east of Forest Hwy 13 on County Road 442, a black-topped road. It is approximately 24 miles northwest of Manistique and 31 miles northeast of Rapid River, and is located on a 60-acre lake.

Colwell Lake is 25 miles northwest of Manistique off M-94 on Clear Lake Road, and is located on a 145-acre lake.

Corner Lake is 20 miles south of Munising on Forest Hwy 13, then 2 miles east on County Road 440, and is located on a 100-acre lake.

Indian River is 20 miles northwest of Manistique on M-94 on the west side of the highway. The campground is situated on a bluff overlooking the Indian River.

Little Bass Lake is 23 miles northwest of Manistique off of M-94; turn left (west) on County Road 437 to Steuben, then left (south) on Bass Lake Road to the campground. It is on an 84-acre lake.

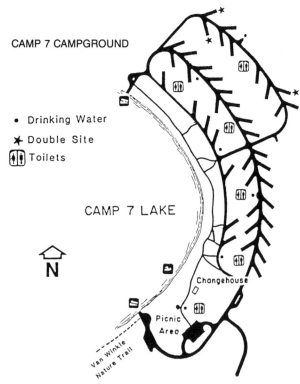

CAMP 7 CAMPGROUND

• Drinking Water
✴ Double Site
🚻 Toilets

CAMP 7 LAKE

Munising Ranger District

For Information

Munising Ranger District
400 E. Munising Ave.
Munising, MI 49862
(906) 387-2512

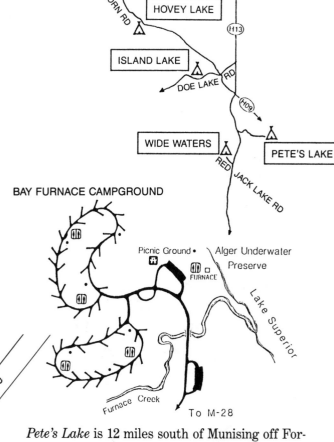

Campground Locations

Au Train Lake is about 10 miles west of Munising. From M-94 at Dixon, travel north on H-03 (Au Train Forest Lake Road) for 3 miles; turn right (east) on Forest Road 2276, then left (north) on Forest Road 2596. The campground can also be reached from Munising by traveling north on M-28 to Au Train, then south for 4 miles on H-03. Au Train, with 830-acres, is the largest inland lake in the area.

Bay Furnace is 5 miles northwest of Munising on M-28, along the south shore of Lake Superior.

Hovey Lake is 8 miles southwest of Munising off M-94; then 4 miles southeast on H-09 (Buckhorn Road). The campground is on the east side of the lake.

Island Lake is 10 miles south of Munising off Forest Hwy 13; turn west (right) on Doe Lake Road and go 2 miles. The campground is on the southeast end of the 32-acre lake.

BAY FURNACE CAMPGROUND

Campgrounds	Number of Sites	Swimming Beach	Hiking Trail	Fishing	Boat Ramp	User Fee
AuTrain Lake*	37	X		X	X	X
Bay Furnace*†	50					X
Hovey Lake	5			X	C	
Island Lake*	45			X	C	X
Pete's Lake*	44	X	X	X	X	X
Widewaters*	34		X	X	X	X

All campgrounds have drinking water and pit toilets.
* On reservation system (1-800-283-CAMP).
† Has dump station.
C—Carry-in boat access.

Pete's Lake is 12 miles south of Munising off Forest Hwy 13, then east on Forest Road 2173 for a short distance. The campground has a 190-acre lake; the 7-mile hiking trail (Bruno's Run) winds through the northern and eastern edges.

Widewaters, on the Indian River, is 13 miles south of Munising off of Forest Hwy 13, then northwest on Red Jack Lake Road (Forest Road 2262) for ½ mile. The 7-mile Bruno's Run Hiking Trail is accessible from the campground.

Rapid River Ranger District

For Information

Rapid River Ranger District
8181 US 2
Rapid River, MI 49878
(906) 474-6442

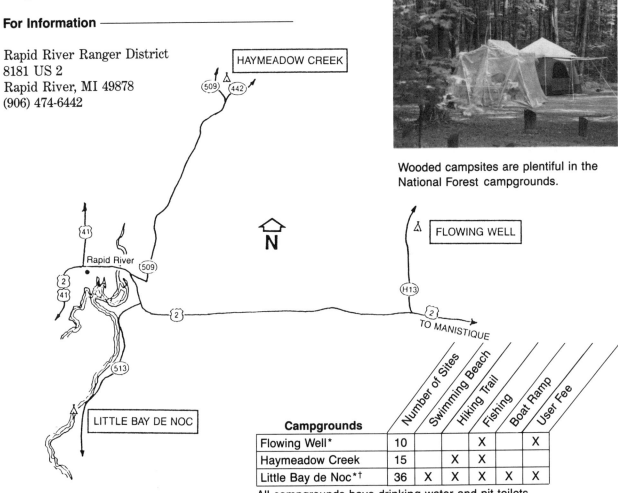

Wooded campsites are plentiful in the National Forest campgrounds.

Campgrounds	Number of Sites	Swimming Beach	Hiking Trail	Fishing	Boat Ramp	User Fee
Flowing Well*	10		X			X
Haymeadow Creek	15		X	X		
Little Bay de Noc*†	36	X	X	X	X	X

All campgrounds have drinking water and pit toilets.
* On reservation system (1-800-283-CAMP).
† 2 group sites available; make reservations with District Ranger.

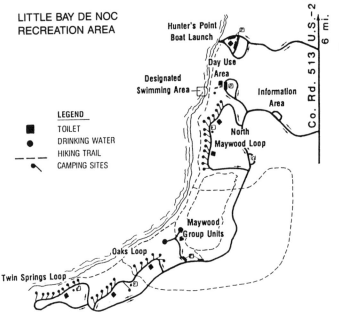

LITTLE BAY DE NOC RECREATION AREA

LEGEND
■ TOILET
● DRINKING WATER
--- HIKING TRAIL
↖ CAMPING SITES

Campground Locations

Flowing Well is 14 miles east of Rapid River on US 2, then north for 3 miles on Forest Hwy 13. The campground is along the banks of the Sturgeon River; the flowing well is 1,160 feet deep and produces 100 gallons of water per minute.

Haymeadow Creek is 11 miles from Rapid City. Take US 2 east from Rapid River for 1.6 miles, turn left on County Road 509, and go north 9.4 miles to the campground. There is a trail from the campground to Haymeadow Falls.

Little Bay de Noc Recreation Area is 9 miles south of Rapid River; go east on US 2, then south on County Road 513 past the Hunter's Point boat launch. The campground is along the sandy shore of Lake Michigan.

St. Ignace Ranger District

For Information

St. Ignace Ranger District
1498 West US 2
St. Ignace, MI 49781
(906) 643-7900

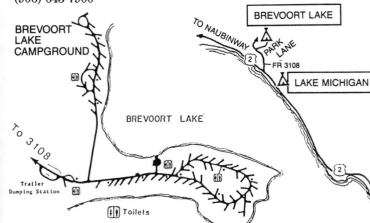

Campground Locations

Brevoort Lake is 20 miles northwest of St. Ignace. From US 2, turn north on the Brevoort Camp Road (FR 3108), then right on Park Lane. The campground is on a 4,233-acre lake that offers many recreational opportunities.

Carp River is 8 miles north of St. Ignace off H-63 (Mackinac Trail). The campground is west of and within a mile of I-75, but there is no exit from I-75 when H-63 crosses under I-75 to run parallel to it on the east. To reach H-63 when approaching from the north, take the M-134 exit; when approaching from the south, take the M-123 exit. The campground is on the Carp River.

Foley Creek is 3 miles north of St. Ignace on H-63 and is adjacent to the Horseshoe Bay Wilder-

ness. When approaching from the north on I-75, take the M-123 exit and travel south on H-63; when approaching from the north on I-75, take the exit north of Evergreen Shores and travel north on H-63.

Lake Michigan is 18 miles northwest of St. Ignace on US 2; the campground is located along the shore of Lake Michigan.

Campgrounds	Number of Sites	Swimming Beach	Hiking Trail	Fishing	Boat Ramp	User Fee
Brevoort Lake*	70	X	X	X	X	X
Carp River	44			X	C	X
Foley Creek	54		X	X		X
Lake Michigan	35					X

All campgrounds have drinking water.
Brevoort Lake and Lake Michigan have flush toilets, Foley Creek and Carp River have pit toilets.
* Has dump station.

All but two of the 22 campgrounds on the Hiawatha National Forest have pit toilets.

Sault Ste. Marie Ranger District

For Information

Sault Ste. Marie Ranger District
4000 I-75 Business Spur
Sault Ste. Marie, MI 49783
(906) 635-5311

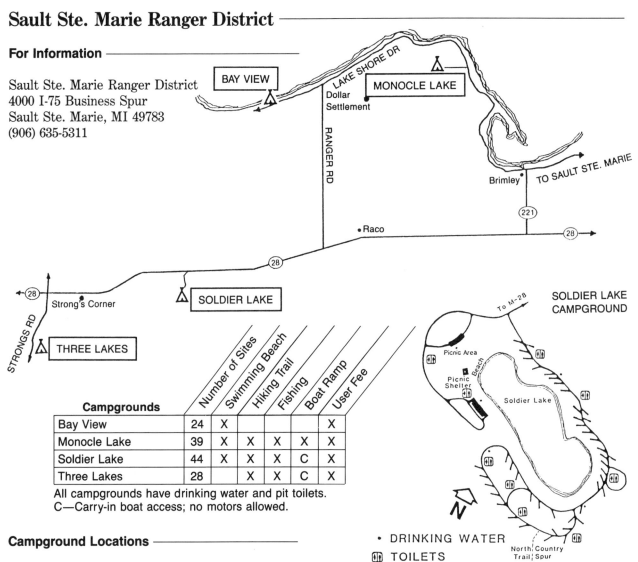

Campgrounds	Number of Sites	Swimming Beach	Hiking Trail	Fishing	Boat Ramp	User Fee
Bay View	24	X				X
Monocle Lake	39	X	X	X	X	X
Soldier Lake	44	X	X	X	C	X
Three Lakes	28		X	X	C	X

All campgrounds have drinking water and pit toilets.
C—Carry-in boat access; no motors allowed.

• DRINKING WATER
◫ TOILETS

Campground Locations

Bay View is 8 miles north of Raco and M-28; go north on Ranger Road for 6 miles to Dollar Settlement, then west (left) on Lake Shore Drive for 2 miles. It is 27 miles northwest of Sault Ste. Marie and accessible via Lake Shore Drive. The campground is along the shores of Lake Superior.

Monocle Lake is 7 miles west and north of Brimley off Lake Shore Drive. Turn left on a forest road before reaching the Point Iroquois Lighthouse. The campground is on a 172-acre lake.

Soldier Lake is 30 miles west of Sault Ste. Marie on M-28. It is on the south side of M-28, less than a mile from the highway. When traveling M-28 from the west, the campground is about 5 miles past Strongs Corner. No motors are permitted on the 15-acre lake.

Three Lakes is south of M-28 at Strongs Corner; turn south on Strongs Road and go 2 miles. The campground is located on 19-acre Walker Lake.

The swimming beach at the 15-acre lake is the main attraction at Soldier Lake campground.

Indian Lake State Park

For Information

Indian Lake State Park
Route 2, Box 2500
Manistique, MI 49854
(906) 341-2355

Location

Indian Lake State Park is composed of two units that are 3 miles apart and separated by the waters of Indian Lake. The 567-acre south shore unit is located 4 miles west of Manistique on County Road 442. It can also be reached off US 2 from Thompson by traveling 3 miles north on M-149, then ½ mile east on County Road 442. To reach the 280-acre west shore unit, continue west on County Road 442, then north on County Road 455. When in the area, visitors should also consider a trip to nearby Palms Book State Park, the site of Michigan's largest spring, gushing over 10,000 gallons of water a minute. This day-use only park is located off of County Road 455 beyond the west shore unit; it may also be reached by traveling to the northern terminus of M-149.

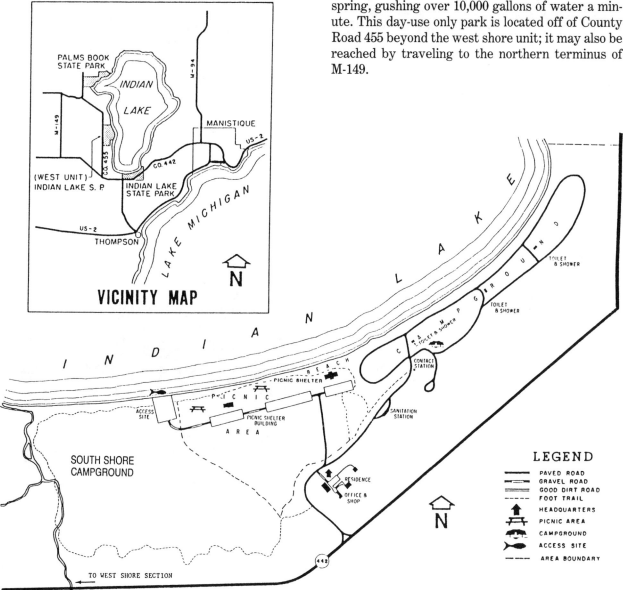

VICINITY MAP

LEGEND

—— PAVED ROAD
—·— GRAVEL ROAD
═══ GOOD DIRT ROAD
----- FOOT TRAIL
HEADQUARTERS
PICNIC AREA
CAMPGROUND
ACCESS SITE
—·—·— AREA BOUNDARY

Facilities & Activities at South Shore Campground

157 modern campsites
  electrical hookups
  flush toilets
  showers
  sanitation station
rent-a-tent/tipi
picnic area
picnic shelter
playground
swimming
beach house
hunting
fishing
boating
boat launch
hiking trails

Facilities & Activities at West Shore Campground

144 modern campsites
  electrical hookups
  flush toilets
  showers
  sanitation station
picnic area
swimming
hunting
fishing
boating
boat launch
hiking

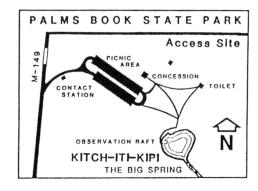

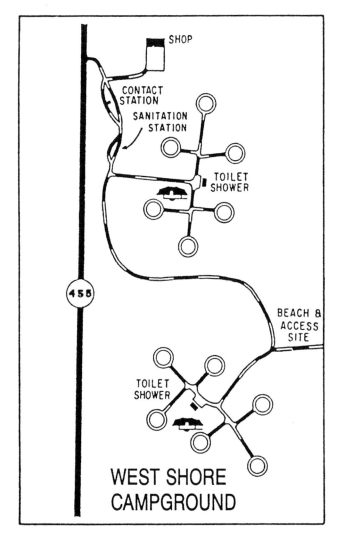

Read and heed! This camper is learning all about "swimmer's itch" from a bulletin board displayed at Indian Lake State Park.

Isle Royale National Park

For Information

Isle Royale National Park
87 North Ripley Street
Houghton, MI 49931-1895
(906) 482-0984

ONT
Canada
Isle Royale NP
N
United States
Grand Portage NM
Copper Harbor
LAKE SUPERIOR
MINN
Houghton
Duluth
Superior
MICH
WIS
17
53
61
41
26
28
2
35
45

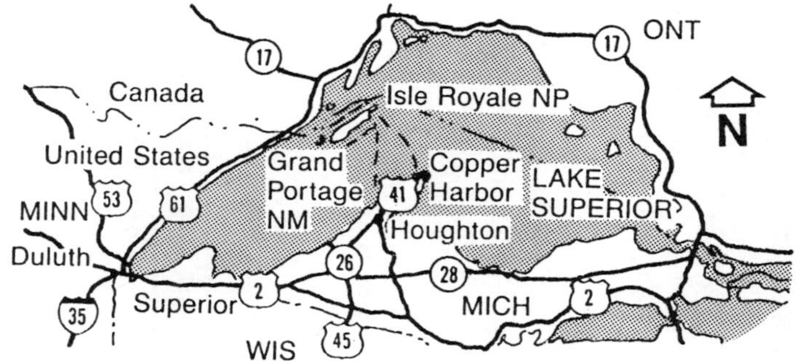

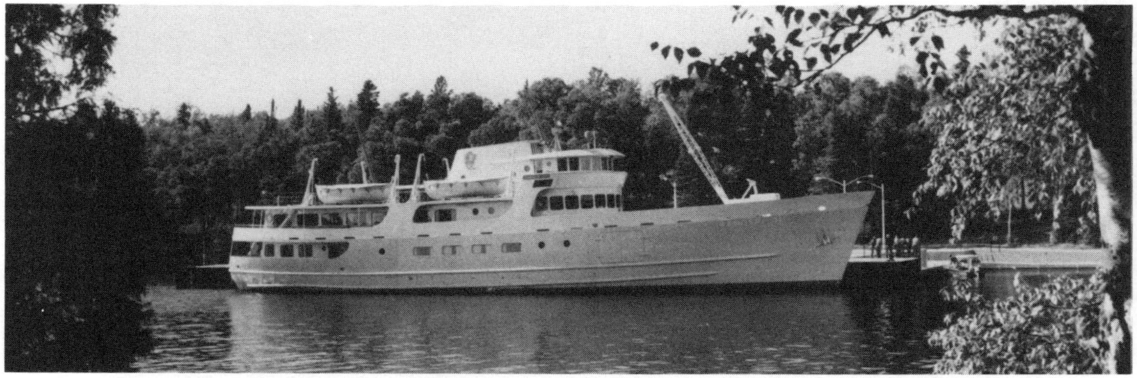

Courtesy Michigan Travel Bureau

Transportation from the mainland to Isle Royale National Park is by boat or floatplane. The government-operated *Ranger III,* pictured here, travels between Houghton and Rock Harbor and operates June 1 through Labor Day.

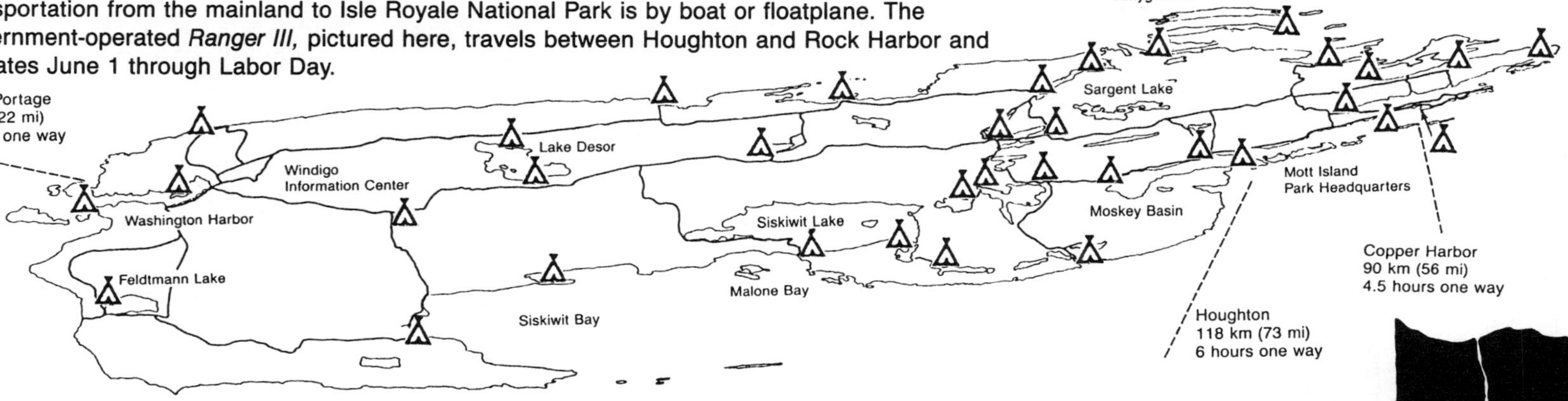

Amygdaloid
Grand Portage
35 km (22 mi)
3 hours one way
Sargent Lake
Lake Desor
Windigo
Information Center
Mott Island
Park Headquarters
Washington Harbor
Siskiwit Lake
Moskey Basin
Feldtmann Lake
Malone Bay
Copper Harbor
90 km (56 mi)
4.5 hours one way
Siskiwit Bay
Houghton
118 km (73 mi)
6 hours one way

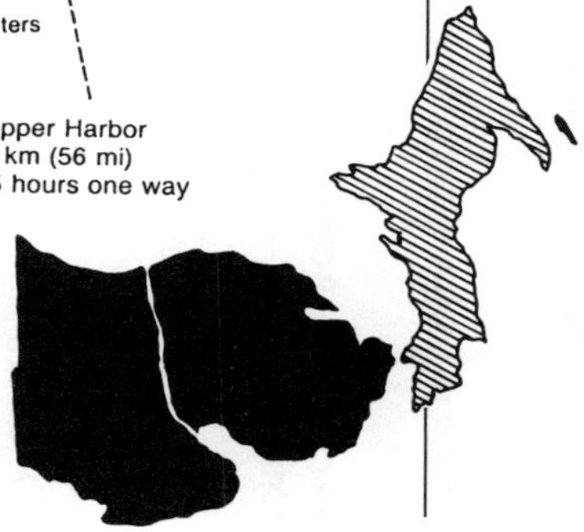

Isle Royale National Park (*continued*)

Location

Isle Royale National Park is located in Lake Superior's northwest corner, just 22 miles off the Minnesota shore. The park is accessible only by boat or floatplane; visitor season is mid-April to the end of October. Transportation from the mainland is from Houghton and Copper Harbor, Michigan and from Grand Portage, Minnesota. Travel on and around the park is by foot, boat, or floatplane; there are no roads or motorized vehicles. Park headquarters and an information center are located at 87 North Ripley Street in Houghton.

About the Park

Isle Royale National Park, with 210 square miles of ridge and valley topography, extends nearly 45 miles from northeast to southwest and is about 9 miles wide. Dozens of smaller islands surround the main island. Moose and wolves share the island with red fox and beaver. Isle Royale has spruce–fir and birch–maple forests, inland lakes, and rocky shores; it is rugged but also fragile. Park visitors should minimize their impact when they travel and practice low-impact techniques when they camp. Numerous points of interest, such as historic copper mines, lighthouses, fisheries, and shipwrecks, are accessible via 166 miles of maintained foot trails and by various boat services.

The park was authorized by Congress in 1931 "to conserve a prime example of Northwoods Wilderness." In 1976 the park was designated part of the National Wilderness Preservation System under the Wilderness Act, and remains today as an example of primitive America. In 1981 it was designated a Biosphere Reserve by the United Nations, giving it international significance.

General Park Information

▲ When planning your visit, contact the park and request the general information brochure, as well as related brochures on the following: *Getting There* (covers transportation), *Camping/Hiking/Boating*, *Drinking Water*, and *Publications*.

▲ The brochures listed above contain information that will aid you in planning your trip. Because of the park's unique wilderness setting,

Courtesy Michigan Travel Bureau

Isle Royale National Park consists of the main island, about 9 miles wide and 45 miles long, surrounded by dozens of smaller islands. The park was authorized by Congress in 1931 "to conserve a prime example of Northwoods Wilderness."

there is an abundance of pertinent information; only the most basic information is cited in this book.

▲ Transportation from the mainland to the park is by boat or floatplane; reservations are always required. The *Getting There* brochure contains detailed information, rates, and schedules on all tour boats.

—The Government-operated *Ranger III* travels between Houghton and Rock Harbor.

—The concession-operated *Isle Royale Queen III* travels between Copper Harbor and Rock Harbor.

—The concession-operated *Wenonah* travels from Grand Portage to Windigo.

—The concession-operated *Voyageur II* (from Grand Portage) circumnavigates Isle Royale, providing drop-off/pick-up service between some 7 points on the island.

—The *M.V. Sandy*, a concession-operated tour boat that operates out of Rock Harbor, provides several options for pick up and drop offs in the area.

—Weather dependent, there is on-demand seaplane service to Isle Royale from Houghton; service is also available between Rock Harbor and Windigo.

▲ Lodge and housekeeping cottages are available at Rock Harbor. For reservations, rates, and information during the summer season, write:

> National Park Concessions, Inc.
> Box 405
> Houghton, MI 49931
> (906) 337-4993.

▲ Rock Harbor also has coffee shop, dining room, store, gift shop, laundry, showers, and marina.

▲ Windigo does not have overnight accommodations but it has a grocery store, camping supplies, snack foods, laundry, and showers.

▲ Canoe rentals, boat rentals, and motor rentals are available at both Rock Harbor and Windigo.

▲ Pets and wheeled vehicles are not allowed within park boundaries.

▲ Swimming is not popular because of the extremely cold water of Lake Superior and the leeches in the warmer inland lakes.

▲ Scuba-diving activities require pre-registration at a ranger station.

▲ Guided nature hikes and evening programs are posted at the ranger stations.

▲ Several 6-day Field Seminars are co-sponsored each summer by the National Park Service and the Isle Royale Natural History Association. Lodging and meals are at the Rock Harbor Lodge; each course is conducted by a professional instructor.

▲ All facilities at Isle Royale have only limited handicapped accessibility; contact the park for specific information.

▲ Mosquitoes, black flies, and gnats can be a problem; bring insect repellent and bug-proof tent netting.

▲ There is no public telephone service on Isle Royale.

▲ Medical services are not available in the park; park visitors should carry a good first-aid kit and be prepared to handle their own emergencies.

▲ A Michigan fishing license is required in all Lake Superior waters; none is required in inland lakes and streams, but Michigan regulations apply.

▲ It is recommended that boats less than 20 feet long do not cross Lake Superior from the Keweenaw Peninsula; boats up to 20 feet long may be transported on the *Ranger III*.

▲ All boaters should carry *Lake Survey Chart 14976*, which may be purchased from the park; they should also have an FM radio of sufficient power to reach shore.

▲ All boats must obtain a permit upon arrival; all must have proper home state registration; overnight docking is allowed only at campgrounds and docks indicated in park map brochure.

▲ Gasoline and oil are sold at Rock Harbor and Windigo; diesel fuel is available only at Rock Harbor.

▲ Mid-summer temperatures rarely exceed 80 degrees; evenings are usually cool; rain is frequent.

Camping Information

▲ Backcountry camping is allowed on a first-come, first-served basis; campsites cannot be reserved.

▲ 3 types of camping are available:

—3-sided shelters (maximum 6 people)

—tent sites (maximum 6 people) for 1 to 3 tents

—group sites (maximum 10 people)

Courtesy Michigan Travel Bureau

When fishing on Isle Royale National Park, a Michigan fishing license is required, as it is for all Lake Superior waters; no license is required for fishing in inland lakes and streams, but Michigan regulations apply.

▲ All campers and boaters are required to get a camping permit upon arrival. Permits are available free at any of the 4 ranger stations.

▲ 36 campgrounds are available. Group campsites are available at 17 of them, 19 of them can accommodate boats, 25 are accessible for canoes, 8 can be reached only by trail.

▲ Long-term camping stays are not available; length of stay ranges from 1 to 5 nights, with an average stay of 3 nights; permits designate the campsites when the itinerary is planned.

▲ There are no entrance or camping fees.

▲ The camping season is from mid-April through October.

▲ Cross-country, off-trail travel is not recommended because of dense vegetation, bogs, and swamps.

▲ More than 166 miles of maintained trails are available; it is recommended that all hikers carry the Isle Royale topographic map.

▲ Open wood fires are prohibited in many campgrounds; bring a self-contained fuel stove.

▲ Any water on Isle Royale not obtained from water-purification systems at Rock Harbor or Windigo may be contaminated; ask for the *Drinking Water* handout for treatment recommendations.

▲ Do not leave personal items, packs, or food unattended; foraging squirrels and red foxes can quickly damage or carry off items.

▲ Campers should practice low-impact wilderness camping methods; all trash must be carried out.

Recreational Activities

backcountry camping
hiking
boat camping
canoeing/boating
boat tours
scuba diving
fishing
wildlife watching
Field Seminars
guided nature hikes
evening ranger programs

Lake Gogebic State Park

For Information

Lake Gogebic State Park
H.C. 1, Box 139
Marenisco, MI 49947
(906) 842-3341

Location

Lake Gogebic State Park is located along the west side of Lake Gogebic, the largest inland lake of the Upper Peninsula. The 361-acre park is on M-64 between US 2 and M-28. When traveling east from Wakefield or west from Watersmeet on US 2, take M-64 north for 9 miles. The park is in the heart of the Ottawa National Forest, an area noted for its many spectacular waterfalls.

Facilities & Activities

165 modern campsites
  electrical hookups
  flush toilets
  showers
  sanitation station
rent-a-tent
picnic area
picnic shelter

playground
swimming
beach house
fishing
boating
boat launch
2-mile hiking trail
cross-country skiing

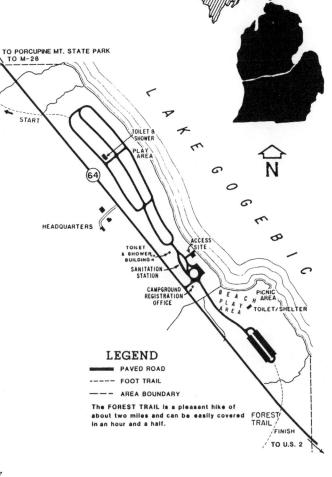

LEGEND
▬▬ PAVED ROAD
----- FOOT TRAIL
-- -- AREA BOUNDARY

The FOREST TRAIL is a pleasant hike of about two miles and can be easily covered in an hour and a half.

The rent-a-tent program, available at more than one-fourth of the state park campgrounds, is designed for people with little or no camping equipment. The tent, along with some equipment, is already set up; other equipment is available for rent.

Lake Superior State Forest

For Information

Lake Superior State Forest
Box 445
Newberry, MI 49868
(906) 293-5131

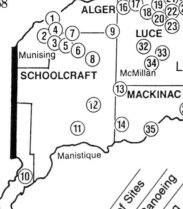

Campgrounds	Number of Sites	Boating/Canoeing	Swimming	Fishing
1. Kingston Lake	14	B	2	W
2. North Gemini Lake	17	B	2	W
3. South Gemini Lake	8	B	2	W
4. Ross Lake	10	B	2	W
5. Canoe Lake	4		3	W
6. Cusino Lake	6	B	1	W
7. Stanley Lake	10	B	3	W
8. Fox River	6	C	3	C
9. East Branch of Fox River	16		3	C
10. Portage Bay	18	B	1	W
11. Merwin Creek	11	C	3	W
12. Mead Creek	10	C	3	W
13. South Manistique Lake	29	B	2	W
14. Milakokia Lake	36	B	2	W
15. Lake Superior	18		1	C
16. Blind Sucker No. 1	13	B	1	W
17. Blind Sucker No. 2	36	B	2	W
18. Pratt Lake	6		2	C
19. Holland Lake	15		2	C
20. Pretty Lake	18	B C	1	C
21. Perch Lake	35	B	1	W
22. Headquarters Lake	8		3	
23. High Bridge	7	C	3	C

Swimming: 1—Sandy beach and bottom.
2—Gravel or rocky bottom with little or no beach.
3—Swimming is not recommended.
Fishing: C—Cold-water species.
W—Warm-water species.

Campground Locations

1. *Kingston Lake*—16 miles northeast of Melstrand via County Road H-58, Au Sable Point Road.
2. *North Gemini Lake*—10 miles northeast of Melstrand via County Road H-58 and Twin Lakes Truck Trail.
3. *South Gemini Lake*—12 miles northeast of Melstrand via County Road H-58 and Twin Lakes Truck Trail.
4. *Ross Lake*—14 miles northeast of Melstrand via County Road H-52 and Crooked Lake Road.
5. *Canoe Lake*—9 miles east of Melstrand via county roads H-528 and 450 and Wolf Lake Road.
6. *Cusino Lake*—11 miles east of Melstrand via county roads H-52 and 450.
7. *Stanley Lake*—15 miles northwest of Seney via County Road 450 and Mahoney Lake Road.
8. *Fox River*—5 miles northwest of Seney via County Road 450.
9. *East Branch of Fox River*—8 miles north of Seney via M-77.
10. *Portage Bay*—10 miles south of Garden via County Road 483 and Portage Bay Road.
11. *Merwin Creek*—9 miles northwest of Gulliver via US 2, county roads 483 and 433.
12. *Mead Creek*—6 miles southwest of Germfask via M-77 and County Road 436.

Lake Superior State Forest (*continued*)

	Number of Sites	Boating/Canoeing	Swimming	Fishing
24. Reed & Green Bridge	4	C	1	C
25. Two Hearted River Canoe Camp	4	C	3	C
26. Mouth of Two Hearted River	45	B C	1	C
27. Pike Lake	23	B	2	W
28. Bodi Lake	20	B	1	W
29. Culhane Lake	22	B	2	W
30. Andrus Lake	25	B	1	C
31. Shelldrake Dam	17	B	3	W
32. Bass Lake	18	B	3	C W
33. Sixteen Creek	12	B C	3	W
34. Natalie	12	B	3	W
35. Big Knob	23		1	
36. Black River	12		3	C
37. Garnet Lake	8	B	2	W
38. Hog Island Point	58	B	1	C
39. Little Brevoort Lake (North)	20	B	2	W
40. Little Brevoort Lake (South)	12	B	2	W
41. Munuscong River	50	B C	3	W
42. Maxton Bay	18	B	3	W

Swimming: 1—Sandy beach and bottom.
2—Gravel or rocky bottom with little or no beach.
3—Swimming is not recommended.
Fishing: C—Cold-water species.
W—Warm-water species.

13. *South Manistique Lake*—6 miles southwest of Curtis via South Curtis Road and Long Point Road.
14. *Milakokia Lake*—7 miles southwest of Gould City via US 2 and Pike Lake Grade.
15. *Lake Superior*—15 miles east of Grand Marais via Grand Marais Truck Trail.
16. *Blind Sucker No. 1*—14 miles east of Grand Marais via Grand Marais Truck Trail.
17. *Blind Sucker No. 2*—16 miles east of Grand Marais via Grand Marais Truck Trail.
18. *Pratt Lake*—28 miles northwest of Newberry via M-123 and county roads 407 and 416.
19. *Holland Lake*—26 miles northwest of Newberry via M-123 and county roads 407 and 416.

20. *Pretty Lake*—27 miles northwest of Newberry via M-123, county roads 407 and 416, and Campground Road; canoe or walk-in.
21. *Perch Lake*—25 miles north of Newberry via M-123 and County Road 407.
22. *Headquarters Lake*—24 miles north of Newberry via M-123 and County Road 407.
23. *High Bridge*—23 miles north of Newberry via M-123 and County Road 407.
24. *Reed & Green Bridge*—31 miles north of Newberry via M-122 and county roads 401 and 410.
25. *Two-Hearted River Canoe Camp*—28 miles north of Newberry.
26. *Mouth of Two-Hearted River*—35 miles northeast of Newberry, via M-123, county roads 500, 414, 412, and 423.
27. *Pike Lake*—29 miles northeast of Newberry via M-123, county roads 500 and 437.
28. *Bodi Lake*—32 miles northeast of Newberry via M-123, county roads 500 and 437.
29. *Culhane Lake*—30 miles northeast of Newberry via M-123 and County Road 500.
30. *Andrus Lake*—6 miles north of Paradise via Wire Road and Vermillion Road.
31. *Shelldrake Dam*—8 miles north of Paradise via Wire Road and Vermillion Road.
32. *Bass Lake*—9½ miles north of McMillan via county roads 415 and 421.
33. *Sixteen Creek*—6 miles northwest of Newberry via M-123 and Charcoal Grade.
34. *Natalie*—4½ miles west of Newberry via county roads 405 and 43A.
35. *Big Knob*—14 miles southwest of Naubinway via US 2 and Big Knob Road.
36. *Black River*—7 miles northeast of Naubinway via US 2 and Black River Road.
37. *Garnet Lake*—1 mile southeast of Garnet.
38. *Hog Island Point*—7 miles east of Naubinway via US 2.
39. *Little Brevoort Lake (North Unit)*—2 miles northeast of Brevort via Carp River Road and Worth Road.
40. *Little Brevoort Lake (South Unit)*—1½ miles southeast of Brevort via US 2.
41. *Munuscong River*—8 miles northeast of Pickford via M-48 and Sterlingville Road.
42. *Maxton Bay*—4½ miles northeast of Drummond via Maxton Plains Road.

McLain State Park

McLain State Park
M-203
Hancock, MI 49930
(906) 482-0278

LEGEND

▬▬▬	PAVED ROAD
=====	POOR DIRT ROAD
- - - -	FOOT TRAIL
🚙	MODERN CAMPGROUND
— - —	AREA BOUNDARY
··········	FITNESS TRAIL
④	EXERCISE STATIONS
	TRAIL LENGTH – 2 MILES

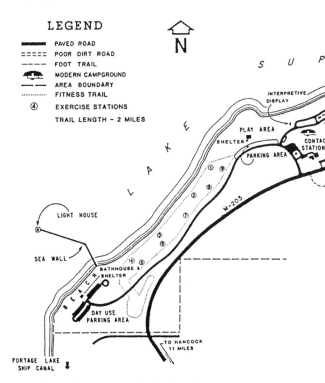

Location

F.J. McLain State Park is located in the heart of Copper Country, 9 miles north of Hancock and 7 miles west of Calumet on M-203. The 417-acre park is on the shoreline of Lake Superior; bluffs overlook a thin strip of beach that is almost 2 miles long.

Facilities & Activities

103 modern campsites
  electrical hookups
  flush toilets
  showers
  sanitation station
9 rustic campsites
  vault toilets
  hand pump
rent-a-tent
1 rustic cabin (sleeps 8)
picnic area
picnic shelter
playground
swimming
beach house and concession
fishing
sea wall for fishing
boating
hiking trail
10 km of cross-country ski trails
fitness trail with exercise stations

Michigan has thousands of miles of cross-country ski trails; on "Cross-Country Day" many parks and resorts offer free admission, clinics, and equipment rental.

Muskallonge Lake State Park

For Information

Muskallonge Lake State Park
Route 1, Box 245
Newberry, MI 49868
(906) 658-3338

LEGEND

- - - - PARK BOUNDARY   ·—·· GRAVEL ROAD
———— PAVED ROAD

🚐 CAMPGROUND   🏊 BEACH

🏢 HEADQUARTERS   🚤 BOAT LAUNCH

🏕 PICNIC AREA   🚽 SANITATION STATION

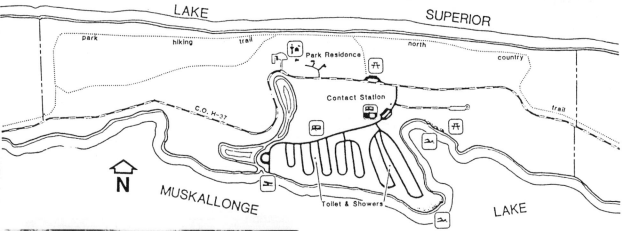

Playgrounds, usually located near the picnic area, provide great family fun.

Location

Muskallonge Lake State Park is located 28 miles north of Newberry; take M-123 north from Newberry to Four Mile Corner, turn left on County Road 407 (also listed as H-37), and follow that road to the park. The 217-acre park is the site of Deer Park, a lumber town of the late 1800s. Lumber was shipped from a large dock that extended into Lake Superior. Muskallonge Lake was a mill pond for logs brought to it by narrow gauge railroad lines. Today, sandy beaches offer swimming in Muskallonge Lake and the stoney shore of Lake Superior lures rockhounds to search for agates and colorful stones.

Facilities & Activities

179 modern campsites
  electrical hookups
  flush toilets
  showers
  sanitation station
picnic area
playground
swimming
beach house
fishing
boating
boat launch
hiking trails
portion of North Country Trail

This lone beach walker is probably searching for agates along the Lake Superior shore.

Ottawa National Forest

For Information

Forest Supervisor's Office
Ottawa National Forest
2100 E. Cloverland Drive
Ironwood, MI 49938
(906) 932-1330 or 1-800-562-1201 (toll free in Upper Peninsula)

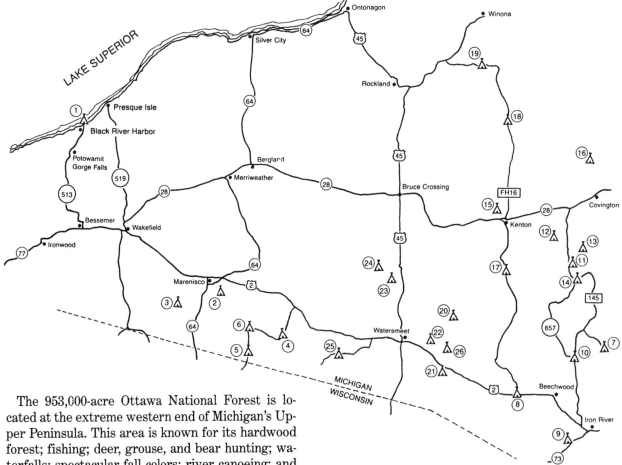

The 953,000-acre Ottawa National Forest is located at the extreme western end of Michigan's Upper Peninsula. This area is known for its hardwood forest; fishing; deer, grouse, and bear hunting; waterfalls; spectacular fall colors; river canoeing; and plentiful winter snows. The Ottawa National Forest is "Waterfall Country"; there are trails to many of the forest's waterfalls while others require map and compass to view. Summers are cool, and snowfall begins in late October or November and lasts until April.

Materials are available from each of the District Ranger offices, as well as from the office of the Forest Supervisor, on recreational opportunities on the Ottawa National Forest. Contact these offices for maps and specific information on items such as fishing, hunting, trails, winter activities, river trips for canoeists, opening and closing dates for campgrounds, and wilderness areas.

Camping

The twenty-six campgrounds of the Ottawa National Forest offer a wide spectrum of camping experiences. All are accessible by road and serve both tent and trailer campers. Most are located on lakes or streams and offer fishing and swimming opportunities. All campgrounds include picnic tables, tent pads, fire grates, and toilet facilities. Most can accommodate trailers up to 22 feet in length. Only 3 campgrounds have no water supply.

The three campgrounds with the most highly developed facilities are Lake Ottawa, Sylvania, and

Ottawa National Forest (*continued*)

Black River Harbor. A nightly fee is charged at most campgrounds for the summer recreation period when full services are provided; several campgrounds are available free of charge. During the early spring and late fall when services are reduced, the fees at some sites are reduced or waived. The seasons vary, but most campgrounds are open by May 15; some open as early as May 1. Most campgrounds close after Labor Day, although some remain open into the fall.

All camping is on a first-come, first-served basis, except at several campgrounds so noted. For these, reservations can be made, for a small additional fee, via check or credit card, through MISTIX at 1-800-283-CAMP. Reservations for the group camping facilities at Marion Lake can be made by calling the Watersmeet Ranger District.

With a few exceptions, the public lands within the boundary of the Ottawa National Forest are open to backcountry camping. Such campers should be prepared to pack in their water supply and pack out their trash. Fires are permitted but use of camp stoves is recommended for remote-area camping. Low-impact camping techniques that leave an area undisturbed are encouraged. Snowmobiling is allowed on all unplowed Forest Service roads unless the road has been designated and signed as being closed to snowmobiles.

Wilderness Areas

There are three areas managed as Wilderness under the National Wilderness Preservation System. Their use is regulated to the extent necessary for their protection and public safety. You will need proper equipment and outdoor skills to safely enjoy many of their unique opportunities. These areas do not include roads so you must travel on foot or by canoe; camping is permitted.

Sturgeon River Gorge Wilderness is located 3 miles north of Sidnaw and 35 miles south of Houghton. Access to this 14,139-acre wilderness is primarily from the south near Sidnaw via M-28, Pequet Lake Road, and Sturgeon Gorge Road. Sturgeon River Campground is just outside the wilderness boundary to the southeast. Major scenic attractions of this wilderness are the Sturgeon River, its rapids and falls, and the Gorge itself.

Sylvania Wilderness is located 3 miles southwest of Watersmeet, adjacent to the Wisconsin/Michigan border. Access to this 18,327-acre wilderness is from County Road 535 off of US 2, west of Waters-

In addition to its canoeing and water-access camping opportunities, the Sylvania Wilderness contains nearly 30 miles of foot trails. Overnight campers must stay at one of the 84 wilderness campsites.

meet. Sylvania's rolling hills and 4,000 acres of deep, clear lakes were shaped by glaciers thousands of years ago. Almost all of Sylvania's 35 lakes are landlocked, fed by springs, bogs, and precipitation. Six of Sylvania's 35 lakes are more than 250 acres in size. The wilderness contains nearly 30 miles of foot trails that are suited for both day hiking and overnight trips.

There are 84 designated campsites in 29 locations bordering many of the larger lakes in the wilderness. A permit is required; register for sites at the Visitor Information Station. Each campsite has an outdoor toilet and 2 or 3 individual camping areas, each with a tent pad, fire grill, and table. Wells or pumps are not provided and lake water is not drinkable, so carry in drinking water or boil lake water at least 5 minutes.

McCormick Wilderness is located about 35 miles east of the main body of the Ottawa National Forest. Marquette is located 50 miles to the east. The 16,850-acre Wilderness is administered by the Kenton Ranger District. The area can be reached by going 3 miles west of Champion on M-28 and then north on County Road 607 for 8 miles. Access to the interior of McCormick Wilderness is limited; a 3-mile foot trail connects County Road 607 with White Deer Lake. More than 100 miles of hiking trails once crossed the area, but these have fallen into disuse and are generally difficult to locate.

The lay of the land at McCormick is varied, ranging from nearly level ground to rocky cliffs and outcrops; there are 18 small lakes. The area straddles the divide between the Lake Superior and Lake Michigan watersheds. The major attractions of the Wilderness are the waterfalls on the Yellow Dog River. The rugged McCormick Wilderness has

Recreational Trails

There's something for everyone in the way of hiking trails on the Ottawa National Forest. The more than 196 miles of hiking and backpacking trails vary widely in character. Some provide short easy walks to points of interest, such as waterfalls and historic sites, while others offer opportunity for challenging cross-country travel.

Some of the forest's most popular trails are located in the Black River Harbor area. These trails provide access to Great Conglomerate, Gorge, Potawatomi, Sandstone, and Rainbow falls and range in length from ¼ to 1½ miles. All trails descend rather steeply from the rim of the Black River gorge to overlook points. Because of its unique character, the trail that serves Gorge and Potawatomi falls was designated a National Recreation Trail in 1978. Developments along it include stairways and observation platforms that overlook the Black River and the two waterfalls.

The *North Country Trail* is a federally legislated National Scenic Trail. When completed, it will extend 3,200 miles from the Appalachian Trail in Vermont to the Lewis and Clark Trail in North Dakota. About 118 miles of the North Country National Scenic Trail cross the Ottawa National Forest. The trail is challenging; it traverses areas of very rugged topography and is often several miles from the nearest motor vehicle access point. Most stream crossings are without bridges. There are no developed campsites available except at Black River Harbor on Lake Superior, Porcupine Mountain Wilderness State Park at Presque Isle, Bob Lake Campground, and Sturgeon River Campground close to the trail's east end. Trailside camping is permitted.

The trail across the Ottawa National Forest is being constructed in segments. For information on the trail, contact the District Ranger responsible for the particular segment of the trail: Bessemer District Ranger for the Black River segment; Bergland District Ranger for the Bergland segment; Kenton District Ranger for the Sturgeon River segment; and Ontonagon District Ranger for the Victoria segments.

Canoeing

More than 300 miles of floatable/canoeable rivers and 500 lakes await the canoeist. M-28 separates two distinct kinds of canoeing opportunities in the Ottawa National Forest. The portion of the Forest lying south of M-28 is relatively flat. Hundreds of small lakes dot the landscape, especially toward the Wisconsin border. Rivers in this portion of the forest range from flat water with moderate currents to small rapids. In contrast, the area lying north of M-28 is rugged, with fast water, rock ledges, and waterfalls that must be portaged.

Some of Michigan's most powerful waterfalls are found in the western part of the Upper Peninsula on the wild Presque Isle River of the Porcupines and the Black River in Ottawa National Forest.

Bessemer Ranger District

For Information

Bessemer Ranger District
500 North Moore Street
Bessemer, MI 49911
(906) 667-0261

Campground Locations

Black River Harbor is 15 miles due north of Bessemer on County Road 513. It is located on Lake Superior, adjacent to a picturesque harbor and waterfalls area (Rainbow, Sandstone, Great Conglomerate, Potawatomi, and Gorge). The recreation area also has an enclosed pavilion, 60 picnic tables, a playground area, space for transient boaters, and a concessionaire.

Bobcat Lake is 3 miles southeast of Marenisco off of US 2 and M-64. Just south of town, go east across from Rose's Canteena; proceed ½ mile until you cross a bridge; then turn south on Saari Road and proceed to the campground.

Henry Lake is southwest of Marenisco off of M-64; go south for 5 miles, turn right on Forest Hwy 123 and go west for 5 miles to the campground.

Langford Lake is 20 miles southeast of Marenisco; go east on US 2 for 12 miles, turn right on County Road 527 (South Thayer Road) and go 5 miles, then left on Langford Lake Road to the campground.

Moosehead Lake is 16 miles southeast of Marenisco; go south on M-64 for 4½ miles; turn left on Forest Hwy 323 and go to Pomeroy Lake Road; turn left and go to the intersection of County Road 525 and Forest Hwy 118; turn right on Forest Hwy 118 and follow signs to the campground.

Pomeroy Lake is southeast of Marenisco; go east on US 2 for 10 miles and turn right on County Road 525 (also called Forest Hwy 318); go 6 miles and turn right on Langford Lake Road (still County Road 525) and follow signs to the campground.

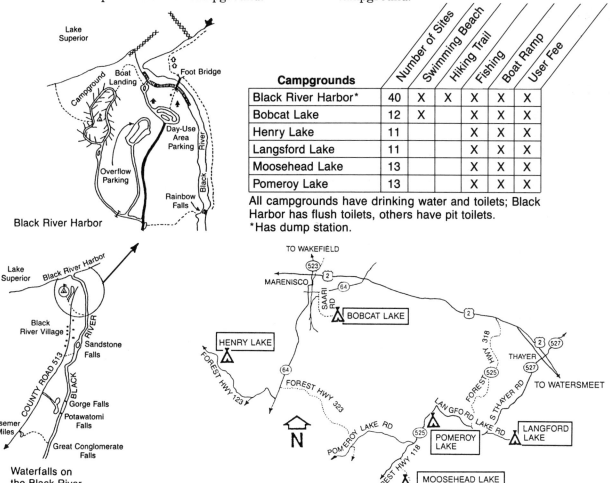

Campgrounds	Number of Sites	Swimming Beach	Hiking Trail	Fishing	Boat Ramp	User Fee
Black River Harbor*	40	X	X	X	X	X
Bobcat Lake	12	X		X	X	X
Henry Lake	11			X	X	X
Langsford Lake	11			X	X	X
Moosehead Lake	13			X	X	X
Pomeroy Lake	13			X	X	X

All campgrounds have drinking water and toilets; Black Harbor has flush toilets, others have pit toilets.
*Has dump station.

Black River Harbor

Waterfalls on the Black River

Iron River Ranger District

For Information

Iron River Ranger District
801 Adams
Iron River, MI 49935
(906) 265-5139

The Ottawa National Forest has 26 campgrounds; each is located on a lake or stream and offers the opportunity to fish.

Campground Locations

Blockhouse Campground is 20 miles north of Iron River via US 2 and County Road 657. Near Gibbs City when County Road 657 turns left, continue on due north on Forest Hwy 137 until Forest Hwy 347 veers right; follow Forest Hwy 347 to the campground.

Golden Lake is 14 miles northwest of Iron River. Travel west on US 2; the campground is less than a mile north of US 2 on Forest Hwy 16.

Lake Ottawa is 7 miles west of Iron River. Go west on US 2 for 1½ miles, then left on M-73 for 1 mile and right on Forest Hwy 101 for 4 miles.

Paint River Forks is 13 miles north of Iron River. Travel west on US 2 for 3 miles, then north on County Road 657 about 1½ miles past Gibbs City.

Campgrounds	Number of Sites	Swimming Beach	Hiking Trail	Fishing	Boat Ramp	User Fee
Blockhouse	2			X		
Golden Lake	22			X	X	X
Lake Ottawa*	32	X	X	X	X	X
Paint River Forks	4			X		

Lake Ottawa has flush toilets, others have pit toilets; Blockhouse and Paint River Forks do **not** have drinking water.
*Has dump station.

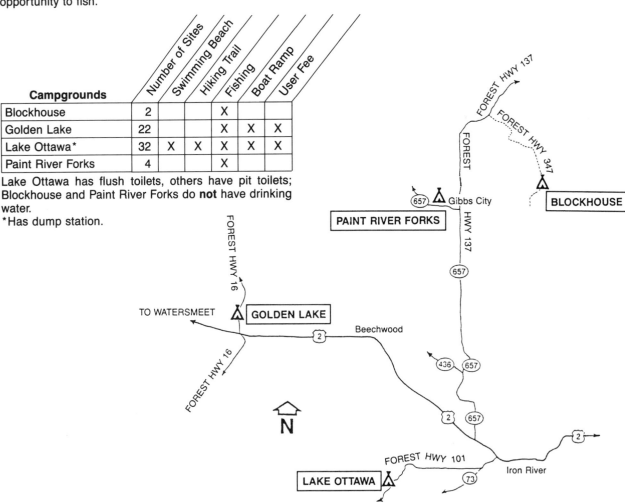

Kenton Ranger District

For Information

Kenton Ranger District
P.O. Box 198
Kenton, MI 49943
(906) 852-3500

You're never too young to wet a line!

Campgrounds	Number of Sites	Swimming Beach	Hiking Trail	Fishing	Boat Ramp	User Fee
Lake Ste. Kathryn*	25	X		X	X	X
Lower Dam	7			X		X
Norway Lake*	28	X	X	X	X	X
Perch Lake–West*	20			X	X	X
Sparrow Rapids	6		X	X		X
Sturgeon River	9			X		X
Tepee Lake	17	X	X	X	X	X

All campgrounds have drinking water and pit toilets.
*On reservation system (1-800-283-CAMP).

Campground Locations

Lake Ste. Kathryn is 8 miles south of Sidnaw and M-28 via the Sidnaw South Road and Forest Hwy 137.

Lower Dam is 7 miles southeast of Kenton; travel south on Forest Hwy 16, then east on Lake Thirteen Road, then south on Lower Dam Road to the campground. Or from Sidnaw, go south on Sidnaw South Road, west on Lake Thirteen Road, then south on Lower Dam Road.

Norway Lake is 8 miles south of Sidnaw and M-28 via the Sidnaw South Road and Norway Lake Road.

Perch Lake is 11 miles south of Sidnaw and M-28. Travel south on the Sidnaw South Road and continue south on Forest Hwy 137. Look for the Perch Lake sign; the campground is about a mile east of Forest Hwy 137.

Sparrow Rapids is 4 miles northwest of Kenton and M-28. Go north on Forest Hwy 16 and turn left (west) within a half mile; this road follows the East Branch of the Ontonagon River to the campground, which is on the left.

Sturgeon River is 7 miles northeast of Sidnaw and M-28. Travel north on Pequet Lake Road; when Markey Lake Road goes left, continue right on Sturgeon Gorge Road to the campground.

Tepee Lake is 7 miles south of Kenton and M-28. Travel south on Forest Hwy 16, then east on Forest Hwy 143 to the campground.

Ontonagon Ranger District

For Information

Ontonagon Ranger District
Ontonagon, MI 49953
(906) 884-2085

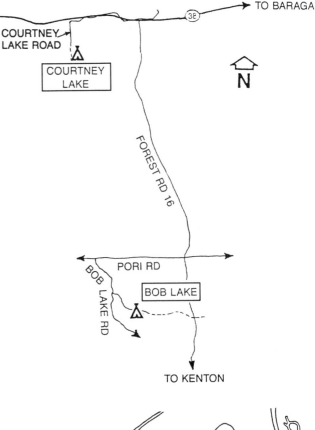

The Ottawa National Forest offers almost 200 miles of hiking and backpacking trails; some are short, easy walks while others offer opportunities for challenging cross-country travel.

Campgrounds	Number of Sites	Swimming Beach	Hiking Trail	Fishing	Boat Ramp	User Fee
Bob Lake	17	X	X	X	X	X
Courtney Lake	21	X		X	X	X

Both campgrounds have drinking water and pit toilets.

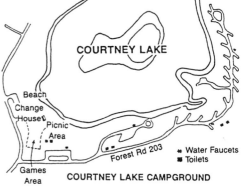

COURTNEY LAKE CAMPGROUND

Campground Locations

Bob Lake is north of Kenton and M-28 and southeast of Greenland and M-38. From M-38, travel south on Forest Hwy 16, turn right (west) on Pori Road, then left on Bob Lake Road, and follow signs to the campground.

Courtney Lake is 8 miles east of Greenland via M-38 and Courtney Lake Road.

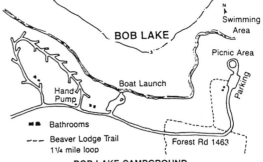

BOB LAKE CAMPGROUND

Watersmeet Ranger District

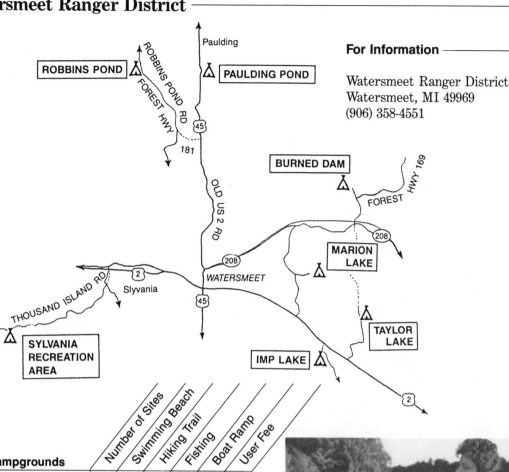

Paulding

ROBBINS POND

PAULDING POND

ROBBINS POND RD

FOREST HWY

45

181

OLD US 2 RD

BURNED DAM

FOREST HWY 169

208

MARION LAKE

208

WATERSMEET

2

Slyvania

45

THOUSAND ISLAND RD

535

SYLVANIA RECREATION AREA

IMP LAKE

TAYLOR LAKE

2

For Information

Watersmeet Ranger District
Watersmeet, MI 49969
(906) 358-4551

Campgrounds	Number of Sites	Swimming Beach	Hiking Trail	Fishing	Boat Ramp	User Fee
Burned Dam	6			X		
Imp Lake	21	X	X	X	X	X
Marion Lake*	30	X	X	X	X	X
Paulding Pond	4			X	X	
Robbins Pond	3			X		
Sylvania**	35	X	X	X	X	X
Taylor Lake	6			X	X	

All campgrounds have drinking water except Burned Dam;
Sylvania has flush toilets, all others have pit toilets.
 * Has a group camping area; maximum 100; available
   by reservation.
** Also has 84 wilderness sites.

Dogs enjoy camping, too, but remember that, at most campgrounds, pets must be kept under immediate control on a leash not exceeding 6 feet.

Campground Locations

Burned Dam is 7 miles northeast of Watersmeet. From US 45, north of Watersmeet, turn east on County Road 208 (Old US 2 Road), then left on Forest Hwy 169.

Imp Lake is 6 miles southeast of Watersmeet just off of US 2; watch for signs; the campground is on the right about a mile off the highway.

Marion Lake is 5 miles east of Watersmeet via US 2 and left on Marion Lake Road; or from County Road 208, turn right on Marion Lake Road.

Paulding Pond is 8 miles north of Watersmeet on US 45; the campground is on the right.

Robbins Pond is 9 miles northwest of Watersmeet via US 45, then left on Robbins Pond Road (Forest Hwy 181).

Sylvania is 8 miles southwest of Watersmeet via US 2 and County Road 535 (Thousand Island Road); follow the signs to the Sylvania Recreation Area.

Taylor Lake is 8 miles southeast of Watersmeet via US 2, then left on Taylor Lake Road; the campground is about 2 miles from the highway.

Pictured Rocks National Lakeshore

A close-up view of the rocks along the National Lakeshore that have been sculpted into arches and other formations.

For Information

Pictured Rocks National Lakeshore
P.O. Box 40
Munising, MI 49862-0040
(906) 387-2607

▲ Campground

Boat launch

Lifeguarded swimming area

Interpretive trail

Handicap access

Inland Buffer Zone

Lakeshore Zone

Trail

Access route to lakeshore

Unpaved road

From this point west, H-58 is unpaved.

Sable Falls

Au Sable Light Station

Grand Sable Dunes

Grand Sable Lake

77

RHODY CREEK

TRUCK TRAIL

LAKE SUPERIOR STATE FOREST

TRUCK TRAIL

HURRICANE

ADAMS TRAIL ROAD

H58

Twelvemile Beach

LAKE SUPERIOR

ROCKS LAKESHORE TRAIL

PICTURED

Beaver Lake

Beaver Basin

From this point east, H-58 is unpaved.

H58

Melstrand

Van Meer

H58

H15

HIAWATHA NATIONAL FOREST

Chapel Basin

ROCKS

LAKESHORE TRAIL

PICTURED

Miners Castle Overlook

MINERS CASTLE ROAD

Munising Falls

Grand Island

Sand Point

Wetmore

94-28

94

Pictured Rocks National Lakeshore *(continued)*

Location

Pictured Rocks National Lakeshore is located on the Lake Superior shore of Michigan's Upper Peninsula. It can be reached either from M-28 and M-94 at Munising or M-77 at Grand Marais. County Road H-58 leads directly into the park. The 72,899-acre park, authorized in October 1966 as the first national lakeshore, consists of the Lakeshore Zone, which is primarily Park Service-owned, and the Inland Buffer Zone, which is in mixed public and private ownership. A U.S. Forest Service/National Park Service visitor information center is located at the intersection of M-28 and County Road H-58 in Munising; it is the prinicipal location to obtain information about the attractions and recreational opportunities of Pictured Rocks.

About the Lakeshore

Pictured Rocks National Lakeshore, only 3 miles wide at its widest point, hugs the Lake Superior shoreline for more than 40 miles. The Pictured Rocks, for which the park is named, rise directly from the lake to heights of 50 to 200 feet and extend northeastward for 15 miles from the town of Munising. This wall of rock has been sculpted into caves, arches, and formations; the play of light upon the cliffs changes with each passing hour. One of the most popular ways to see the Pictured Rocks is by boat. From June to mid-October, tour boats leave Munising daily.

Beyond the Pictured Rocks is a sand-and-pebble strand known as Twelvemile Beach, and at the northern end of the park are the Au Sable Light Station, Grand Sable Banks, and Grand Sable Dunes. Much of the land is covered with a mixture of northern hardwoods, pine, hemlock, spruce, and fir along with small lakes, ponds, and streams. Pictured Rocks National Lakeshore is known as a "four season" recreation area; each season offers its own unique recreational opportunities in a spectacular environment of cliffs, beaches, sand dunes, waterfalls, and forests.

General Park Information

▲ The visitor information center is open year-round; phone (906) 387-3700.
▲ The Munising Falls Interpretive Center is open daily during the summer season; located

The wall of rocks rises directly from Lake Superior to heights of 50 to 200 feet.

at the beginning of Sand Point Road, it has exhibits describing natural and cultural history of the park.
▲ The Grand Sable Visitor Center is open Wednesday through Sunday during the summer; it is located on County Road H-58 just west of Grand Marais.
▲ The Grand Marais Maritime Museum is open on Saturday and Sunday during the summer; located on Coast Guard Point in Grand Marais, it has exhibits on the early years of shipping, shipwrecks, lighthouses, etc.
▲ The park headquarters office is open year-round, Monday through Friday; it is located on Sand Point, northeast of Munising.
▲ Throughout the summer, the park offers a wide range of interpretive programs.
▲ From June to mid-October, commercially operated scenic cruises leave Munising daily; the

complete trip is more than 37 miles and takes 2½ to 3 hours.

▲ Scuba diving is popular in the Alger Underwater Preserve, which extends from Au Train (west of Munising) to Au Sable Point; the preserve contains large colorful rocks, weed beds with fish, and a dozen shipwrecks. (See *Diving and Snorkeling Guide to the Great Lakes* by Kathy Johnson and Greg Lashabrook; Pisces Books, Houston, TX, 1991, for more detailed information on scuba diving in this area.)

▲ For information on the scenic boat cruises, as well as for charter boats for scuba-diving trips, contact the Alger Chamber of Commerce, P.O. Box 405, Munising, MI 49862, phone (906) 387-2138.

Courtesy Michigan Travel Bureau

There's no doubt about it . . . fishing in Michigan is indeed a year-round sport.

▲ The inland lakes and streams offer a variety of fishing opportunities; in winter, ice fishing is good on Munising Bay and most inland lakes; a Michigan fishing license is required.

▲ Hunting is permitted; a Michigan hunting license is required; ask for the brochure on fishing & hunting.

▲ The Beaver Lakes and Grand Sable Lake offer opportunities for canoeing and small boating; launch ramps are located at Munising and Grand Marais for access to Lake Superior for motor boats large enough to handle the rough water.

▲ The 42.8-mile Lakeshore Trail, a component of the North Country National Scenic Trail, runs along the shore the entire length of the park.

▲ A network of hiking and interpretive trails, as well as many old logging roads, provide numerous hiking possibilities; ask for the brochure on day hikes.

▲ Insect repellant is a must if you plan to come in the late spring or early summer; blackflies and mosquitoes are out in force.

▲ Poison ivy is alive and well in the park; learn what it looks like and caution others with you.

▲ Some Lakeshore cliffs are up to 200 feet high; stay back from cliff edges and overhangs as the sandstone outcroppings are unstable.

▲ Autumn is one of the best times to hike, explore the beaches, and to camp at either the vehicle-accessible or backcountry campsites.

▲ Heavy snows close park roads from about November to May; campers may still enter the park on designated snowmobile routes, or by crosscountry skiing or snowshoeing.

▲ An average annual snowfall of 200 inches provides a winter wonderland for winter campers and snowshoers.

▲ Cross-country skiers have access to 17 miles of groomed and tracked trails as well as "out back" bushwhacking.

▲ Snowmobilers can traverse 50 miles of designated routes.

Camping Information

Car Camping

▲ 3 campgrounds are accessible by car: Little Beaver Lake (8 sites), Twelvemile Beach (37 sites), and Hurricane River (22 sites).

▲ All campgrounds have picnic tables, grills, toilets, and water; water is available only from early May to mid-November.

Pictured Rocks National Lakeshore *(continued)*

▲ All campgrounds are available on first-come, first-served basis; a fee is charged.

▲ You must register upon arrival; stays are limited to 14 days.

▲ Handicapped-accessible campsites and toilets are available at each campground.

▲ Other public campgrounds in the local area can be found in Hiawatha National Forest and the Lake Superior State Forest.

Backcountry Camping

▲ Camping is permitted only at designated campsites within established backcountry campgrounds or at specified group sites.

▲ 13 campgrounds and 7 group sites are spaced every 2 to 5 miles along the Lakeshore Trail.

▲ Only 2 sites have toilets; water is not available.

▲ Water should be treated; only water obtained from park water systems can be assumed safe for drinking.

▲ Use of backpacking stoves is encouraged; campfires are allowed only in communal metal fire rings; beach fires are not permitted.

▲ Campers should practice low-impact, wilderness camping methods; all trash must be carried out.

▲ Permits are required; thirty percent of the individual sites and all of the group sites are available by advance reservation. Phone (906) 387-3700 for reservations and information.

▲ Party size for each campsite is limited to 8; groups consisting of 9–20 can be accommodated in designated group campsites.

▲ Only foot and boat traffic is permitted in the backcountry; motorized or wheeled vehicles, pets, and domestic pack animals are prohibited.

▲ Those planning to camp in the backcountry should obtain the *Backcountry Camping* handout; it shows the locations of the designated campgrounds as well as regulations governing the backcountry.

Courtesy Michigan Travel Bureau

Michiganders claim that the snow in Michigan is "different" because of the "lake-effect"; one thing is certain—the visual effect is outstanding!

Recreational Activities

camping
picnicking
hiking
swimming
canoeing/boating
fishing
hunting
ranger-led interpretive programs
commercial boat tours
scuba diving
winter camping
cross-country skiing
snowshoeing
ice fishing
snowmobiling

Pictured Rocks National Lakeshore is known as a "four season" recreation area; even winter camping is popular.

Porcupine Mountains Wilderness State Park

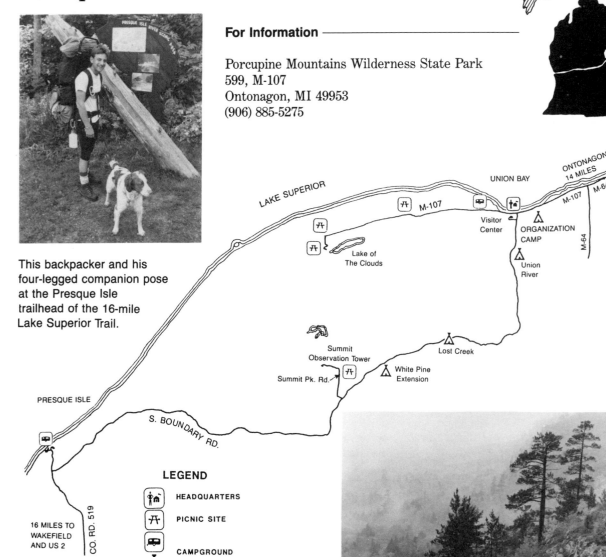

This backpacker and his four-legged companion pose at the Presque Isle trailhead of the 16-mile Lake Superior Trail.

For Information

Porcupine Mountains Wilderness State Park
599, M-107
Ontonagon, MI 49953
(906) 885-5275

ONTONAGON 14 MILES

UNION BAY

LAKE SUPERIOR

M-107

M-64

Visitor Center

ORGANIZATION CAMP

Lake of The Clouds

Union River

Summit Observation Tower

Lost Creek

Summit Pk. Rd.

White Pine Extension

PRESQUE ISLE

S. BOUNDARY RD.

CO. RD. 519

16 MILES TO WAKEFIELD AND US 2

LEGEND

👤🏠	HEADQUARTERS
🏕	PICNIC SITE
🚐 ⛺	CAMPGROUND

The "Porkies" exhibit a special mystique in a heavy fog; the park is one of the few remaining large wilderness areas in the Midwest.

Courtesy Michigan Travel Bureau

Location

Porcupine Mountains Wilderness State Park is 15 miles west of Ontonagon; take M-64 to Silver City, then M-107 to the park. This 63,000-acre park is one of the few remaining large wilderness areas in the Midwest. All park visitors should plan to begin at the Visitor Center near the junction of M-107 and South Boundary Road. There you will be able to view interesting displays and a slide show, and obtain maps and information that will help you plan your visit to the "Porkies." There are several campgrounds: a modern campground is at Union Bay, a semi-modern campground is at the mouth of the Presque Isle River, and three rustic camping areas are located along the South Boundary Road.

Porcupine Mountains Wilderness State Park (*continued*)

Facilities & Activities at the Union Bay Area ——

100 modern campsites
  electrical hookups
  flush toilets
  showers
  sanitation station
Interpretive Center
picnic area
picnic shelter
playground
hunting
fishing
boating
boat launch
access to more than 90 miles of hiking/backpacking
  trails
snowmobiling
40.2 km of cross-country ski trails
cross-country ski rental
downhill ski area

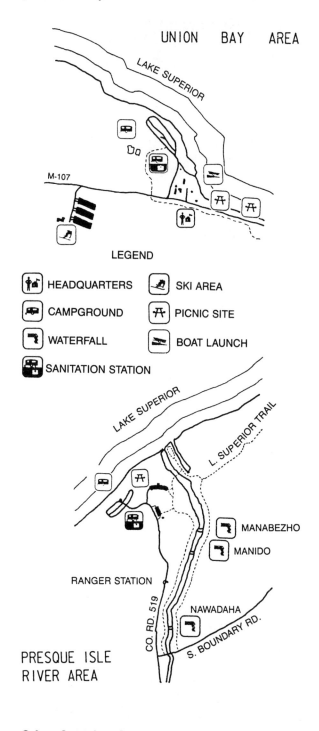

UNION BAY AREA

LAKE SUPERIOR

M-107

LEGEND

👤 HEADQUARTERS		🎿 SKI AREA	
🚐 CAMPGROUND		🏕 PICNIC SITE	
🏞 WATERFALL		🚤 BOAT LAUNCH	
🚐 SANITATION STATION			

LAKE SUPERIOR

L. SUPERIOR TRAIL

MANABEZHO

MANIDO

RANGER STATION

NAWADAHA

CO. RD. 519

S. BOUNDARY RD.

PRESQUE ISLE
RIVER AREA

The three waterfalls in the Presque Isle River Area are
accessible via hiking trails from the campground.

Facilities & Activities at the Presque Isle River Area ——

88 semi-modern campsites
  flush toilets
  showers
  sanitation station
picnic area
playground
hunting
fishing
boating
access to more than 90 miles of hiking/backpacking
  trails

Other Camping Areas ——

16 rustic cabins (each sleeps 2–8)
organization campground (rustic)
3 rustic campgrounds (vault toilet & hand pump)
  3 campsites at Union River
  3 campsites at Lost Creek
  8 campsites at White Pine Extension

Straits State Park

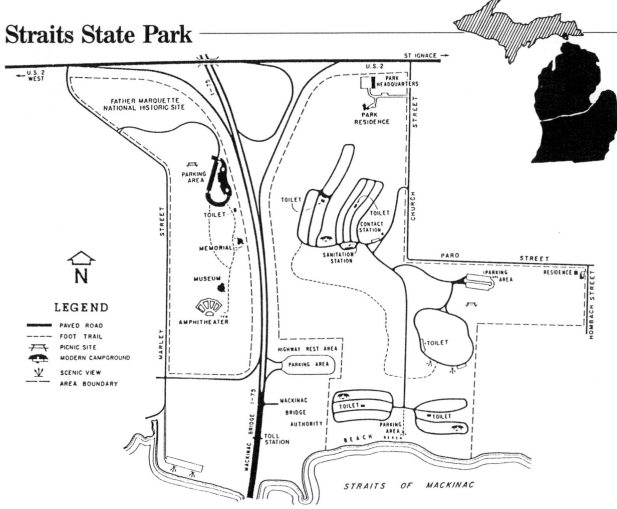

Location

Straits State Park is located in St. Ignace off of Church Street, just south of US 2. The 181-acre park lies to the immediate east of I-75, while Father Marquette National Historic Site lies to the immediate west of I-75, accessible from US 2 via Marley Street. The two parks afford fine views of the Mackinac bridge, straits, and islands.

For Information

Straits State Park
720 Church Street
St. Ignace, MI 49781
(906) 643-8620

Straits State Park's beach is on the Straits of Mackinac; it affords a great view of the Mackinac bridge.

Facilities & Activities

322 modern campsites
  electrical hookups
  flush toilets
  showers
  sanitation station
organization campground
museum, memorial structure, and amphitheater at
  the Father Marquette National Historic Site
picnic area
playground
swimming
boating
hiking trail

Tahquamenon Falls State Park

The Tahquamenon River flows through the state park, creating the Upper Falls and the Lower Falls. A maximum flow of more than 50,000 gallons of water per second has been recorded cascading over the Upper Falls, pictured here.

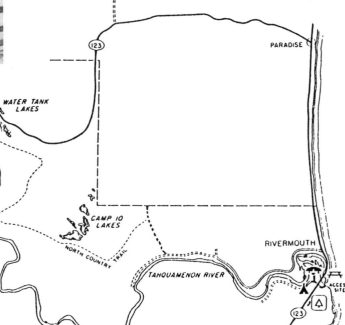

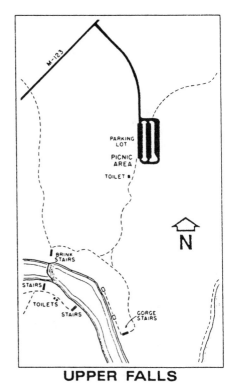

UPPER FALLS

For Information

Tahquamenon Falls State Park
Star Route 48, Box 225
Paradise, MI 49768
(906) 492-3415

Location

Tahquamenon Falls State Park is the second largest state park in Michigan; it extends over 13 miles and contains more than 35,000 acres. There are three developed units within the park: the Upper Falls unit, the Lower Falls unit, and the Rivermouth unit. All three units are accessible from M-123. The Upper Falls is one of the largest waterfalls east of the Mississippi River; it has a drop of nearly 50 feet and is more than 200 feet across. This unit does not have a campground; the Lower Falls unit has 2 modern campgrounds, and the Rivermouth unit has both a modern and a rustic campground. Backpack camping areas are also available.

Tahquamenon Falls State Park (*continued*)

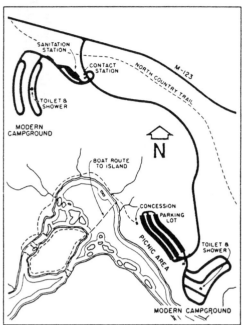

LOWER FALLS

Facilities & Activities at Lower Falls Campground

183 modern campsites
  electrical hookups
  flush toilets
  showers
  sanitation station
picnic area
picnic shelter
playground
concession
hunting
fishing
rowboat/canoe rental
hiking trails
portion of North Country Trail
snowmobiling
cross-country skiing

Facilities & Activities at Rivermouth Campground

76 modern campsites
  electrical hookups
  flush toilets
  showers
  sanitation station

60 rustic campsites
  vault toilets
  hand pump
organization campground
picnic area
picnic shelter
hunting
fishing
boating
boat launch
hiking
snowmobiling
cross-country skiing

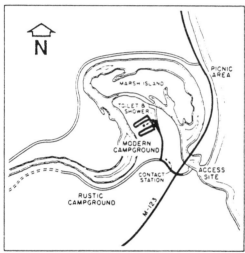

RIVERMOUTH

The Lower Falls, four miles downstream from the Upper Falls, are not as large but are equally beautiful.

Twin Lakes State Park

LEGEND

—— PAVED ROAD
▭▭ GRAVEL ROAD
------ FOOT TRAIL
— — AREA BOUNDARY
⊼ PICNIC SITE
🚍 MODERN CAMPGROUND

N

HOUGHTON
28 MILES

LAKE

ROLAND

CONTACT STATION

BEACH HOUSE

BOAT RAMP

TOILET

BEACH

PICNIC SHELTER

SANITATION STATION

TOILET

NATURE TRAIL

STATE FOREST SNOWMOBILE TRAIL M-26

PARK RESIDENCE

HEADQUARTERS

Two hikers, with their dogs on leashes, enjoy a stroll along the nature trail.

For Information

Twin Lakes State Park
M-26, Twin Lakes Route
Toivola, MI 49965
(906) 288-3321

Location

Twin Lakes State Park is located on M-26, 28 miles southwest of Houghton and 3 miles northeast of Winona. Heavily wooded, the 175-acre park is located on the shoreline of Lake Roland, known as one of the warmest inland lakes in the Upper Peninsula.

Facilities & Activities

62 modern campsites
  electrical hookups
  flush toilets
  showers
  sanitation station
picnic area
picnic shelter
playground
swimming
beach house
fishing
boating
boat launch
hiking trail
snowmobiling
cross-country skiing

Van Riper State Park

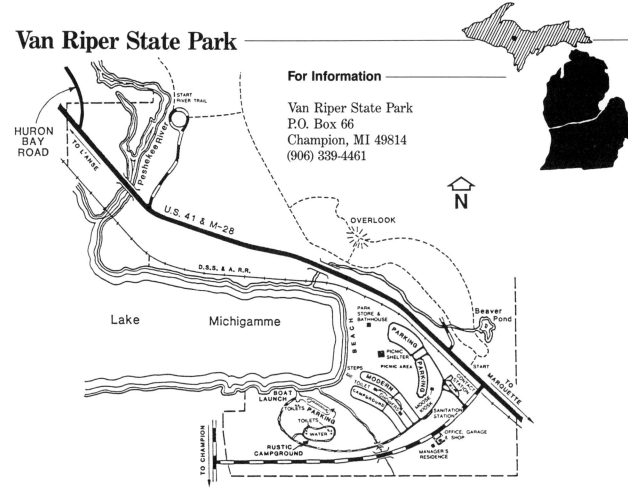

Location

Van Riper State Park is located 31 miles west of Marquette, or a mile beyond Champion on US 41/M-38. The 1,200-acre park contains ½ mile of frontage on the east end of Lake Michigamme with a fine sand beach, and 1½ miles of frontage on the Peshekee River.

The fine sand and moderate water temperature make the swimming beach at Van Riper the place to be on a summer afternoon.

Facilities & Activities

151 modern campsites
  electrical hookups
  flush toilets
  showers
  sanitation station
75 rustic campsites
  vault toilets
  hand pump
rent-a-tent
organization campground
picnic area
picnic shelter
playground
swimming
bathhouse and park store
hunting
fishing
boating
boat launch
hiking trails

Wells State Park

For Information

Wells State Park
M-35
Cedar River, MI 49813
(906) 863-8747

Now this is something you don't see very often . . . four bicycles on one rack!

COUNTY ROAD 352

M-35

PARK
ENTRANCE

N

LEGEND

▬▬▬	SURFACE ROAD
....	FOOT TRAIL
🚐	CAMPGROUND
🏚	FRONTIER CABIN
🏖	BEACH
🚻	RESTROOMS
🛉	HEADQUARTERS
🏠	PICNIC SHELTER
⛱	PICNIC AREA
🚽	SANITATION STATION
🏛	STATE LAND

Location

J. W. Wells State Park is located 30 miles southwest of Escanaba, or a mile beyond Cedar River on M-35. The 974-acre, densely wooded park has 3 miles of beach frontage on Lake Michigan's Green Bay.

Facilities & Activities

176 modern campsites
  electrical hookups
  flush toilets
  showers
  sanitation station
organization campground
6 rustic cabins (each sleeps 8 or 12)
picnic area
picnic shelter
playground
swimming
beach house
hunting
fishing
boating
hiking trails
snowmobiling
cross-country skiing

Every camper could wish for a campsite this neat!

Region 2

Colonial Fort Michilimackinac State Park, located at the northern tip of the Lower Peninsula, features a reconstructed fort and a maritime museum. The park has a picnic area but no camping facilities.

Aloha State Park

For Information

Aloha State Park
4347 Third Street
Cheboygan, MI 49721
(616) 625-2522

Location

Aloha State Park is located 9 miles south of Cheboygan via M-27 and M-33. From M-33, turn west on M-212 and travel ¾ miles to the park entrance. The 91-acre park is adjacent to beautiful Mullett Lake, which is part of a 35-mile inland waterway starting at Lake Huron. Both Mullett and Burt Lakes are part of the waterway.

Facilities & Activities

300 modern campsites
   electrical hookups
   flush toilets
   showers
   sanitation station
rent-a-tent
picnic area
picnic shelter
playground
swimming beach
fishing
fishing piers
fish cleaning station
boating
boat launch
boat basin

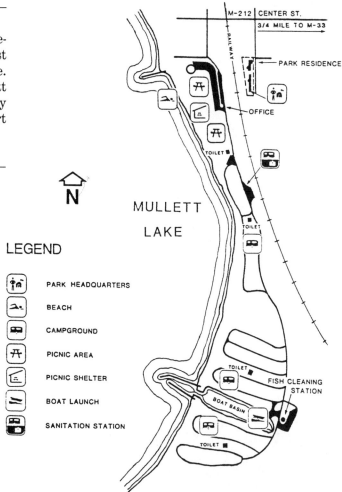

LEGEND

🏫	PARK HEADQUARTERS
🏊	BEACH
🚐	CAMPGROUND
🎋	PICNIC AREA
🏠	PICNIC SHELTER
〰	BOAT LAUNCH
🚐	SANITATION STATION

MULLETT LAKE

Bicycles provide a great means of transportation, particularly when the campground is located a distance from the recreation area.

Au Sable State Forest

For Information

Au Sable State Forest
Route 1, Box 146
Mio, MI 48647
(517) 826-3211

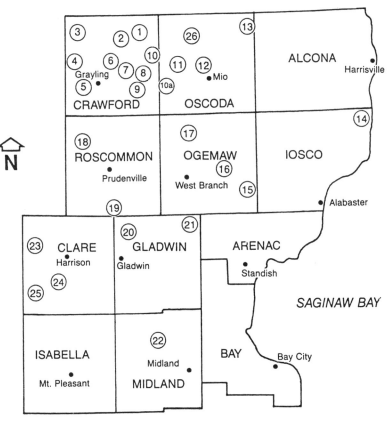

Campground Locations

1. *Shupac Lake*—2 miles north of Lovells via Twin Bridge Road.
2. *Jones Lake*—9 miles east of Frederic via County Road 612.
3. *Upper Manistee River*—6½ miles west of Frederic via County Road 612.
4. *Manistee River Bridge*—8 miles west of Grayling via M-72.
5. *Lake Margrethe*—5 miles west of Grayling via M-72.
6. *Au Sable River Canoe Camp*—7 miles east of Grayling via North Down River Road and Headquarter's Road.
7. *Burton's Landing*—4½ miles east of Grayling via M-72 and Burton's Landing Road.
8. *Keystone Landing*—6 miles east of Grayling via M-72 and Keystone Landing Road.
9. *Canoe Harbor*—14 miles southeast of Grayling via M-72.

Safely secured in a life jacket, this little guy is now ready for a boat ride.

Au Sable State Forest (*continued*)

Campgrounds	Number of Sites	Boating/Canoeing	Swimming	Fishing
1. Shupac Lake	30	B	1	W
2. Jones Lake	42	B	2	W
3. Upper Manistee River	30	C	3	C
4. Manistee River Bridge	23	C	3	C
5. Lake Margrethe	40		1	W
6. Au Sable River Canoe Camp	20	C	3	C
7. Burton's Landing	12	C	3	C
8. Keystone Landing	18	C	3	C
9. Canoe Harbor	45	C	3	C
10. White Pine Canoe Camp		C	3	C
10a. Rainbow Bend	12	C	3	C
11. Parmalee Bridge	7	C	3	C
12. Mio Pond	24	C	2	W
13. McCollum Lake	32	B	2	W
14. Van Etten Lake	62	B	2	W
15. Hardwood Lake	22	B	2	W
16. Rifle River	40	C	3	C
17. Ambrose Lake	30	B	2	W
18. Houghton Lake	50	B	2	W
19. House Lake	41		1	W
20. Trout Lake	35	B	2	C
21. Wildwood	18		3	W
22. Black Creek	22		3	W
23. Temple	25	C	3	W
24. Pike Lake	32		3	W
25. Mud Lake	8	B	3	W
26. Muskrat Lake	10	C	3	W

Swimming: 1—Sandy beach and bottom.
2—Gravel or rocky bottom with little or no beach.
3—Swimming is not recommended.
Fishing: C—Cold-water species.
W—Warm-water species.

Unlike a backpacker's tent, you can stand up to dress in this type of tent.

10. *White Pine Canoe Camp*—12 miles east of Grayling via M-72 and McMaster's Bridge Road; on Au Sable, canoe group campsites.
10a. *Rainbow Bend*—15 miles east of Grayling via M-72 and McMaster's Bridge Road.
11. *Parmalee Bridge*—5 miles north of Luzerne via County Road 489.
12. *Mio Pond*—3 miles northwest of Mio via M-33 and Popps Road.
13. *McCollum Lake*—8½ miles northwest of Curran via M-65 and McCollum Lake Road.

14. *Van Etten Lake*—4½ miles northwest of Oscoda via US 23 and F-41 (Old M-171).
15. *Hardwood Lake*—13½ miles southeast of West Branch via M-55 and County Road 21.
16. *Rifle River*—11 miles southeast of Rose City via M-33 and Peters Road.
17. *Ambrose Lake*—11 miles north of West Branch via County Road 15 and County Road 20.
18. *Houghton Lake*—6 miles northwest of Houghton Lake Headquarters via West Shore Drive.
19. *House Lake*—2½ miles northeast of Meredith via Meredith Grade.
20. *Trout Lake*—3 miles northeast of Meredith via Meredith Grade.
21. *Wildwood*—13 miles south of West Branch via M-30 and Wildwood Shores Road.
22. *Black Creek*—3 miles northwest of Sanford via Saginaw Road and West River Road.
23. *Temple*—10½ miles west of Harrison via M-61.
24. *Pike Lake*—9½ miles northwest of Farwell via M-115.
25. *Mud Lake*—11 miles east of Evart via US 10, M-66, Grand Road, and Brown Road.
26. *Muskrat Lake*—12 miles northwest of Mio via M-72, County Road 608, and Richardson Road.

Bay City State Park

For Information

Bay City State Park
3582 State Park Drive
Bay City, MI 48706
(517) 684-3020

LEGEND

🚐	CAMPGROUND
⛺	ORGANIZATION CAMPGROUND
🚻	TOILET SHOWER BUILD.
🚐	SANITATION STATION
🏕	PICNIC AREA
🏖	BEACH
🏢	HEADQUARTERS
P	PARKING

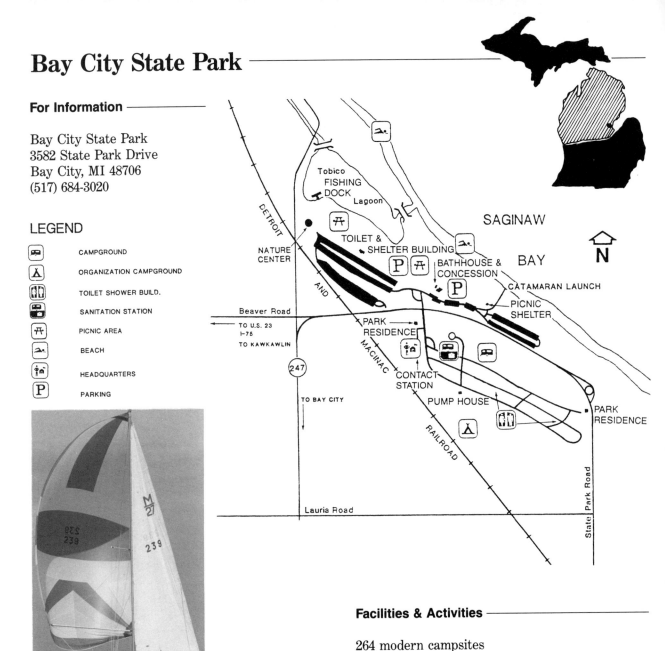

Catching the wind with friends on Saginaw Bay—perfect summertime fun.

Location

Bay City State Park is located 5 miles north of Bay City, and from US 10 may be reached by traveling north on M-13/M-247 (Euclid Road). Access is also from I-75; take exit 168 and travel east on Beaver Road to the park entrance. The 196-acre park is on Saginaw Bay on Lake Huron; Tobico Lagoon is a popular site for birders.

Facilities & Activities

264 modern campsites
  electrical hookups
  flush toilets
  showers
  sanitation station
rent-a-tent
organization campground
Nature Center
picnic area
picnic shelter
playground
swimming beach
beach house and concession
fishing
fishing dock at Tobico Lagoon
boating
hiking trails/observation towers in Tobico Lagoon
  area

Burt Lake State Park

Beaches and sand volleyball just go together.

For Information

Burt Lake State Park
P.O. Box 609
Indian River, MI 49749
(616) 238-9392

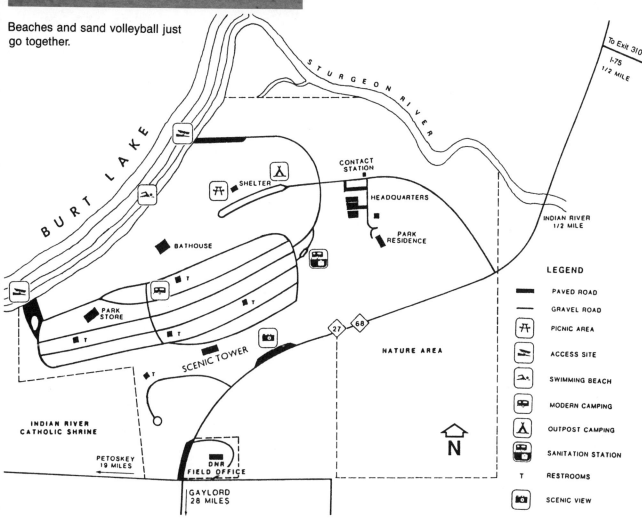

LEGEND

▬	PAVED ROAD
—	GRAVEL ROAD
🎎	PICNIC AREA
✈	ACCESS SITE
🏊	SWIMMING BEACH
🚐	MODERN CAMPING
⛺	OUTPOST CAMPING
🚐	SANITATION STATION
T	RESTROOMS
📷	SCENIC VIEW

Location

Burt Lake State Park is ½ mile south of Indian River and 1 mile from I-75. Take exit 310 and travel west on M-68 to the park entrance. This 405-acre park is located on the south shore of Burt Lake and bordered on the north by the Sturgeon River. Burt Lake is part of a 35-mile inland waterway, which starts at Lake Huron.

Facilities & Activities

375 modern campsites
  electrical hookups
  flush toilets
  showers
  sanitation station
rent-a-tipi
organization campground
picnic area
picnic shelter

playground
swimming beach
beach house
park store
fishing
boating
2 boat launches
boat rental
cross-country skiing

Cheboygan State Park

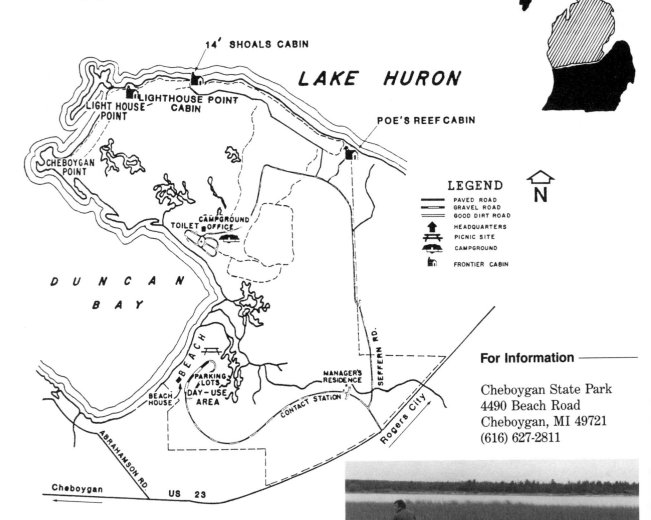

LEGEND
- —— PAVED ROAD
- === GRAVEL ROAD
- === GOOD DIRT ROAD
- ⬆ HEADQUARTERS
- ⛱ PICNIC SITE
- ⛺ CAMPGROUND
- 🏠 FRONTIER CABIN

N

14' SHOALS CABIN

LAKE HURON

LIGHTHOUSE POINT CABIN

LIGHT HOUSE POINT

POE'S REEF CABIN

CHEBOYGAN POINT

TOILET CAMPGROUND OFFICE

DUNCAN BAY

BEACH

MANAGER'S RESIDENCE

PARKING LOTS DAY-USE AREA

BEACH HOUSE

SEFFERN RD.

CONTACT STATION

ABRAHAMSON RD.

Rogers City

Cheboygan

US 23

For Information

Cheboygan State Park
4490 Beach Road
Cheboygan, MI 49721
(616) 627-2811

Problems? Looks like low tide to me!

Facilities & Activities

78 modern campsites
  electrical hookups
  flush toilets
  showers
  sanitation station
organization campground
3 rustic cabins (each sleeps 8)
picnic area
picnic shelter
playground
swimming beach
beach house
hunting
fishing
boating
boat launch (hand-carried)
6 miles of hiking trails
cross-country skiing

Location

Cheboygan State Park is located 4 miles east of Cheboygan on US 23. The 1,200-acre park is a peninsula, with Lake Huron on the east and Duncan Bay on the west. The campground and the day-use area are both located on Duncan Bay but are some 4 miles apart. A network of trails enables hikers to explore the beach, dunes, lighthouse ruins, and a swamp area.

Clear Lake State Park

For Information

Clear Lake State Park
P.O. Box 51, N. M-33
Atlanta, MI 49709
(517) 785-4388

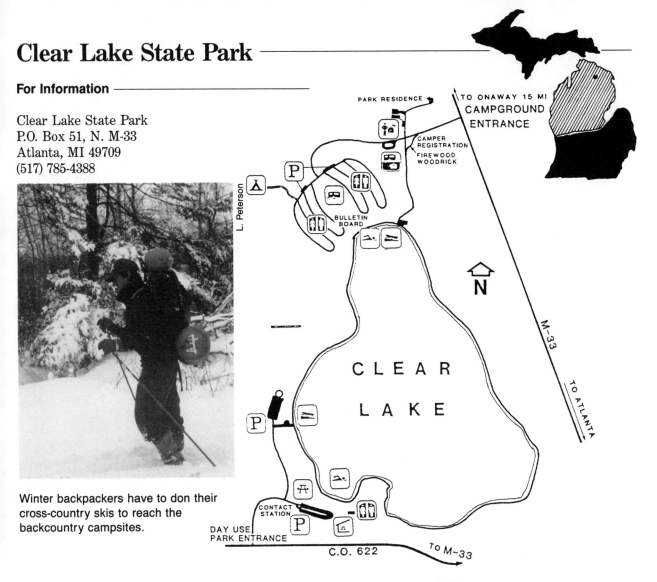

Winter backpackers have to don their
cross-country skis to reach the
backcountry campsites.

LEGEND

P	PARKING	
	PICNIC SHELTER	
	PICNIC AREA	
	BEACH	

	BOAT LAUNCH
	TOILET SHOWER BUILDING
	MODERN CAMPGROUND
	ORGANIZATION CAMPGROUND
	HEADQUARTERS
	SANITATION STATION

Location

Clear Lake State Park is located north of Atlanta, Michigan on M-33. The campground and the day-use area have separate entrances; the day-use park entrance is 6 miles north of Atlanta on M-33 then west on County Road 622; the campground entrance is an additional 5 miles north on M-33. The 290-acre park claims to be geographically situated halfway between the north pole and the equator on the 45th parallel.

Facilities & Activities

200 modern campsites
  electrical hookups
  flush toilets
  showers
  sanitation station
rent-a-tent
organization campground
picnic area
picnic shelter
playground
swimming beach
beach house
hunting
fishing
boating
2 boat launches
hiking trails
portion of the Clear Lake–Jackson Lake Trail
access to snowmobile and cross-country ski trails

Fisherman's Island State Park

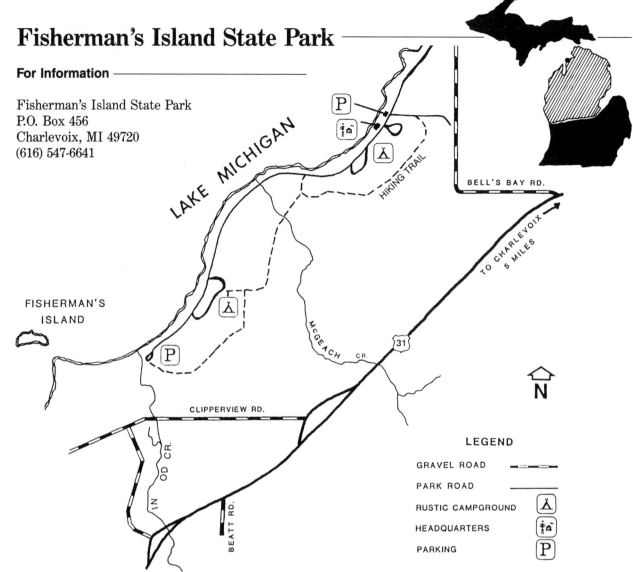

For Information

Fisherman's Island State Park
P.O. Box 456
Charlevoix, MI 49720
(616) 547-6641

LEGEND

GRAVEL ROAD	
PARK ROAD	
RUSTIC CAMPGROUND	
HEADQUARTERS	
PARKING	

Location

Fisherman's Island State Park is located 5 miles southwest of Charlevoix off of US 31. Turn west on Bell's Bay Road and travel 2½ miles to the park entrance. The 2,678-acre park has several miles of undeveloped Lake Michigan shoreline that is a haven for gemstone enthusiasts in search of the Petoskey stone.

Facilities & Activities

90 rustic campsites
  vault toilets
  hand pump
picnic area
swimming beach
hunting
fishing
hiking trails

Riding a bicycle on the sandy beach can be a challenge, so these sidewalks really help!

Harrisville State Park

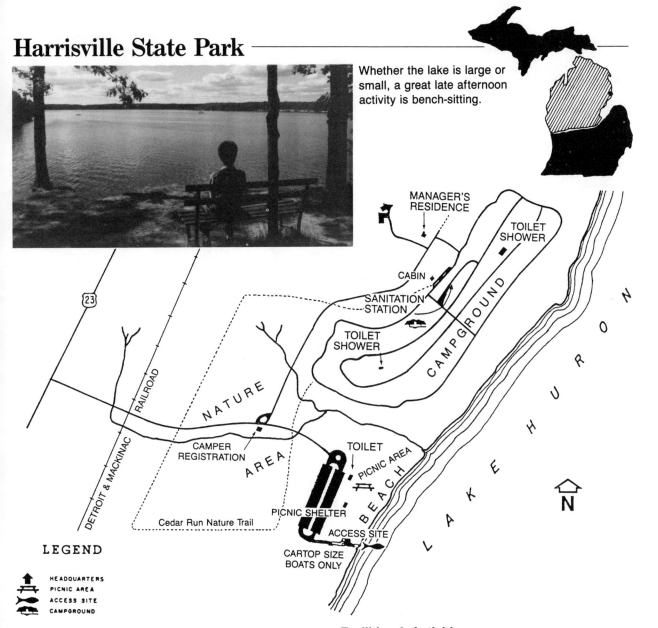

Whether the lake is large or small, a great late afternoon activity is bench-sitting.

LEGEND

HEADQUARTERS
PICNIC AREA
ACCESS SITE
CAMPGROUND

(Map labels: MANAGER'S RESIDENCE, TOILET SHOWER, CABIN, SANITATION STATION, TOILET SHOWER, CAMPGROUND, LAKE HURON, US 23, RAILROAD, DETROIT & MACKINAC, NATURE AREA, CAMPER REGISTRATION, Cedar Run Nature Trail, TOILET, PICNIC AREA, PICNIC SHELTER, BEACH, ACCESS SITE, CARTOP SIZE BOATS ONLY, N)

For Information

Harrisville State Park
P.O. Box 326
Harrisville, MI 48740
(517) 724-5126

Location

Harrisville State Park is located ½ mile south of Harrisville on US 23. This 94-acre park has a sandy beach on Lake Huron that is bordered by tall cedars and pines; the 1-mile long Cedar Run Nature Trail allows campers to explore this forest community.

Facilities & Activities

229 modern campsites
  electrical hookups
  flush toilets
  showers
  sanitation station
rent-a-tent
organization campground
1 rustic cabin (sleeps 4)
picnic area
picnic shelter
playground
swimming beach
fishing
boating
boat access (hand-carried)
nature trail

Hartwick Pines State Park

For Information

Hartwick Pines State Park
Route 3, Box 3840
Grayling, MI 49738
(517) 348-7068

LOGGING CAMP

PARK STORE

CONTACT STATION

HEADQUARTERS

SHELTER & TOILET

SANITATION STATION

CHAPEL

BRAILLE TRAIL

THE PINES

N

MONARCH PINE

TOILET

INTERPRETIVE CENTER

CAMPGROUND

93

TO EXIT 259 AT I-75

HARTWICK LAKE

Location

Hartwick Pines State Park is located 7½ miles north of Grayling; from I-75, take exit 259 and travel northeast on M-93 for 3 miles to the park entrance. With 9,672 acres, Hartwick Pines is the largest state park in the Lower Peninsula. The park's high rolling hills, built up by ancient glaciers, overlook the broad expanse of the valley of the east branch of the Au Sable River and four small lakes within the park. The principal feature of the park is the forest of virgin pines. Other attractions include the logging museum, a historic logging camp, and the 155-foot tall white pine known as "The Monarch."

Facilities & Activities

42 modern campsites
  electrical hookups
  flush toilets
  showers
  sanitation station
21 semi-modern campsites
  flush toilets
  showers
  sanitation station
organization campground
Interpretive Center
picnic area
picnic shelter
playground
park store
hunting
fishing
hiking trails
snowmobiling
28.2 km of cross-country ski trails

Hoeft State Park

For Information

Hoeft State Park
US 23 North
Rogers City, MI 49779
(517) 734-2543

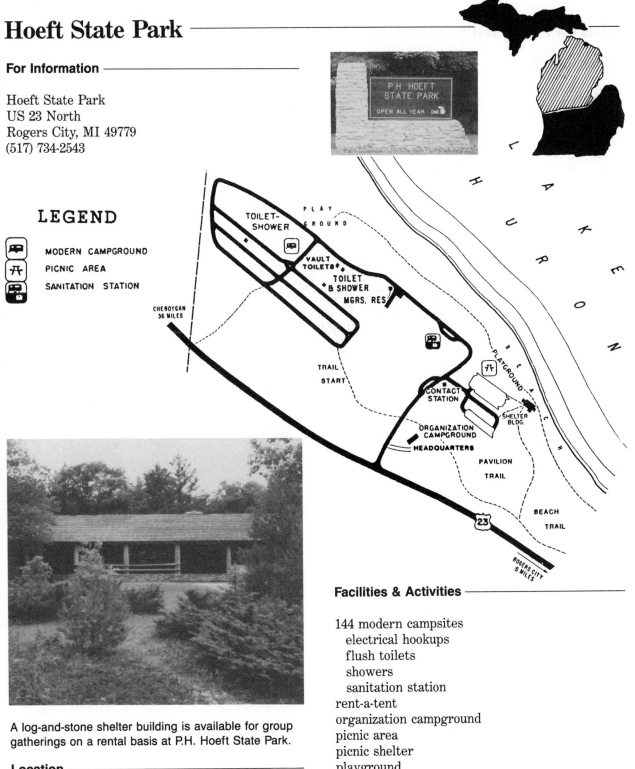

LEGEND

🚐 MODERN CAMPGROUND

🎋 PICNIC AREA

🚐 SANITATION STATION

CHEBOYGAN 36 MILES

PLAY GROUND

TOILET-SHOWER

VAULT TOILETS

TOILET & SHOWER

MGRS. RES.

TRAIL START

CONTACT STATION

ORGANIZATION CAMPGROUND

HEADQUARTERS

PLAYGROUND

SHELTER BLDG.

PAVILION TRAIL

BEACH TRAIL

US 23

ROGERS CITY 5 MILES

LAKE HURON

BEACH

A log-and-stone shelter building is available for group gatherings on a rental basis at P.H. Hoeft State Park.

Location

P.H. Hoeft State Park is located 5 miles northwest of Rogers City on US 23. The 301-acre park is in Huron Dunes country. With more than a mile of Lake Huron shoreline, the park has 2 buoyed beaches, one in the day-use area and one in the campground.

Facilities & Activities

144 modern campsites
  electrical hookups
  flush toilets
  showers
  sanitation station
rent-a-tent
organization campground
picnic area
picnic shelter
playground
swimming beach
beach house
hunting
fishing
boating
4½ miles of hiking trails
groomed cross-country ski trails

Huron National Forest

For Information

Forests Supervisor's Office
Huron-Manistee National Forests
421 S. Mitchell Street
Cadillac, MI 49601
(616) 775-2421
1-800-999-7677 (nationwide)

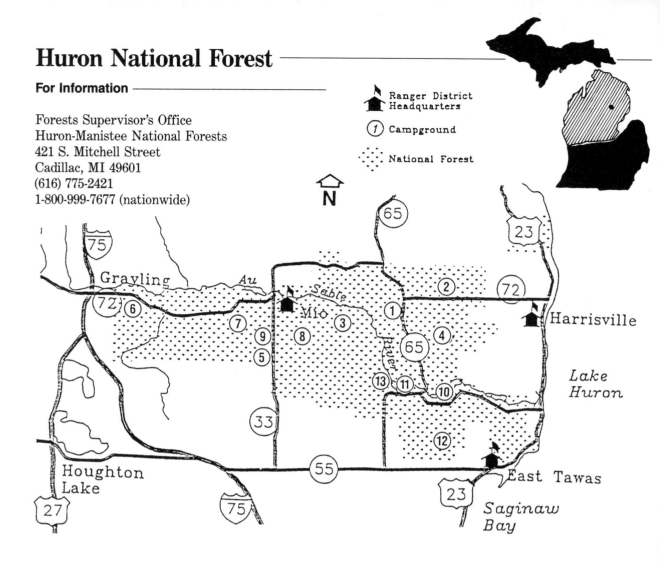

Huron National Forest extends over 431,800 acres in the northeastern part of the Lower Peninsula. It was established by presidential proclamation in 1909, only four years after the organization of the Forest Service as part of the U.S. Department of Agriculture. The Huron National Forest was originally known as the Michigan Forest. In 1871 wildfires swept from Manistee on Lake Michigan to Lake Huron, and in 1881 the thumb area of Michigan suffered heavy forest losses. After the establishment of the National Forest, reforestation and watershed management followed fire control. Today, the Huron National Forest provides timber for wood products, quality water resources, wildlife habitat, and a variety of recreational opportunities. The Forest is accessible from the north and south via I-75, US 23, M-33, and M-65, and from the west via M-72.

Lumbermen's Monument, dedicated in 1932, is the site of a nine-foot bronze logger that commemorates the pioneer loggers who first opened this land to man's industry. Located 13 miles northwest of East Tawas, the monument overlooks the river valley. A visitor center at the monument houses interpretive displays that explore the rich logging legacy of the Au Sable River.

Materials are available from each of the three District Ranger offices, as well as from the office of the Forest Supervisor, on recreational opportunities in the Huron National Forest. Contact them for maps and specific information on fishing, hunting, trails, winter activities, river trips for canoeists, opening and closing dates for campgrounds, and so forth.

Camping

The Huron National Forest has 12 developed campgrounds with more than 250 camping units for individuals and families; in addition, four areas are designated as group campgrounds. These campgrounds offer a wide spectrum of camping experiences. All are accessible by better unpaved or paved roads and serve both tent and trailer campers. Owners of large trailers should contact the appropriate District Ranger office for trailer restrictions. Most campgrounds are located on lakes or streams and many offer fishing and swimming opportunities as well. All campgrounds include picnic tables, tent pads, fire grates, water, and toilet facilities. No electrical hookups or showers are provided.

Kneff Lake Campground is the most highly developed facility in the Huron National Forest as it has flush toilets. A nightly fee is charged at all but one campground for the summer recreation period when full services are provided; the 10-site individual/family camping area at the Luzerne Trail Camp is free of charge. During the early spring and late fall when services are reduced, the fees at some sites are reduced or waived. The seasons vary, but the managed season for most campgrounds is from Memorial Day weekend through Labor Day, although some remain open later into the fall. Check with the District Ranger office regarding dates that the area may be open outside the managed season.

All developed campgrounds have a limit of 14 days' stay. In addition, group size should be limited to 8 people and 2 vehicles per campsite. All camping is on a first-come, first-served basis; reservations may not be made. However, reservations for group camping facilities should be made by calling the appropriate District Ranger office. Fees are charged for most of the group campgrounds. Some campgrounds are operated by private concessioners under a special use permit issued by the Forest Service. Signs will be posted near the fee collection facility stating a particular site is under concessioner management.

Dispersed area camping is generally available anywhere in the forest outside the boundaries of any developed recreation site or outside any area that has been closed to camping. No facilities are provided and no fees are charged. The maximum stay is 16 days. Low-impact camping techniques that leave an area undisturbed are encouraged. All refuse should be taken back home by the camper.

Primitive camping opportunities exist at four locations in the Huron National Forest. Most primitive campsites have minimal facilities and may provide only a pit toilet or a hand pump. Drinking water may not be available for the entire season, so plan to bring your own. There is no charge for using primitive sites. The Harrisville Ranger District has three primitive sites: the McKinley Trail Camp, walk-in camps (not accessible by vehicle) at Hoist Lake and Reid Lake, and the Luzerne Trail Camp on the Mio Ranger District.

Recreational Trails

Huron National Forest has approximately 150 miles of trails suitable for hiking. Some trails are specifically for hiking, while some allow other summer uses such as horseback riding. In addition, there are cross-country ski trails, which make for ideal non-winter hiking. Approximately 85 miles of the Michigan Shore-to-Shore Hiking and Riding Trail between Lake Huron and Lake Michigan are in the Huron National Forest. Free handout sheets and maps are available on hiking trails. Most of the hiking trails are linear trails; generally, the cross-country ski trails and the interpretive trails consist of loops of varying lengths. There are also more than 200 miles of motorized trails for cycles and snowmobiles.

A picnic table, tent pad, and fire grate are provided at each site in national forest campgrounds.

Canoeing

The Au Sable River is a major tributary to Lake Huron and the only major river in the Huron National Forest. A 23-mile segment of the main stream of the Au Sable River was designated a National Scenic River on October 4, 1984. The Mio Ranger District has been charged with the administration of the Scenic River corridor. The segment begins one mile below Mio Pond and ends just below the Forest Service Road 4001 bridge. More than 75 miles of the river are suitable for canoeing; commercial liveries rent canoes. Contact the Forest Supervisor's office for handouts and maps of the four segments of the river and the canoe liveries that operate in these areas.

REGION 2

Harrisville Ranger District

For Information

Harrisville Ranger District
US 23
Harrisville, MI 48740
(517) 724-5431

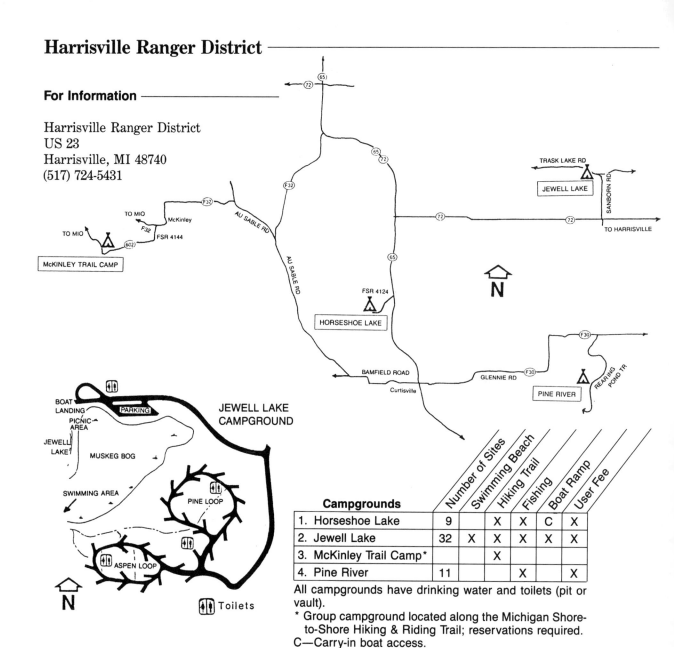

Campgrounds	Number of Sites	Swimming Beach	Hiking Trail	Fishing	Boat Ramp	User Fee
1. Horseshoe Lake	9		X	X	C	X
2. Jewell Lake	32	X	X	X	X	X
3. McKinley Trail Camp*			X			
4. Pine River	11			X		X

All campgrounds have drinking water and toilets (pit or vault).

* Group campground located along the Michigan Shore-to-Shore Hiking & Riding Trail; reservations required.

C—Carry-in boat access.

Campground Locations

Horseshoe Lake is about 4 miles northwest of Glennie; go north on M-65 for 3½ miles, then left on FSR 4124 for 1 mile to the campground. The 16-acre lake is a designated trout lake.

Jewell Lake is west of Harrisville off of M-72. Travel west on M-72 for 14½ miles, then north on Sanborn Road for 1.7 miles, then left on Trask Lake Road for 7/10 mile, then left on FSR 4601. The nearest community is Barton City, about ½ mile northwest. The 193-acre lake is good for perch, bluegill, rock bass, and pike.

McKinley Trail Camp is about 9 miles east of the community of Mio via County Road 602 or Forest Road F-32. It is northwest of Glennie and

can be reached two ways: one way is to take Bamfield Road west for 4 miles, turn right on Au Sable River Road and travel 7 miles, then left on Road F-32 and go 6 miles, then left on FSR 4144 for ¾ mile, then right on County Road 602 for 2 miles to the camp access road. Road F-32 can also be reached by traveling north of Glennie on M-65/M-72 and turning left on F-32, which takes you to FSR 4144.

Pine River is about 9½ miles east of Glennie. Leave M-65 at Glennie and follow F-30 east for 9 miles to Rearing Pond Trail (FSR 4121); turn right and go 2.3 miles to the entrance (on the right). Located near the Pine River, it offers some of the finest trout fishing around.

. . . backpacking, via cross-country skis, in the winter . . .

The seasons in Michigan are well defined and ideal for outdoor excursions . . . whether it's hiking the trails in the fall of the year . . .

. . . or camping at one of the agency campgrounds in the summer.

Michiganders enjoy various means of transportation when they recreate . . . iceboating . . .

. . . bicycling . . .

. . . and sailboarding . . . is anyone directing traffic?

The water of Lake Superior may be too cold for swimming but it's ideal for wading at Porcupine Mountains Wilderness State Park (see page 52).

The campground at Lake Michigan Recreation Area adjoins Lake Michigan and is adjacent to the Nordhouse Dunes Wilderness Area; both are on the Manistee National Forest (see page 90).

The 100-acre lake at Metamora-Hadley Recreation Area provides an excellent swimming beach, as well as fishing and boating opportunities. The beach concession has boat and canoe rentals (see page 135).

77

L. Peterson

M. Little

Potawatomi Falls is just one of a series of magnificent waterfalls near Black River Harbor Recreation Area on the Ottawa National Forest (see page 40).

Cross-country ski trails run just about everywhere; the opportunities are as varied as the terrain.

M. Little

The Upper Falls at Tahquamenon Falls State Park is one of the largest waterfalls east of the Mississippi River; it has a drop of more than 50 feet and is more than 200 feet across (see page 55).

M. Little

Massive coastal sand dunes tower above Lake Michigan at Sleeping Bear Dunes National Lakeshore. This view is from an overlook along the Pierce Stocking Scenic Drive (see page 111).

78

There appears to be no age limit as to who can use the playground equipment that is provided at all state parks.

Rowboats can be rented at Tahquamenon Falls State Park in order to paddle to an island for closer views of the Lower Falls (see page 55).

Authentic Indian replica tipis are available at several state parks and are equipped similar to a tent.

The Traverse City State Park campground is adorned with towering trees, producing lots of welcome shade for campers (see page 116).

Courtesy Michigan Travel Bureau

More than one hundred lighthouses remain in existence along Michigan's coastline

M. Little

You can find more than 150 waterfalls across the length and breadth of the rugged Upper Peninsula.

M. Little

Michigan has many excellent canoe streams; several state parks have canoe rental concessions.

Courtesy Michigan Travel Bureau

Touched by four of the five Great Lakes, Michigan is a sailor's delight!

This view across the Lake of the Clouds at Porcupine Mountains Wilderness State Park reveals only a portion of one of the few remaining large wilderness areas in the Midwest.

Sled-dog competition is gaining in popularity, particularly in the Upper Peninsula.

Young State Park has 1½ miles on beautiful Lake Charlevoix, but these youngsters prefer fishing at the small pond called Mirrow Lake (see page 119).

There is no wonder that so many folks prefer the fall of the year to hike and camp; the colors are magnificent!

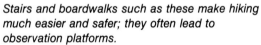

The special mystique of a lighthouse at sunset cannot be described by mere words!

Stairs and boardwalks such as these make hiking much easier and safer; they often lead to observation platforms.

One of the most popular ways to see the Pictured Rocks National Lakeshore is by boat. From June to mid-October, tour boats leave Munising daily (see page 48).

Mio Ranger District

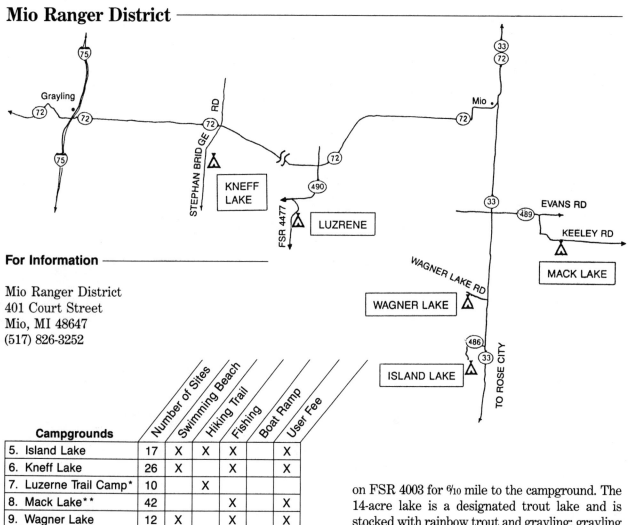

For Information

Mio Ranger District
401 Court Street
Mio, MI 48647
(517) 826-3252

Campgrounds	Number of Sites	Swimming Beach	Hiking Trail	Fishing	Boat Ramp	User Fee
5. Island Lake	17	X	X	X		X
6. Kneff Lake	26	X		X		X
7. Luzerne Trail Camp*	10		X			
8. Mack Lake**	42			X		X
9. Wagner Lake	12	X		X		X

All campgrounds have drinking water and vault toilets;
Kneff Lake also has flush toilets.

  * Also has a group campground; located along the
Michigan Shore-to-Shore Hiking & Riding Trail; 325
capacity; reservations required.

** Also has a group camping area (White Pine Loop);
maximum 15; reservations available.

Campground Locations

Island Lake is off of M-33, 10 miles south of Mio
and 6 miles north of Rose City. From Mio,
travel south for 10 miles on M-33; turn west on
County Road 486 and go about 7/10 mile to the
campground. Fish for perch, bluegill, and largemouth and rock bass.

Kneff Lake is 8 miles east of Grayling. From the
junction of Business I-75 and M-72 in Grayling,
travel east on M-72 for 6½ miles; turn right on
Stephan Bridge Road and go 1.4 miles, then left
on FSR 4003 for 6/10 mile to the campground. The
14-acre lake is a designated trout lake and is
stocked with rainbow trout and grayling; grayling
must be released.

Luzerne Trail Camp is off of M-72, west of Mio
and south of Luzerne. From Luzerne, travel
south on County Road 490 for 2 miles, then
south on FSR 4477 for 3/4 mile. The trail is managed primarily for hiking and horseback riding.
The individual/family camping area is open
year-round; the group camping area is open by
permit only.

Mack Lake is southeast of Mio off of M-33. From
Mio, travel south on M-33 for about 4 miles,
turn east onto County Road 489, and go 4¼
miles to the campground. The lake is a 174-acre
shallow lake with a muck bottom; mostly perch,
bullheads, bass, pike, and sunfish are found
here.

Wagner Lake is off of M-33, about 7 miles south of
Mio and 9 miles north of Rose City. From Mio,
travel south on M-33 for 7 miles, then west on
Wagner Lake Road (FSR 4211) for 1.2 miles.
The 26-acre lake, surrounded by National For-
est, is good bluegill, bass, and perch fishing.

Tawas Ranger District

For Information

Tawas Ranger District
326 Newman Street, Federal Building
East Tawas, MI 48730
(517) 362-4477

Campgrounds	Number of Sites	Swimming Beach	Hiking Trail	Fishing	Boat Ramp	User Fee
10. Monument	20					X
11. Rollways	19		X			X
12. Round Lake	33	X		X	X	X
13. South Branch Trail Camp*	25		X			X

All campgrounds have drinking water and pit toilets.
* Also has a group campground; located along the Michigan Shore-to-Shore Hiking & Riding Trail; 250 capacity; reservations required.

Campground Locations

Monument is about 13 miles northwest of Tawas City. From M-55 at Tawas Monument Road; turn left and go 11 miles to River Road; turn right and go ¼ mile to entrance on left. The campground is near Lumberman's Monument Visitor Center on River Road Scenic Byway.

Rollways is 7 miles north of Hale and southwest of Glennie off of M-65. From the junction of M-55 with M-65, travel north 14 miles (through Hale) to Rollaway Road; turn left and go ¼ mile to the entrance on the right.

Round Lake is 9 miles northwest of Tawas City. From the intersection of M-55 with Plank Road (on the northwest side of Tawas City), follow Plank Road northwest for 7 miles, then go left on Indian Lake Road for ¼ mile, then right on Latham Road for ½ mile. When approaching from the west, leave M-55 about 6 miles east of its intersection with M-65; turn north on Sand Lake Road and go 6½ miles to Indian Lake Road; turn left and go 2½ miles to Latham Road, then left for ½ mile to the campground. The lake is 89 acres, with fishing for largemouth bass, pike, and sunfish; the Sand Lake community is ½ mile away.

South Branch Trail Camp is off of Rollaway Road about 2 miles beyond Rollways Campground (see location information for Rollways). The trail is managed primarily for hiking and horseback riding. The individual/family camping area is open year-round; the group camping area is open by permit only.

Interlochen State Park

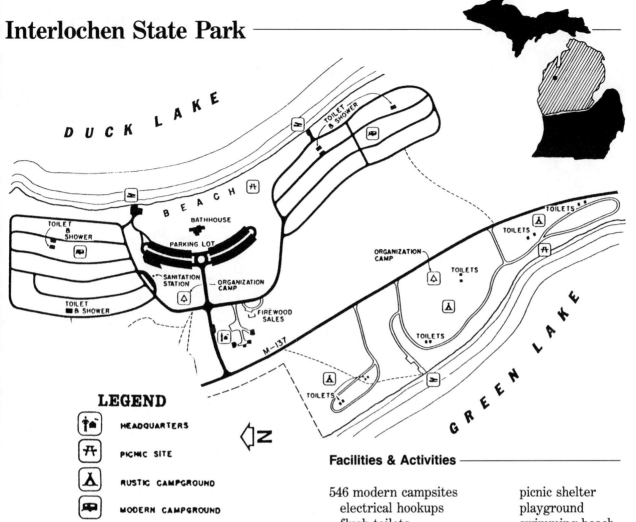

LEGEND

👪	HEADQUARTERS
🎋	PICNIC SITE
🛖	RUSTIC CAMPGROUND
🚐	MODERN CAMPGROUND
🚤	ACCESS SITE

For Information

Interlochen State Park
South M-137
Interlochen, MI 49643
(616) 276-9511

Facilities & Activities

546 modern campsites
  electrical hookups
  flush toilets
  showers
  sanitation station
71 rustic campsites
  vault toilets
  hand pump
rent-a-tent/tipi
3 organization campgrounds
picnic area

picnic shelter
playground
swimming beach
beach house
park store
fishing
boating
3 boat launches
boat rental
nature trail

Location

Interlochen State Park is located 15 miles southwest of Traverse City off of US 31. From US 31, turn south on M-137 and travel 1 mile beyond Interlochen to the park entrance. With towering virgin white pine, the 187-acre park is located on a thin strip of land between Duck Lake and Green Lake. The park, located next to the renowned Interlochen National Music Camp, has almost a mile of shoreline.

Have you ever noticed that adults stretch out and kids get on all fours when they get on a beach?

Leelanau State Park

Courtesy Michigan Travel Bureau

. . . just another camping family that believes in togetherness.

For Information

Leelanau State Park
Route 1, Box 49
Northport, MI 49670
(616) 386-5422

LAKE MICHIGAN

LIGHTHOUSE · BEACH · LIGHTHOUSE POINT

PICNIC AREA

CAMPGROUND

PARK OFFICE

CATHEAD BAY RD.

BELL RD.

CATHEAD BAY

OVERLOOK

PURKISS ROAD

COUNTY ROAD 629

GRAND TRAVERSE BAY

RUSCHKE RD.

BEACH ACCESS

LEG LAKE

OBSERVATION DOCK

TRAIL PARKING

COUNTY ROAD 629

LEGEND

Paved Road

Gravel Road

------ Trail

WOOLSEY AIRPORT (TWP)

MUD LAKE

OTTIS ROAD

OTTIS ROAD

N

DENSMORE ROAD

To Northpoint

Location

Leelanau State Park, located 10 miles north of Northport on County Road 629, is separated into two sections. The campground, picnic area, and the historic Grand Traverse Lighthouse are on the tip of the Leelanau Peninsula, while the undeveloped part of the park lies along Cathead Bay. Most of the park's best beaches and all of its trails are in this undeveloped section. Trail parking for access to this area is at the end of Densmore Road.

Facilities & Activities

50 rustic campsites
  vault toilets
  hand pump
picnic area
playground
swimming
hunting
fishing
network of hiking trails
9.7 km of cross-country ski trails

Ludington State Park

For Information

Ludington State Park
P.O. Box 709, M-116
Ludington, MI 49431
(616) 843-8671

LAKE MICHIGAN

HAMLIN LAKE

LOST LAKE

TO POINT SABLE LIGHTHOUSE

COAST GUARD TRAIL

LOGGING TRAIL

RIDGE TRAIL

BEECHWOOD TRAIL

LOST LAKE TR.

BEECHWOOD CAMPGROUND

COAST GUARD TRAIL

CEDAR CAMPGROUND

RIDGE TRAIL

DUNE TRAIL

PARK STORE

PINES CAMPGROUND

BIG SABLE RIVER

SABLE RIVER

BATHHOUSE & CONCESSION

VISITOR CENTER

SKYLINE TRAIL

HAMLIN DAM

BEACHHOUSE & CONCESSION

BIKE PATH

M-116

N

REGION 2

LEGEND

t	TOILET		HEADQUARTERS	
s	SHELTER		SANITATION STATION	
T	TOILET BUILDING		BOAT LAUNCH	
S	TOILET SHOWER BUILDING		FISH CLEANING STATION	
	SCENIC VIEW		BEACH	

Location

Ludington State Park is located 8 miles north of Ludington, at the end of M-116 between Lake Michigan and Hamlin Lake. The park encompasses 5,300 acres of virgin conifer and hardwood forests, hills, ravines, and lofty dunes. There are 2 excellent beaches, one on Lake Michigan and one on Hamlin Lake. An outstanding feature of the park is its trail system; one of the 11 marked trails leads to the picturesque Point Sable Lighthouse.

Facilities & Activities

3 modern campgrounds with 398 campsites
  electrical hookups
  flush toilets
  showers
  sanitation station
organization campground
Visitor Center
picnic area
playground
swimming beaches
2 beach houses with concessions
park store
hunting
fishing
fish-cleaning station
boating
boat launch
boat rentals at Hamlin Lake
canoeing
paved bike trails
18-mile network of hiking trails
16 miles of cross-country ski trails

Mackinaw State Forest

For Information

Mackinaw State Forest
Box 576
Gaylord, MI 49735
(517) 732-3541

Mackinaw City

Cheyboygan

LAKE HURON

BEAVER ISLAND ①

EMMET ④

CHEBOYGAN

⑥

⑦

⑧ Rogers City

N

LAKE MICHIGAN

Charlevoix

③

⑤

PRESQUE ISLE

⑨

CHARLEVOIX
②

⑪

㉘

⑩

⑫

⑬

⑱

㉔

㉕

⑭

Alpena

ANTRIM

2a

Gaylord

MONTMORENCY

㉓

Hillman

㉖

⑮

OTSEGO

⑰

⑳

㉑

㉒

ALPENA

Elk Rapids

⑯

⑲

㉗

Campground Locations

1. *Beaver Island*—7 miles south of St. James via East Side Road.
2. *Graves Crossing*—10 miles north of Mancelona via US 131 and M-66.
2a. *Pinney Bridge*—13 miles west of Gaylord on M-32 to US 131, and southeast to Dead Man's Hill Road; walk-in sites on the Jordan Valley Pathway.
3. *Weber Lake*—7½ miles northwest of Wolverine via Wolverine Road and Prue Road.
4. *Maple Bay*—3½ miles east of Brutus via Brutus Road.
5. *Haakwood*—2 miles north of Wolverine via Old US 27, then east on Campground Road.
6. *Twin Lakes*—6 miles southeast of Alverno via Black River Road and Twin Lakes Road.
7. *Black Lake*—11 miles northeast of Onaway via M-211, County Road 489, Black Mountain Road, and Donva Road.
8. *Ocqueoc Falls*—10 miles northeast of Onaway via M-68 and Millersburg Road.
9. *Shoepac Lake*—12 miles southeast of Onaway via M-33 and Tomahawk Lake Highway.
10. *Tomahawk Lake*—11 miles southeast of Onaway via M-33 and Tomahawk Lake Highway.
11. *Pine Grove*—12 miles southeast of Wolverine via Wolverine Road and Webb Road.

Boaters always appreciate a good launch ramp.

Mackinaw State Forest *(continued)*

Campgrounds	Number of Sites	Boating/Canoeing	Swimming	Fishing
1. Beaver Island	25	B	1	C
2. Graves Crossing	10	C	3	C
2a. Pinney Bridge	10			
3. Weber Lake	18		3	C W
4. Maple Bay	36	B	1	W C
5. Haakwood	18	C	3	C
6. Twin Lakes	12		3	W
7. Black Lake	50	B	1	W
8. Ocqueoc Falls	14		3	C
9. Shoepac Lake	28	B	3	W C
10. Tomahawk Lake	42	B	1	W
11. Pine Grove	6		3	C
12. Pickerel Lake	39	B	1	C
13. Pigeon River	19		3	C
14. Pigeon Bridge	10		3	C
15. Round Lake	6		3	W
16. Lake Marjory	10	B	3	W
17. Big Bear Lake	43	B	1	W
18. Town Corner	12	B	2	W
19. Little Wolf Lake	28		1	C W
20. McCormick Lake	8	B	3	C
21. Big Oaks	23	B	3	C W
22. Avery Lake	14	B	2	W
23. Lake 15	12	B	2	C W
24. Jackson Lake	24	B	2	W
25. Ess Lake	29	B	1	W
26. Thunder Bay River	10	B	3	W
27. Ossineke	42	B	1	C
28. Elk Hill	5	C	3	C

Swimming: 1—Sandy beach and bottom.
      2—Gravel or rocky bottom with little or no beach.
      3—Swimming is not recommended.
Fishing: C—Cold-water species.
      W—Warm-water species.

12. *Pickerel Lake*—10 miles east of Vanderbilt via Sturgeon Valley Road and Pickerel Lake Road.
13. *Pigeon River*—13 miles east of Vanderbilt via Sturgeon Valley Road and Osmund Road.

Screened shelters offer protection from the rain as well as the bugs.

14. *Pigeon Bridge*—11 miles east of Vanderbilt via Sturgeon Valley Road.
15. *Round Lake*—14 miles southeast of Vanderbilt via Sturgeon Valley Road and Round Lake Road.
16. *Lake Marjory*—1¼ miles southeast of Waters via Old US 27.
17. *Big Bear Lake*—1½ miles southwest of Vienna via Principal Meridian Road and Little Bear Lake Road.
18. *Town Corner*—Inquire at District Headquarters, Gaylord. Phone (517) 732-3541.
19. *Little Wolf Lake*—3 miles southeast of Lewiston via County Road 489 and Wolf Lake Road.
20. *McCormick Lake*—10 miles southwest of Atlanta via M-32 and McCormick Lake Road.
21. *Big Oaks*—10 miles southwest of Atlanta via County Road 487 and Avery Lake Road.
22. *Avery Lake*—9 miles southwest of Atlanta via County Road 487 and Avery Lake Road.
23. *Lake 15*—3 miles southwest of Atlanta.
24. *Jackson Lake*—6 miles north of Atlanta via M-33.
25. *Ess Lake*—16 miles northeast of Atlanta via M-33 and County Road 624.
26. *Thunder Bay River*—9 miles southwest of Alpena via M-32 and Indian Reserve Road.
27. *Ossineke*—1 mile east of Ossineke.
28. *Elk Hill*—13½ miles east of Vanderbilt via Sturgeon Valley Road and Osmund Road.

Manistee National Forest

Forests Supervisor's Office
Huron-Manistee National Forests
421 S. Mitchell Street
Cadillac, MI 49601
(616) 775-2421
1-800-999-7677 (nationwide)

Camping

Manistee National Forest, covering 531,700 acres in the northwestern quarter of the Lower Peninsula, was established in 1938. After more than 50 years of protection and management, most of the land is covered with a new maturing forest. The forest, accessible via US 10, US 31, US 131, or M-37, has the Pere Marquette National Scenic River, several state scenic rivers, and 4½ miles of Lake Michigan shoreline, plus shoreline on numerous other lakes and streams.

Materials are available from each of the four District Ranger offices, as well as from the office of the Forest Supervisor, on recreational opportunities in the Manistee National Forest. Contact these offices for maps and specific information on items such as fishing, hunting, trails, winter activities, river trips for canoeists, and opening and closing dates for campgrounds.

The Manistee National Forest has 18 developed campgrounds with more than 425 camping units for individuals and families; in addition, six areas are designated as group campgrounds. These campgrounds offer a wide spectrum of camping experiences. All are accessible by better unpaved or paved roads and serve both tent and trailer campers. Owners of large trailers should contact the appropriate District Ranger office for trailer restrictions. Most campgrounds are located on lakes or streams and many also offer fishing and swimming opportunities. All campgrounds include picnic tables, tent pads, fire grates, water, and toilet facilities. No electrical hookups or showers are provided.

The six campgrounds with the most highly developed facilities are: Peterson Creek, Sand Lake, Udell Hills, Lake Michigan, Nichols Lake, and Pines Point, as they have flush toilets. A nightly fee

Manistee National Forest (*continued*)

is charged at all campgrounds for the summer recreation period when full services are provided. During the early spring and late fall when services are reduced, the fees at some sites are reduced or waived. The seasons vary, but the managed season for most campgrounds is from Memorial Day weekend through Labor Day, although some open as early as April 1 and remain open until December 1. Check with the District Ranger regarding dates that the area may be open outside the managed season.

All developed campgrounds have a 14-day limit on the length of the time you may stay. In addition, the request is made that the group size be limited to 8 people and 2 vehicles per campsite. With one exception, all camping is on a first-come, first-served basis; reservations are taken for some units in the Lake Michigan Recreation Area. For a small additional fee, a campsite can be reserved via check or credit card through Mistix at 1-800-283-CAMP. However, reservations for group camping facilities should be made by calling the appropriate District Ranger office. Fees are charged for most of the group campgrounds. Some campgrounds are operated by private concessioners under a special use permit issued by the Forest Service. Signs will be posted near the fee collection facility stating a particular site is under concessioner management.

Dispersed area camping is generally available anywhere in the forest outside the boundaries of any developed recreation site, or area under closure to camping. No facilities are provided and no fees are charged. The maximum limit of stay is 16 days. Low-impact camping techniques that leave an area undisturbed are encouraged. All refuse should be taken back home by the camper.

Primitive camping opportunities exist at some 14 locations on the Manistee National Forest. Most primitive campsites have minimal facilities and may provide only a pit toilet or a hand pump. Drinking water may not be available for the entire season, so plan to bring your own. Self-contained campers are necessary at some of the primitive camping areas. There is no charge for using primitive sites. Contact the District Ranger office for the location of these areas.

Wilderness Areas

Manistee National Forest has one area managed as wilderness under the National Wilderness Preservation System. It is the only designated wilder-

The Manistee National Forest boasts 4½ miles of Lake Michigan shoreline. The Nordhouse Dunes Wilderness lies along an undeveloped portion of this shoreline; the northern boundary of the wilderness area is accessed from the Lake Michigan Recreation Area.

ness in Michigan's lower peninsula. Its use is regulated to the extent necessary for its protection and public safety.

The *Nordhouse Dunes Wilderness* is located 12 miles southwest of Manistee; the southern edge of the dunes is accessed by Nurnberg Road, while the northern boundary is accessed from the Lake Michigan Recreation Area. Although somewhat small when it comes to wilderness (only 3,450 acres), the Nordhouse Dunes is a unique area. The most striking features of the area are the approximately 7,300 feet of undeveloped Lake Michigan shoreline and the parallel sand dunes. Most are Nipissing Dunes, approximately 3,500 to 4,000 years old. The dunes stand about 140 feet high and surround small parcels and plateaus of woody vegetation.

There is a limited trail system within the wilderness. However, the trails are only minimally signed. The interior dunes provide opportunities for more solitude, primitive recreation, and physical challenge. There is no water source in the dunes, so water must be carried. Due to the fragile nature of Nordhouse Dunes, camping and campfires are discouraged in the open sand areas.

Hiking in the sand dunes is much easier when you stay on the boardwalks.

The campground at Lake Michigan Recreation Area has 4 loops; reservations are taken for some sites.

Recreational Trails

Manistee National Forest has more than 90 miles of trails suitable for hiking. Some trails are specifically for hiking, while some allow other summer uses such as horseback riding. In addition, there are cross-country ski trails, which make ideal non-winter hiking trails. The forest is now constructing the North Country National Scenic Trail, which extends from Vermont to North Dakota with about 150 miles within the Manistee National Forest. More than half of this trail has been completed in the forest. Free handout sheets and maps are available on hiking trails. Most of the hiking trails are linear trails; generally, the cross-country ski trails and the interpretive trails consist of loops of varying lengths. There are also more than 550 miles of motorized trails for cycles and snowmobiles.

Canoeing

Eight rivers offer about 246 miles of canoeing within the boundaries of the Manistee National Forest. The rivers range from 20 feet to 80 feet wide and meander through deeply cut sand and clay banks to wide flat flood plains. Many rivers have commercial canoe liveries operating on them, where you can usually rent canoes for your trip. Handouts and detailed maps are available that explain features of the river, describe access points, and list the canoe liveries in the area. All are available from any of the District Ranger offices or from the Forest Supervisor's Office. The eight rivers are: Big Manistee (2 segments), Pine River, Little Manistee, Big Sable, Pere Marquette, Big South Branch of the Pere Marquette, White, and Little Muskegon.

Baldwin Ranger District

For Information

Baldwin Ranger District
650 N. Michigan Ave.
Baldwin, MI 49304
(616) 745-4631

Campgrounds	Number of Sites	Swimming Beach	Hiking Trail	Fishing	Boat Ramp	User Fee
1. Bowman Bridge*	20		X		CL	X
2. Highbank Lake	9	X	X	X	C	X
3. Gleasons Landing*	4			X		X
4. Old Grade*	20			X		X
5. Timber Creek	9		X			X

All campgrounds have drinking water and toilets (pit or vault).
* All have group campgrounds; Bowman Bridge has 4 sites for 20 each.
C—Carry-in boat access; CL—Canoe landing.

Campground Locations

Bowman Bridge is about 4½ miles west of Baldwin on Carrs Road. In Baldwin, from the junction of US 10 east with M-37, go ⁴⁄10 of a mile south, then right on 7th Street for 5 blocks, then left on Cherry Street for 1½ blocks, then right on 52nd Street (Carrs Road) and west for 4⅓ miles to the site. The campground adjoins the Pere Marquette National Scenic River and has a canoe landing; it also provides access to the North Country Trail.

Highbank Lake is off of M-37, 9 miles south of Baldwin and west from Lilley. Travel south from Baldwin and turn right on 15 Mile Road in Lilley and go ½ mile, then turn right on Roosevelt Drive and go 1½ miles. The lake has 20 surface acres; the North Country Trail provides hiking.

Gleasons Landing is 3 miles southwest of Baldwin; see directions for Bowman Bridge for reaching 52nd Street (Carrs Road). Travel west on Carrs Road for 2⅕ miles to Jenks Road, turn south and travel ½ mile to Shortcut Road, then go southwest for ⁶⁄10 mile to 60th Street, then west for ½ mile to Brooks Road, then south for ⁶⁄10 mile to the site. The campground is located right on the Pere Marquette National Scenic River.

Old Grade is about 11½ miles north of Baldwin. Travel on M-37 for 11 miles, then left on FSR 5190. The campground is on the Little Manistee River, although the river is too shallow for canoeing at this location.

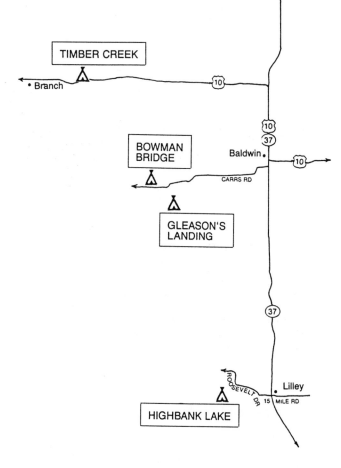

Timber Creek is just off of US 10, about 10 miles west of Baldwin and 2 miles east of the small community of Branch. Go north on FSR 5198. Tank Creek flows through the campground, and a dam impounds a small pond. The North Country Trail is nearby.

REGION 2

Cadillac Ranger District

For Information

Cadillac Ranger District
1800 W. M-55
P.O. Box 409
Cadillac, MI 49601
(616) 775-8539

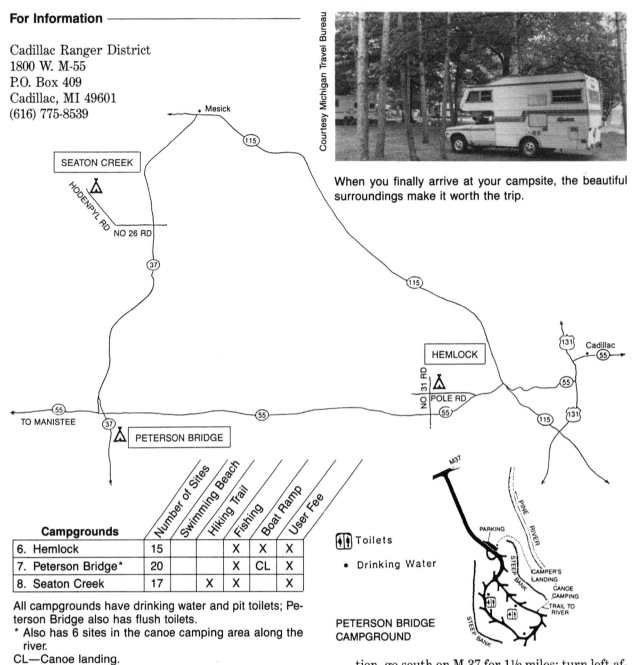

Courtesy Michigan Travel Bureau

When you finally arrive at your campsite, the beautiful surroundings make it worth the trip.

Campgrounds	Number of Sites	Swimming Beach	Hiking Trail	Fishing	Boat Ramp	User Fee
6. Hemlock	15			X	X	X
7. Peterson Bridge*	20			X	CL	X
8. Seaton Creek	17	X		X		X

Toilets
• Drinking Water

PETERSON BRIDGE
CAMPGROUND

All campgrounds have drinking water and pit toilets; Peterson Bridge also has flush toilets.
* Also has 6 sites in the canoe camping area along the river.
CL—Canoe landing.

Campground Locations

Hemlock is 5 miles west of Cadillac. From the junction of M-55 and M-115 (west of Cadillac), travel west on M-55 for 1³/₁₀ miles to Pole Road; turn right and go 1²/₅ miles. The campground adjoins Lake Mitchell, a 2,580-acre prime fishing lake.

Peterson Bridge is off of M-37, just south of M-55 between Cadillac and Manistee. From this junc-

tion, go south on M-37 for 1½ miles; turn left after crossing the bridge. The campground adjoins the Pine River, an outstanding canoeing and trout-fishing river.

Seaton Creek is about 7 miles southwest of Mesick. Travel south on M-37 from Mesick for 6 miles, turn right on No. 26 Road for 1⁷/₁₀ miles, then right on Hodenpyl Road for 1³/₁₀ miles, then right on FSR 5993 for ½ mile. The campground adjoins Seaton Creek and is at the upper end of the backwater of Hodenpyl Dam Pond on the Big Manistee River.

Manistee Ranger District

For Information

Manistee Ranger District
1658 Manistee Hwy.
Manistee, MI 49660
(616) 723-2211

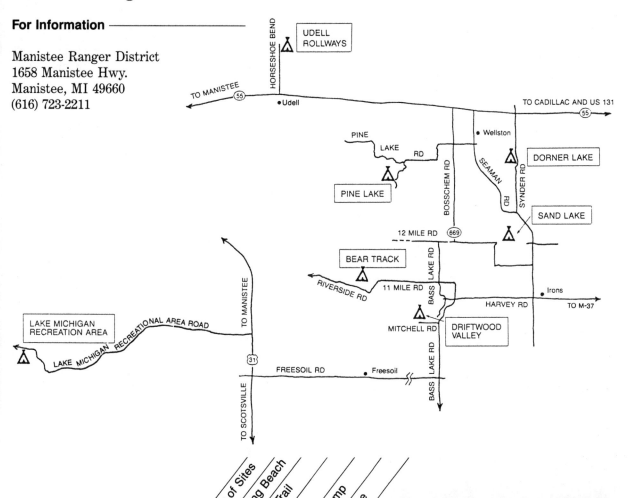

Campgrounds	Number of Sites	Swimming Beach	Hiking Trail	Fishing	Boat Ramp	User Fee
9. Bear Track*	16		X			X
10. Dorner Lake	8			X	X	X
11. Driftwood Valley*	21		X	X		X
12. Lake Michigan Recreation Area*†	98	X	X	X		X
13. Pine Lake	12	X		X	X	X
14. Sand Lake	45	X		X	X	X
15. Udell Rollways	23					X

All campgrounds have vault toilets; Lake Michigan Recreation Area, Sand Lake, and Udell Rollways also have flush toilets.

† Some sites available on reservation system (1-800-283-CAMP).

* Group campgrounds: Bear Track (4 sites, 50 capacity); Driftwood Valley (1 site, 30 capacity); Lake Michigan R.A. (3 sites, 100 capacity); make reservations.

Guess who brought too much gear?

Manistee Ranger District (*continued*)

Lake Michigan Recreation Area

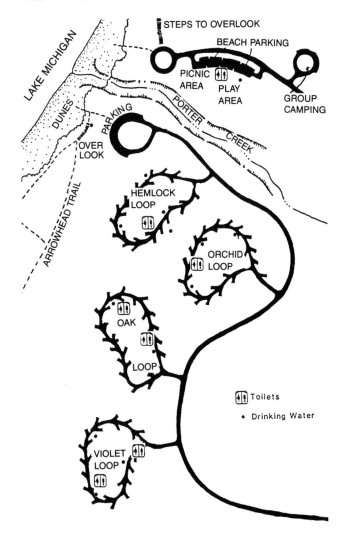

STEPS TO OVERLOOK

BEACH PARKING

LAKE MICHIGAN

DUNES

PORTER CREEK

PICNIC AREA

PLAY AREA

GROUP CAMPING

PARKING

OVER LOOK

ARROWHEAD TRAIL

HEMLOCK LOOP

ORCHID LOOP

OAK

LOOP

VIOLET LOOP

Toilets

• Drinking Water

Campground Locations ——————

Bear Track is southwest of the community of Wellston; Wellston is just south of M-55. Leave M-55 just west of Wellston and go south on M-669 (Bosschem Road) for 4 miles to 12 Mile Road, then west ½ mile, then south on Bass Lake Road for 1 mile to 11 Mile Road, then west

for 2½ miles to FSR 5202 (Riverside Drive). Turn right and go ½ mile to the entrance. The campground adjoins the Little Manistee River and the North Country Trail.

Dorner Lake is southeast of the community of Wellston. From the junction of M-55 with M-669 (Bosschem Road) near Wellston, go east for 2 miles, then right on Snyder Road for 1½ miles. Dorner Lake has 49 surface acres and is popular for yellow perch, pumpkin seed, black crappie, and bluegill.

Driftwood Valley is south of Wellston and accessible from several directions. From Wellston, go south on M-669 (Bosschem Road) for 4 miles to 12 Mile Road, right for ½ mile, then left (south) on Bass Lake Road for about 3 miles. Turn right on FSR 5357 (Mitchell Road) and go ¾ mile. From the west, turn east off of US 31 at its junction with Freesoil Road and go east for 15 miles (through Freesoil) to the stop sign on Bass Lake Road. Turn left and go 1¾ miles north to FSR 5357; then go left for ¾ mile. The campground is adjacent to the Little Manistee River and the North Country Trail.

Lake Michigan Recreation Area is about 13 miles southwest of Manistee. From the junction of US 31 with M-55 in Manistee, take US 31 south for 10 miles, then turn right on Lake Michigan Recreation Area Road and go 8 miles. The campground adjoins Lake Michigan and the Nordhouse Dunes Wilderness Area.

Pine Lake is about 3½ miles southwest of Wellston. From M-55, take M-669 (Bosschem Road) south for 1.1 miles, then turn right on Pine Lake Road and continue for 2.6 miles. Pine Lake is 156 acres, with good largemouth bass, brown trout, bluegill, rock bass, yellow perch, and golden shiner.

Sand Lake is south of Wellston but the nearest community is Dublin, about 1 mile north. From M-55 at Wellston, go south on Seaman Road for 4½ miles through Dublin to the entrance road, then right on FSR 5728 to the campground. Sand Lake is 50 acres and is known for its excellent swimming beach.

Udell Rollways is about 8 miles northwest of Wellston. Go west from Wellston on M-55 to the small community of Udell; turn right on Horseshoe Bend Road, go 1¾ miles. The campground overlooks the Manistee River, but the river is not easily accessible due to a high, steep bank.

White Cloud Ranger District

For Information

White Cloud Ranger District
12 North Charles St.
White Cloud, MI 49349
(616) 689-6696

These youngsters are sharpening their fishing skills.

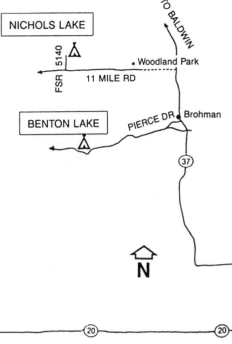

Campgrounds	Number of Sites	Swimming Beach	Hiking Trail	Fishing	Boat Ramp	User Fee
16. Benton Lake	24	X	X	X	X	X
17. Nichols Lake	28	X	X	X	X†	X
18. Pines Point	33		X		CL	X

All campgrounds have drinking water and vault toilets;
Nichols Lake and Pines Point also have flush toilets.
† Boat launch is located ½ mile from campground.
CL—Canoe launch.

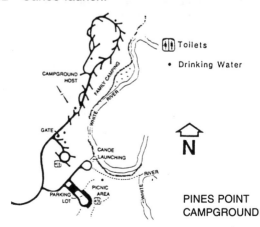

PINES POINT
CAMPGROUND

Campground Locations

Benton Lake is off of M-37 at the community of Brohman, which is south of Baldwin and north of White Cloud. From Brohman, travel west on Pierce Drive for 4½ miles. The North Country Trail is close; the lake has 33 surface acres.

Nichols Lake is 3 miles west of Woodland Park. At a point 2 miles north of Brohman on M-37, turn west on 11 Mile Road and travel 4½ miles. Turn right on FSR 5140 to reach the campground. The lake has 160 surface acres; the North Country Trail is accessible.

Pines Point is about 8½ miles southwest of Hesperia (located at the junction of M-20 and M-120). From Hesperia, go south on M-120 (Maple Island Road) for 1 mile to Garfield Road. Turn right (west) and go 5 miles; turn left on 168th Avenue (FSR 5118) and follow the blacktop for 2½ miles. The campground adjoins the South Branch of the White River, a canoe route.

Mears State Park

For Information

Mears State Park
Pentwater, MI 49449
(616) 869-2051

Most sites at Mears will accommodate any type of camping equipment.

Location

Charles Mears State Park is located off of Business US 31, just 4 blocks from downtown Pentwater. Overlooking beautiful Lake Michigan, the park encompasses 50 partially wooded acres.

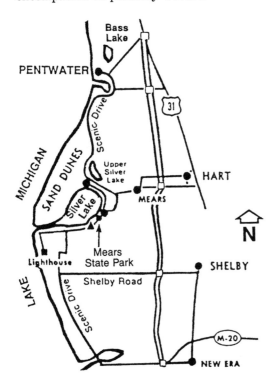

Mears State Park has a unique campground, surrounded by low-lying sand dunes.

Facilities & Activities

180 modern campsites
  electrical hookups
  flush toilets
  showers
  sanitation station
organization campground
picnic area
picnic shelter

playground
swimming beach
beach house and store
fishing
fish-cleaning station
boating
hiking trail

Mitchell State Park

For Information

Mitchell State Park
6093 East M-115
Cadillac, MI 49601
(616) 775-7911

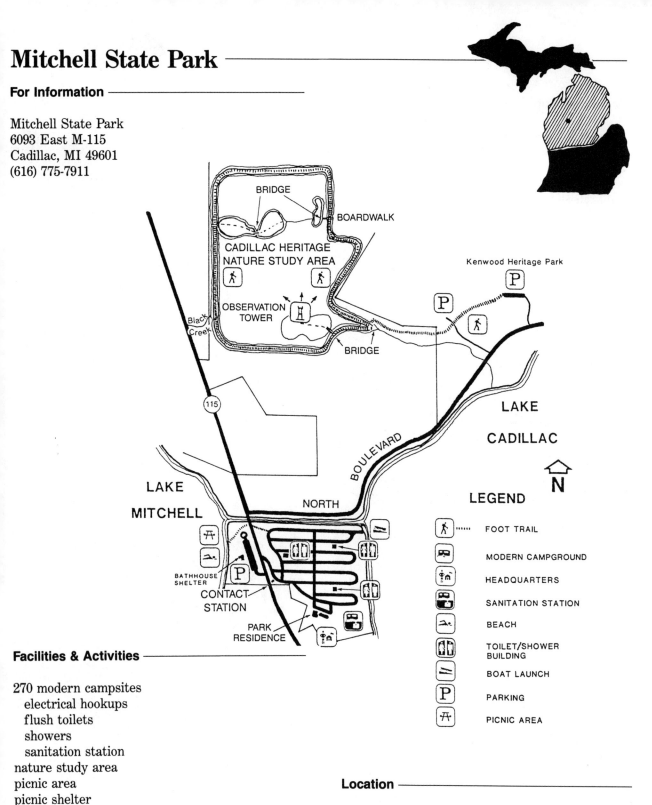

Facilities & Activities

270 modern campsites
  electrical hookups
  flush toilets
  showers
  sanitation station
nature study area
picnic area
picnic shelter
playground
swimming beach
beach house
fishing
boating
boat launch
hiking trails

Location

Wm. Mitchell State Park is located 4 miles west of Cadillac on M-115 at M-55. The 334-acre park is located between Lake Mitchell and Lake Cadillac; the lakes are connected by a ¼-mile canal. The Heritage Nature Study Area is nearby; a hiking trail, boardwalk, and observation tower provide opportunities to view a variety of wildlife.

Mitchell State Park   **99**

Newaygo State Park

For Information

For information April through November:
Newaygo State Park
2793 Beech Street
Newaygo, MI 49337
(616) 856-4452

For information December through March:
Silver Lake State Park
Route 1, Box 254
Mears, MI 49436
(616) 873-3083

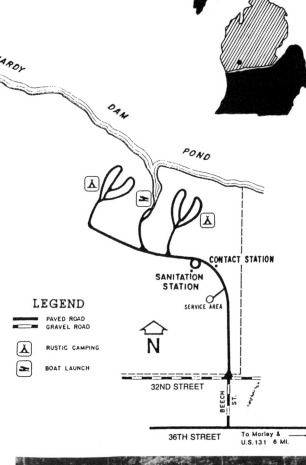

LEGEND

━━━ PAVED ROAD
▭ GRAVEL ROAD

△ RUSTIC CAMPING

⛵ BOAT LAUNCH

N

CONTACT STATION
SANITATION STATION
SERVICE AREA

32ND STREET
BEECH ST.
36TH STREET
To Morley &
U.S. 131   6 MI.

Fishing sites along the bank of Hardy Dam Pond are accessible from Newago State Park.

Location

Newaygo State Park is located on Hardy Dam Pond, a lake created by the impoundment of the Muskegon River. The 257-acre park may be reached from one of several directions, but it helps to have a good road map. From Newaygo, travel north on M-37, then east on 40th Street, which dead-ends into Pine Avenue; jog left and then right to get on 36th Street. When you cross the dam, you know you're getting close. Continue on 36th Street and turn left on Beech Street. You should be seeing park signs by now. From US 131 north of Grand Rapids, take the Morley exit and travel west on Jefferson Road. When you cross into Newaygo County from Mecosta County, Jefferson Road becomes 36th Street. Turn right on Beech Street to the park entrance. The park is not staffed year-round.

Hardy Dam Pond was created by the impoundment of the Muskegon River; the lake sees a lot of action from all sizes and types of boats.

Facilities & Activities

99 rustic campsites
  vault toilets
  hand pump
hunting

fishing
boating
boat launch
hiking

North Higgins Lake State Park

For Information

North Higgins Lake State Park
11511 W. Higgins Lake Drive
Roscommon, MI 48653
(517) 821-6125

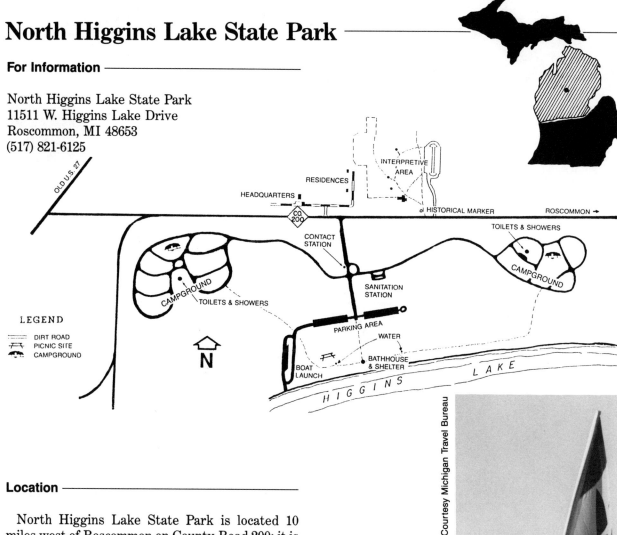

LEGEND

- - - - DIRT ROAD
🏕 PICNIC SITE
🏕 CAMPGROUND

N

Location

North Higgins Lake State Park is located 10 miles west of Roscommon on County Road 200; it is accessible from the west via the Military Road exit from US 27 or from the east via exit 244 from I-75. The 429-acre park, one of the most popular recreation lakes in the state, has 1,500 feet of shoreline along Higgins Lake. The Interpretive Area is the site of the CCC Museum; the Civilian Conservation Corps was responsible for planting millions of trees during the Great Depression.

Facilities & Activities

218 modern campsites
  electrical hookups
  flush toilets
  showers
  sanitation station
organization campground
Interpretive Area
picnic area
picnic shelter
playground

swimming beach
beach house
hunting
fishing
boating
boat launch
network of hiking trails
nature and fitness trail
snowmobile trail
24 km of cross-country ski trails

This windsurfer is on a tack that will bring him all the way to the shore.

Courtesy Michigan Travel Bureau

REGION 2

Onaway State Park

Onaway State Park
Route 1, Box 188
Onaway, MI 49765
(517) 733-8279

LEGEND

↤ ACCESS SITE
P PARKING
禾 PICNIC AREA

N

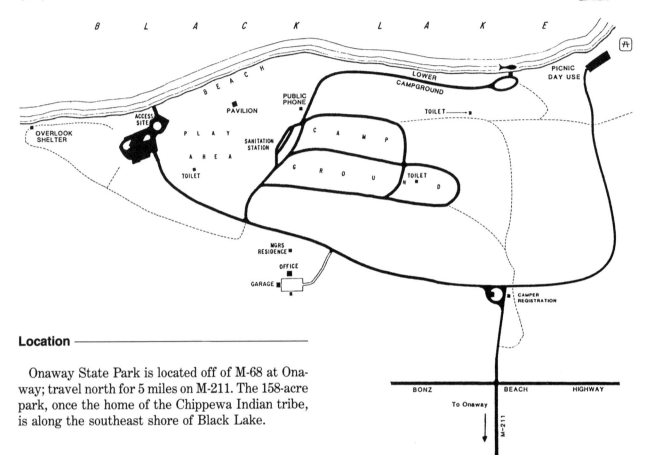

Location

Onaway State Park is located off of M-68 at Onaway; travel north for 5 miles on M-211. The 158-acre park, once the home of the Chippewa Indian tribe, is along the southeast shore of Black Lake.

The lower campground at Onaway State Park borders the lake, which is a real convenience for campers with boats.

Facilities & Activities

103 modern campsites
  electrical hookups
  flush toilets
  showers
  sanitation station
picnic area
picnic shelter
playground
swimming beach
beach house
fishing
boating
boat launch
hiking trails

Orchard Beach State Park

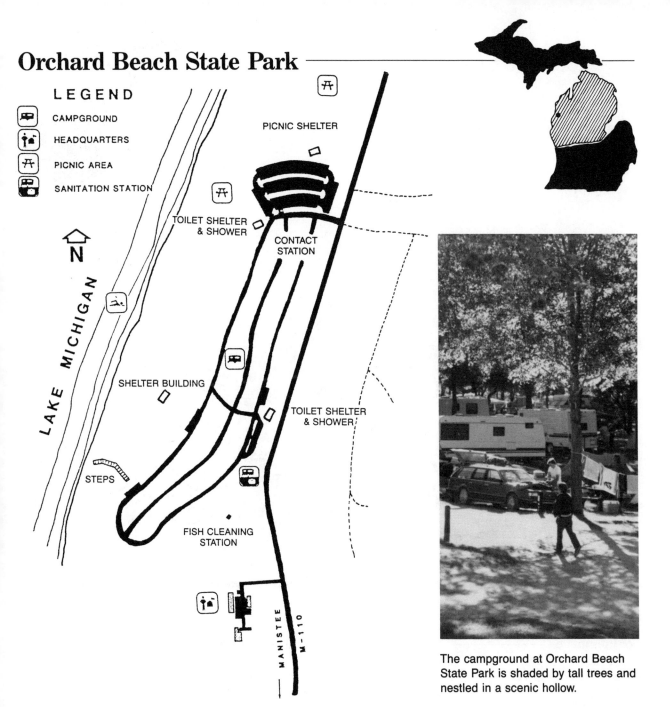

LEGEND

- CAMPGROUND
- HEADQUARTERS
- PICNIC AREA
- SANITATION STATION

N

LAKE MICHIGAN

PICNIC SHELTER

TOILET SHELTER & SHOWER

CONTACT STATION

SHELTER BUILDING

TOILET SHELTER & SHOWER

STEPS

FISH CLEANING STATION

MANISTEE M-110

The campground at Orchard Beach State Park is shaded by tall trees and nestled in a scenic hollow.

For Information

Orchard Beach State Park
2064 Lakeshore Road
Manistee, MI 49660
(616) 723-7422

Location

Orchard Beach State Park is located 2 miles north of Manistee on M-110 from US 31. The 201-acre park is set on a bluff overlooking Lake Michigan.

Facilities & Activities

175 modern campsites
  electrical hookups
  flush toilets
  showers
  sanitation station
picnic area
picnic shelter
playground
swimming beach
network of hiking trails
cross-country skiing

Otsego Lake State Park

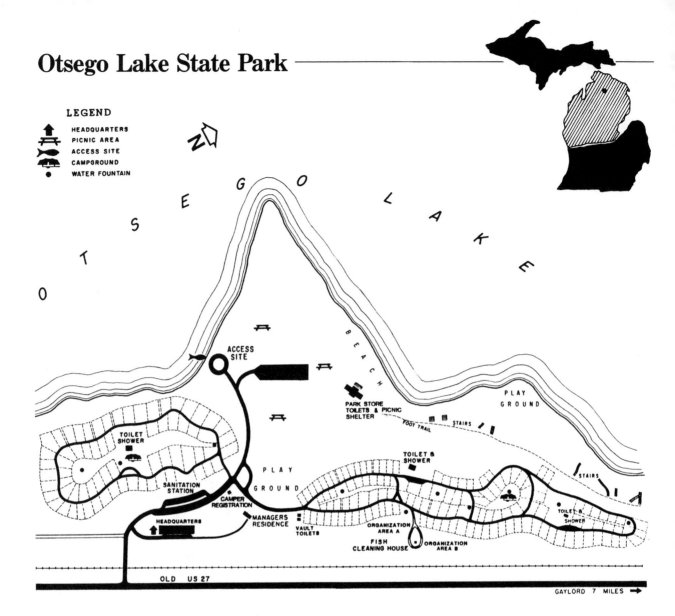

LEGEND
- HEADQUARTERS
- PICNIC AREA
- ACCESS SITE
- CAMPGROUND
- WATER FOUNTAIN

For Information

Otsego Lake State Park
Route 3
Gaylord, MI 49735
(517) 732-5485

Location

Otsego Lake State Park is located 7 miles south of Gaylord on Old US 27. The easiest approach from I-75 is to take exit 270 and travel west to Waters; then turn north onto Old US 27 and follow the park signs. The 62-acre park is on Lake Otsego and has a wide, sandy beach and a line of low bluffs that overlook the water.

Facilities & Activities

203 modern campsites
  electrical hookups
  flush toilets
  showers
  sanitation station
rent-a-tent
2 organization campgrounds
picnic area
playground
swimming beach
beach house and park store
fishing
fish-cleaning house
boating
boat launch
hiking

Pere Marquette State Forest

For Information

Pere Marquette State Forest
Route 1
Cadillac, MI 49601
(616) 775-9727

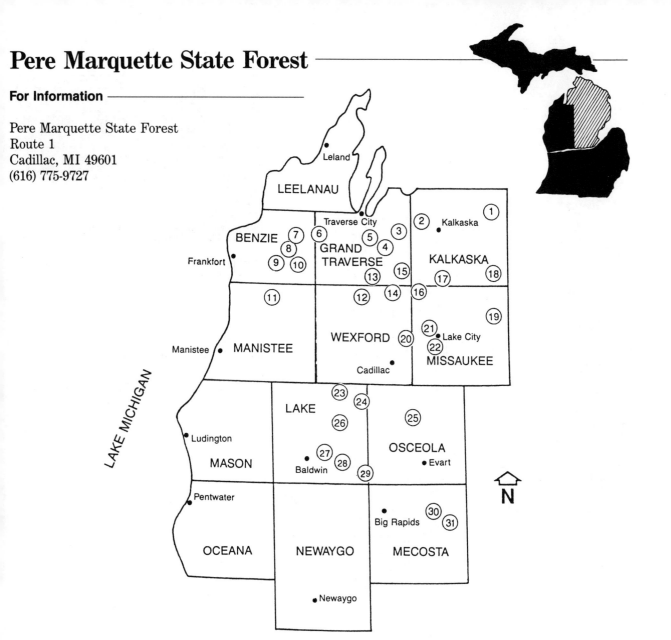

Campground Locations

1. *Pickerel Lake*—13½ miles northeast of Kalkaska via County Road 612 and Sunset Trail Road.
2. *Guernsey Lake*—8 miles west of Kalkaska via Island Lake Road and Campground Road.
3. *Forks*—7 miles south of Williamsburg via Williamsburg Road, Supply Road, and River Road.
4. *Scheck's Place*—12 miles southwest of Williamsburg via Williamsburg Road, Supply Road, and Brown Bridge Road.
5. *Arbutus No. 4*—10 miles southeast of Traverse City via Garfield Road, Potter Road, Four Mile Road, and North Arbutus Lake Road.
6. *Lake Dubonnet*—5 miles northwest of Interlochen State Park via M-137, US 31, and Wildwood Road.
7. *Lake Ann*—2 miles southwest of Lake Ann via Almira Road and Reynolds Road.
8. *Veterans Memorial*—3½ miles east of Honor via US 31.
9. *Platte River*—2½ miles southeast of Honor via US 31 and Goose Road.
10. *Grass Lake*—10 miles northeast of Thompsonville via County Road 669 and Wallin Road.
11. *Healy Lake*—7½ miles southwest of Copemish via County Road 669 and Piagany Road and the entrance road.
12. *Indian Crossing*—6½ miles northeast of Sherman via Road 14 and Campground Road.

(continued)

Pere Marquette State Forest (*continued*)

You're looking at the author's camping rig set up for a one-night stay at Platte River campground.

Campgrounds	Number of Sites	Boating/Canoeing	Swimming	Fishing
1. Pickerel Lake	12	B	2	W
2. Guernsey Lake	26	B	2	C W
3. Forks	8	C	3	C
4. Scheck's Place	31	C	3	C
5. Arbutus No. 4	50	B	1	W
6. Lake Dubonnet	50	B	3	W
7. Lake Ann	30	B	1	W
8. Veterans Memorial	24	C	3	C
9. Platte River	26	C	3	C
10. Grass Lake	15	B C	3	W
11. Healy Lake	24	B	1	W
12. Indian Crossing	19	C	3	C
13. Baxter Bridge	15	C	3	C
14. Old US 131	19	C	3	C
15. Spring Lake	32		2	W
16. Chase Creek	6	C	3	C
17. Smithville	15	C	3	C
18. C.C.C. Bridge	23	C	3	C
19. Reedsburg Dam	42	B	2	W
20. Long Lake	5	B	3	W
21. Goose Lake	54	B	1	W
22. Long Lake	16	B	1	W
23. Lincoln Bridge	9	C	3	C
24. Silver Creek	29	C	3	C
25. Sunrise Lake	17	B	2	C W
26. Carrieville	26		3	C
27. Bray Creek	10		3	C
28. Little Leverentz	7		3	W
29. Big Leverentz	10		3	W
30. Tubbs Island	9	B	3	W
31. Tubbs Lake	21	B	3	W

Swimming: 1—Sandy beach and bottom.
              2—Gravel or rocky bottom with little or no beach.
              3—Swimming is not recommended.
Fishing: C—Cold-water species.
              W—Warm-water species.

13. *Baxter Bridge*—12 miles northwest of Manton via M-42 and Road 31.
14. *Old US 131*—6 miles north of Manton on US 131.

15. *Spring Lake*—1½ miles southwest of Fife Lake via US 131.
16. *Chase Creek*—7½ miles northeast of Manton via US 131, Road 12, and Road 45½.
17. *Smithville*—½ mile northwest of Smithville via M-66.
18. *C.C.C. Bridge*—20 miles southeast of Kalkaska via M-72 and Sunset Trail Road.
19. *Reedsburg Dam*—5 miles northwest of Houghton Lake via M-55 and County Road 300.
20. *Long Lake*—8 miles northeast of Cadillac via US 131 and Campground Road.
21. *Goose Lake*—2½ miles northwest of Lake City via M-66 and Goose Lake Road.
22. *Long Lake*—3½ miles northwest of Lake City via M-66 and Goose Lake Road.
23. *Lincoln Bridge*—7 miles north of Luther via State Road and Ten Mile Road.
24. *Silver Creek*—5½ miles north of Luther via State Road.
25. *Sunrise Lake*—6 miles east of LeRoy via Sunset Lake Road and Fifteen Mile Road.
26. *Carrieville*—3 miles west of Luther via Old M-63 and Kings Highway.
27. *Bray Creek*—1½ miles northeast of Baldwin via M-37, North Street, Maryville Road and 40th Street.
28. *Little Leverentz*—2 miles northeast of Baldwin via US 10 and Campground Road.
29. *Big Leverentz*—2 miles northeast of Baldwin via US 10.
30. *Tubbs Island*—7 miles southwest of Barryton via M-66, Seventeen Mile Road, and 45th Avenue.
31. *Tubbs Lake*—6½ miles southwest of Barryton via M-66, Seventeen Mile Road, and 45th Avenue.

Petoskey State Park

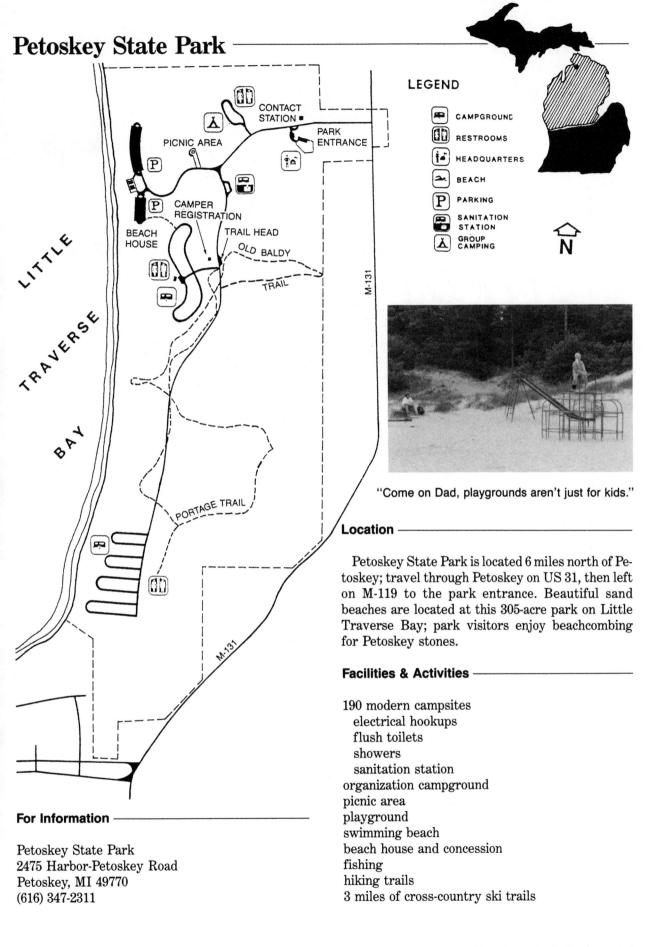

LEGEND

🏕 CAMPGROUND
🚻 RESTROOMS
👤 HEADQUARTERS
🏊 BEACH
Ⓟ PARKING
🚐 SANITATION STATION
⛺ GROUP CAMPING

N

LITTLE TRAVERSE BAY

PICNIC AREA

CONTACT STATION

PARK ENTRANCE

CAMPER REGISTRATION

BEACH HOUSE

TRAIL HEAD

OLD BALDY TRAIL

M-131

PORTAGE TRAIL

M-131

"Come on Dad, playgrounds aren't just for kids."

Location

Petoskey State Park is located 6 miles north of Petoskey; travel through Petoskey on US 31, then left on M-119 to the park entrance. Beautiful sand beaches are located at this 305-acre park on Little Traverse Bay; park visitors enjoy beachcombing for Petoskey stones.

Facilities & Activities

190 modern campsites
  electrical hookups
  flush toilets
  showers
  sanitation station
organization campground
picnic area
playground
swimming beach
beach house and concession
fishing
hiking trails
3 miles of cross-country ski trails

For Information

Petoskey State Park
2475 Harbor-Petoskey Road
Petoskey, MI 49770
(616) 347-2311

REGION 2

Rifle River Recreation Area

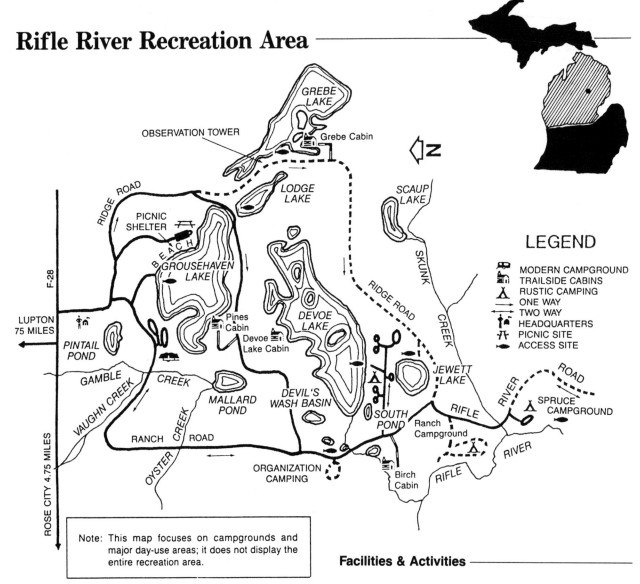

Note: This map focuses on campgrounds and major day-use areas; it does not display the entire recreation area.

For Information

Rifle River Recreation Area
2550 East Rose City Road
Lupton, MI 48635
(517) 473-2258

Location

Rifle River Recreation Area is located 15 miles northeast of West Branch off of M-33 at Rose City; at Rose City, travel 4¾ miles east on F-28 (Rose City Road). The entry to the recreation area is ¾ mile south of Lupton. This 4,329-acre wilderness area is in the Ogemaw State Forest. There are 10 scenic lakes, miles of stream suitable for fly fishing, and the headwaters of Rifle River, a state-designated Scenic Natural River.

Facilities & Activities

80 modern campsites at Grousehaven Lake
  electrical hookups
  flush toilets
  showers
  sanitation station
101 rustic campsites (51 at Devoe Lake; 25 at Ranch; 25 at Spruce)
  vault toilets
  hand pump
organization campground
4 rustic cabins (each sleeps 6)
day-use facilities at Grousehaven Lake & Devoe picnic area & swimming beach
hunting
fishing (lake & stream)
boating (no motors)
canoe/boat launches
12 miles of hiking trails
snowmobiling
cross-country skiing

Silver Lake State Park

Silver Lake State Park
Route 1, Box 254
Mears, MI 49436
(616) 873-3083

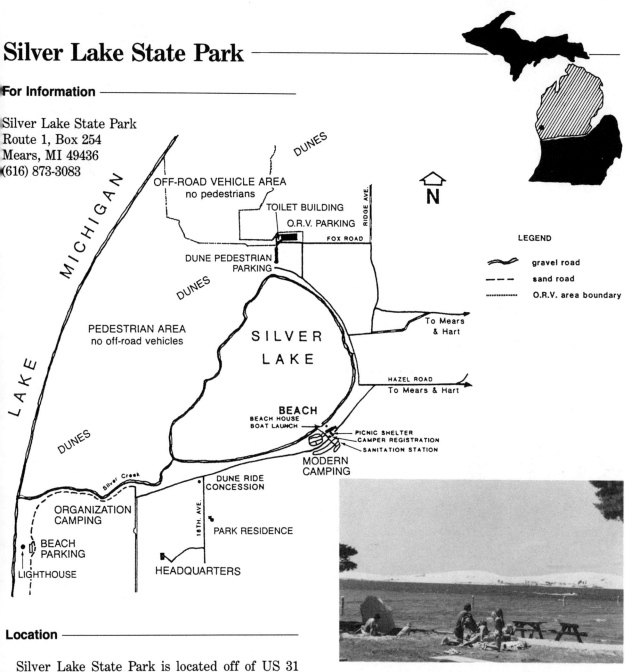

LEGEND

~~~ gravel road

- - - sand road

.... O.R.V. area boundary

The dune area at the state park is across Silver Lake and is quite visible from the swimming beach.

Location

Silver Lake State Park is located off of US 31 along the shoreline of Lake Michigan. The park may be reached by traveling west from either the Mears/Hart or Shelby exits from US 31. Directions are given here for the Shelby exit: travel 6 miles west to County Road B-15 (16th Avenue), then north for 5 miles to the park entrance. The 2,762-acre park is located on Silver Lake but contains almost 4 miles of Lake Michigan shoreline. This is dune country, so the lack of trees is quite noticeable. The north end of the park is a designated ORV (off-road-vehicle) area, the only park in the state with such an area. A dune-ride concession is located in the south end of the park. The historic Little Point Sable Lighthouse is the site of one of the park's day-use areas.

Facilities & Activities

249 modern campsites
  electrical hookups
  flush toilets
  showers
  sanitation station
organization campground
picnic area
picnic shelter
playground

swimming beaches
beach house
hunting
fishing
boating
boat launch
hiking
designated ORV area
snowmobiling

REGION 2

Sleeping Bear Dunes National Lakeshore

For Information

Sleeping Bear Dunes National Lakeshore
P.O. Box 277
Empire, MI 49630
(616) 326-5134

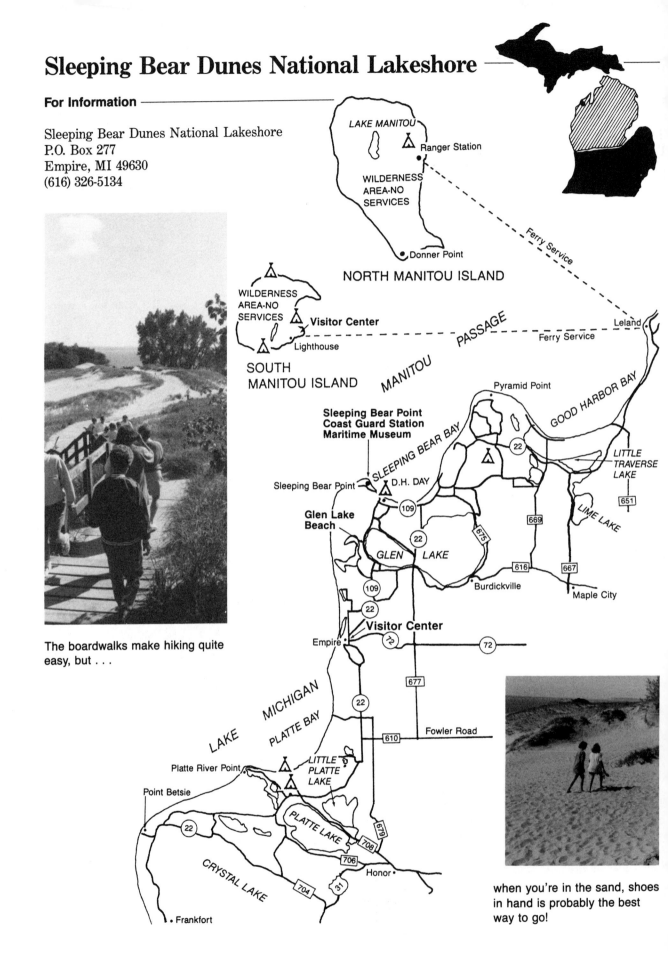

The boardwalks make hiking quite easy, but . . .

when you're in the sand, shoes in hand is probably the best way to go!

Location

Sleeping Bear Dunes National Lakeshore lies on the northwestern shore of Michigan's lower peninsula, a hilly region fringed with massive coastal sand dunes and dotted with clear lakes. The 71,132-acre national lakeshore, established in October 1977, is comprised of the mainland and two tranquil and secluded islands that are located several miles offshore. The main road through the park is M-22, accessible from the south via M-115 through Frankfort, and from the east via M-72 through Traverse City to Empire. The visitor center and park headquarters are located in the same building at the junction of M-22 and M-72 in Empire. Commercial ferry service to both islands is from Leland, northeast of the park on M-22.

The views of the dunes, sand bluffs, and Lake Michigan are spectacular from the numerous overlooks along the trail.

About the Lakeshore

The landscape at Sleeping Bear Dunes National Lakeshore is diverse, with birch-lined streams, dense beech–maple forests, and rugged bluffs towering as high as 460 feet above Lake Michigan. The sand dunes are the product of a long and complex geological and botanical history. Prevailing westerly winds blowing across the lake build two kinds of dunes: beach dunes that develop on low-lying shores of Lake Michigan, and perched dunes that sit high above the shore on plateaus. Pushed by the wind, some dunes migrate; sometimes the shifting sands bury trees.

Nature and history exhibits, a slide program, and book sales are available at the visitor center; the center is open daily all year. Exhibits can also be seen at the Sleeping Bear Point Coast Guard Station Maritime Museum and at several outdoor locations on the mainland and on South Manitou Island.

You'll drive through this bridge when you take the Pierce Stocking Scenic Drive; the 7.4-mile drive is a "must" for all park visitors.

General Park Information

▲ Summer schedules of guided walks and evening programs are available at the visitor center or campgrounds.

▲ The 7.1-mile Pierce Stocking Scenic Drive is open from mid-May to early November, weather permitting; pick up a self-guiding brochure at the drive entrance.

▲ Trailers are prohibited on the scenic drive; bicycles are permitted.

▲ Trailhead locations for 11 summer hikes are marked on the park brochure; trail maps are available at the visitor center.

▲ Hunting is allowed in season under state regulations.

▲ The park's lakes and rivers offer opportunities for swimming, boating, and fishing.

▲ Canoes can be rented on the Platte and Crystal Rivers.

▲ Anglers can fish for trout, pike, bass, and salmon; a Michigan fishing license is required.

▲ About 80 miles of trails are marked in the winter for cross-country skiing; obtain map at the visitor center.

▲ Snowmobiling is prohibited except on rights-of-way along some state and county roads.

▲ Summers are cooler and winters milder along the lakeshore than in nearby inland areas because of Lake Michigan's moderating influence.

▲ Do not drive off established roads in the park.

▲ Always keep your pet on a leash; pets are not allowed on the Dune Climb, Glen Lake Beach, or the Manitou Islands.

▲ Campfires are permitted only in campground and picnic area fireplaces.

▲ Poison ivy is abundant in the park; heed the warning "leaflets of three, let it be."

▲ Commercial ferry service to both Manitou islands is from Leland; ask the visitor center for the information brochures on South and North Manitou.

▲ South Manitou Island is an eight-square-mile, 5,260-acre island; it has many points to visit; there is no food service on the island, so take a lunch.

▲ The trip to South Manitou Island takes 1½ hours and the boat docks on the island for 4 hours.

▲ Trips to South Manitou Island are daily in the summer (June–August); in May, September, and October, there are no trips on Tuesdays and Thursdays.

▲ Four open-aired vehicles are available for a 1½-hour tour of South Manitou Island; these may be arranged with the crew during the cruise.

▲ North Manitou Island is 7¾ miles long by 4¼ miles wide and has 20 miles of shoreline. The 15,000-acre island is managed as wilderness; the primary visitor activities are primitive camping, hiking, backpacking, and hunting.

▲ The trip to North Manitou Island takes 1 hour 10 minutes and has no layover; it has an immediate turnaround departure for Leland.

▲ Trips to North Manitou Island are on Sunday, Wednesday, and Friday in the summer; for fall schedules (September–November), including hunting season, check with park headquarters.

Mainland

▲ There are 2 campgrounds on the mainland; fees are charged at both.
  —Platte River, in the southern end, has 160 sites for tents and R.V.s; water, flush toilets, showers, trailer dumping station, electrical hookups at some sites.
  —D.H. Day, in the northern portion, has 88 sites for tents and R.V.s; water, vault toilets, trailer dumping station, no electrical hookups.

▲ Open year-round on a first-come, first-served basis.

▲ Maximum stay of 14 days between Memorial Day and Labor Day.

▲ Limit of 1 vehicle and a family or 4 unrelated people per campsite.

▲ A group campground is located near Glen Lake Beach; advance reservations must be made with park headquarters; vault toilets but no water at the campsites; no fee.

▲ Other campgrounds in the local area include 3 state parks, 4 state forests, and several privately operated (handout available).

▲ There are 2 backcountry campgrounds on the mainland:
  —White Pine is reached by a 2.7-mile trail from the Platte River Campground.
  —Valley View is 2 miles northeast of Glen Arbor, reached via a 1-mile trail from Hyland Road.

▲ Free backcountry use permits are required; obtain at visitor center, headquarters, and campgrounds.

▲ There is no potable water at either backcountry area.

South Manitou Island

▲ South Manitou Island is reached by a 1½-hour trip on a passenger ferry from Leland.

▲ There are 3 backcountry campgrounds on South Manitou Island: Bay, Weather Station, and Popple, each designed to handle a maximum of 6 campers.

▲ Free backcountry use permits are required; obtain from rangers on island.

▲ Several larger group campsites are designed to hold 25 campers each.

▲ Group sites are available on a reservation basis only; phone the park headquarters.

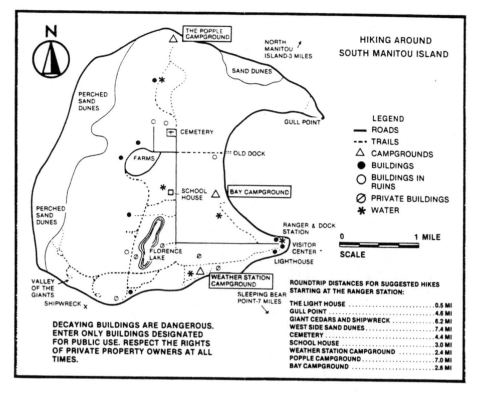

Map legend and details:

HIKING AROUND SOUTH MANITOU ISLAND

THE POPPLE CAMPGROUND
NORTH MANITOU ISLAND-3 MILES
SAND DUNES
PERCHED SAND DUNES
GULL POINT
CEMETERY
FARMS
OLD DOCK
SCHOOL HOUSE
BAY CAMPGROUND
PERCHED SAND DUNES
RANGER & DOCK STATION
VISITOR CENTER
FLORENCE LAKE
LIGHTHOUSE
VALLEY OF THE GIANTS
SHIPWRECK
WEATHER STATION CAMPGROUND
SLEEPING BEAR POINT-7 MILES

LEGEND
— ROADS
--- TRAILS
△ CAMPGROUNDS
● BUILDINGS
○ BUILDINGS IN RUINS
⊘ PRIVATE BUILDINGS
✳ WATER

0   1 MILE
SCALE

ROUNDTRIP DISTANCES FOR SUGGESTED HIKES STARTING AT THE RANGER STATION:

THE LIGHT HOUSE .... 0.5 MI
GULL POINT .... 4.6 MI
GIANT CEDARS AND SHIPWRECK .... 6.2 MI
WEST SIDE SAND DUNES .... 7.4 MI
CEMETERY .... 4.4 MI
SCHOOL HOUSE .... 3.0 MI
WEATHER STATION CAMPGROUND .... 2.4 MI
POPPLE CAMPGROUND .... 7.0 MI
BAY CAMPGROUND .... 2.6 MI

DECAYING BUILDINGS ARE DANGEROUS. ENTER ONLY BUILDINGS DESIGNATED FOR PUBLIC USE. RESPECT THE RIGHTS OF PRIVATE PROPERTY OWNERS AT ALL TIMES.

▲ Campers should practice low-impact, wilderness camping methods.

▲ Mosquitoes are common in the summer; poison ivy is abundant; be prepared for adverse weather.

▲ Travel light as there is no transportation for your camp gear.

▲ Water is available at 4 locations.

▲ Open fires are permitted in community fire rings only; dead and down wood may be used; backpack-style cooking stoves are recommended.

▲ For more detailed information, obtain the map/brochure on South Manitou Island available from the park.

North Manitou Island

▲ North Manitou Island is reached by a 1-hour, 10-minute trip on a passenger ferry from Leland.

▲ Wilderness camping regulations are in effect on North Manitou Island.

▲ There are 8 designated sites in the Village Campground.

▲ The remainder of the island is open to camping with certain restrictions.

▲ Campsites are limited to 2 tents and 6 persons.

▲ Free backcountry use permits are required; obtain from rangers on island.

▲ Raccoons are very troublesome; food should be suspended at night.

▲ Travel in the wilderness area is by foot only.

▲ Potable water is available only at the Ranger Station and the Village Campground.

▲ Open fires are prohibited in the wilderness area; use backpack-style cooking stoves; open fires are permitted in community fire rings in designated campgrounds.

▲ For camping restrictions and information, obtain the map/brochure on North Manitou Island; available from the park.

Recreational Activities

camping
picnicking
hiking
swimming
canoeing/boating
fishing
hunting
cross country skiing
7.4-mile scenic drive
summer ranger programs
summer ranger-guided tours
commercial ferry ride to islands

REGION 2

South Higgins Lake State Park

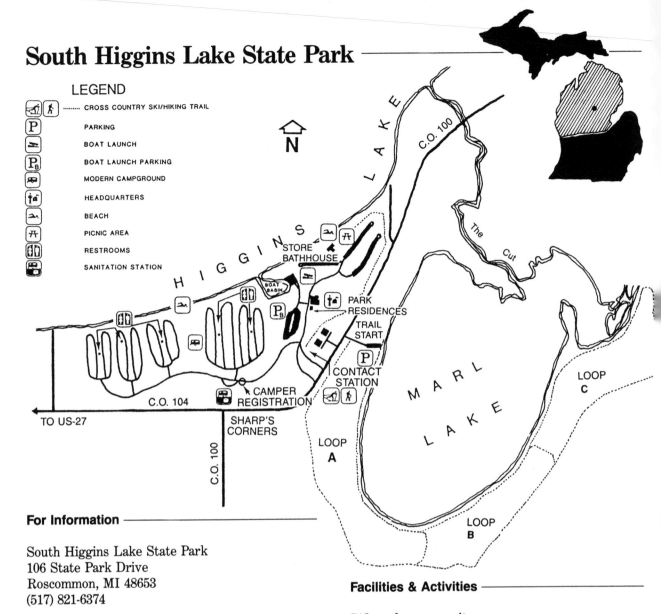

LEGEND

......	CROSS COUNTRY SKI/HIKING TRAIL
P	PARKING
	BOAT LAUNCH
P_B	BOAT LAUNCH PARKING
	MODERN CAMPGROUND
	HEADQUARTERS
	BEACH
	PICNIC AREA
	RESTROOMS
	SANITATION STATION

For Information

South Higgins Lake State Park
106 State Park Drive
Roscommon, MI 48653
(517) 821-6374

Location

   South Higgins Lake State Park is located on the south shore of Higgins Lake, south of Grayling. Access to this 1,007-acre park is via US 27 from the west and via I-75 from the east. When traveling US 27, take the Higgins Lake exit and travel east; follow Higgins Lake Road (County Road 104) to Sharps Corner where it becomes County Road 100; continue on this road to the park entrance. When traveling on I-75, take exit 239 and head west on M-18; turn right immediately on Robinson Lake Road; the next turn is south (left) on Higgins Cut Road (County Road 100); continue south on this road to the park. South Higgins Lake State Park has more than 1 mile of fine beach, wooded campgrounds, and a shallow 300-acre marl-bottom lake for fishing.

Facilities & Activities

512 modern campsites
  electrical hookups
  flush toilets
  showers
  sanitation station
organization campground
picnic area
playground
swimming beach
beach house and park store
hunting
fishing
boating
boat basin
boat launch
boat rentals (canoes, rowboats, small motorboats, pontoons, paddle boats)
11 miles of hiking trails
11 miles of cross-country ski trails

Tawas Point State Park

For Information

Tawas Point State Park
686 Tawas Beach Road
East Tawas, MI 48730
(517) 362-5041

Location

Tawas Point State Park is located 3½ miles southeast of East Tawas; from US 23, travel east on Tawas Point Road and follow the park signs. This 183-acre park, at the tip of a sand spit, has 2 miles of beautiful white sandy beaches, with Tawas Bay to the west and Lake Huron to the south and east. A Coast Guard foghorn and the historic Tawas Bay Lighthouse are part of the scene. The park is a favorite spot for birders during the fall and spring migrations.

Facilities & Activities

210 modern campsites
 electrical hookups
 flush toilets
 showers
 sanitation station
organization campground
picnic area
picnic shelter
playground
swimming beach
beach house
fishing
nature trail

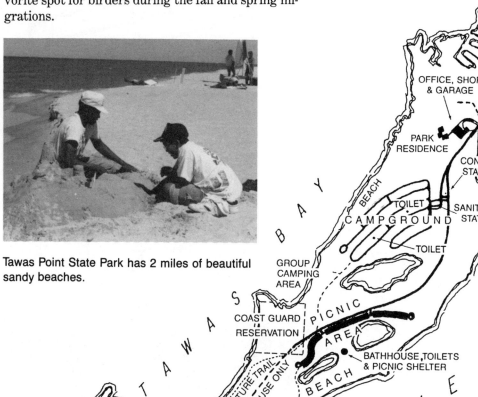

Tawas Point State Park has 2 miles of beautiful sandy beaches.

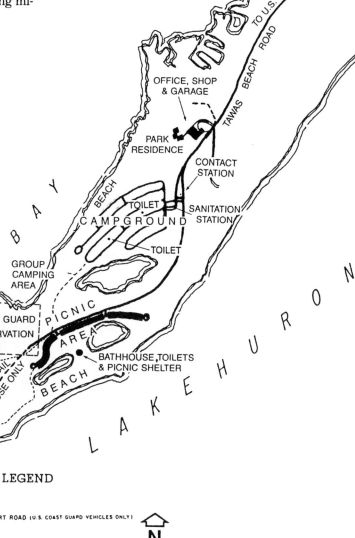

OFFICE, SHOP & GARAGE

PARK RESIDENCE

CONTACT STATION

TAWAS BEACH ROAD

TO U.S. 23

BEACH

TOILET

SANITATION STATION

CAMPGROUND

TOILET

TAWAS BAY

GROUP CAMPING AREA

COAST GUARD RESERVATION

PICNIC AREA

BATHHOUSE, TOILETS & PICNIC SHELTER

BEACH

SANDY HOOK NATURE TRAIL

U.S.C.G. USE ONLY

LAKE HURON

U.S.C.G. FOG HORN

LEGEND

- - - DIRT ROAD (U.S. COAST GUARD VEHICLES ONLY)

- - - - - FOOT TRAIL

N

Traverse City State Park

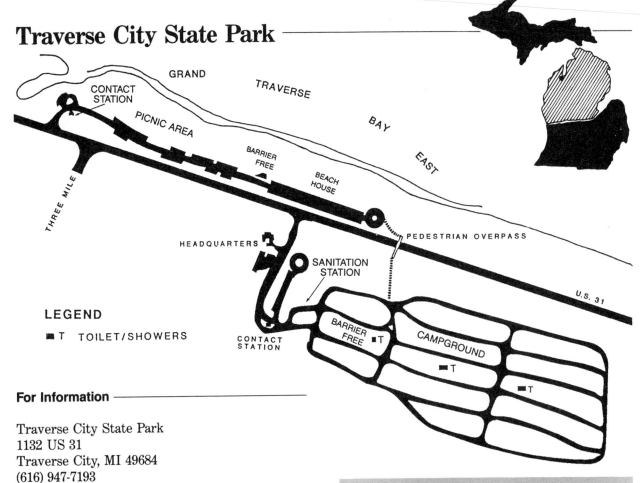

LEGEND

■T TOILET/SHOWERS

For Information

Traverse City State Park
1132 US 31
Traverse City, MI 49684
(616) 947-7193

Location

Traverse City State Park is located 2 miles east of Traverse City on US 31. The campground of this 343-acre urban park is on the south side of US 31 and the day-use area of the park is on the north side of US 31. There is a pedestrian overpass between the two areas. The ¼-mile beach front is on the East Arm of Grand Traverse Bay.

Facilities & Activities

343 modern campsites
  electrical hookups
  flush toilets
  showers
  sanitation station
organization campground
picnic area
playground
swimming beach
beach house
fishing

Grand Traverse Bay is a great place to sail; the state park is on the east arm of the bay.

Wilderness State Park

Wilderness State Park
Carp Lake, MI 49718
(616) 436-5381

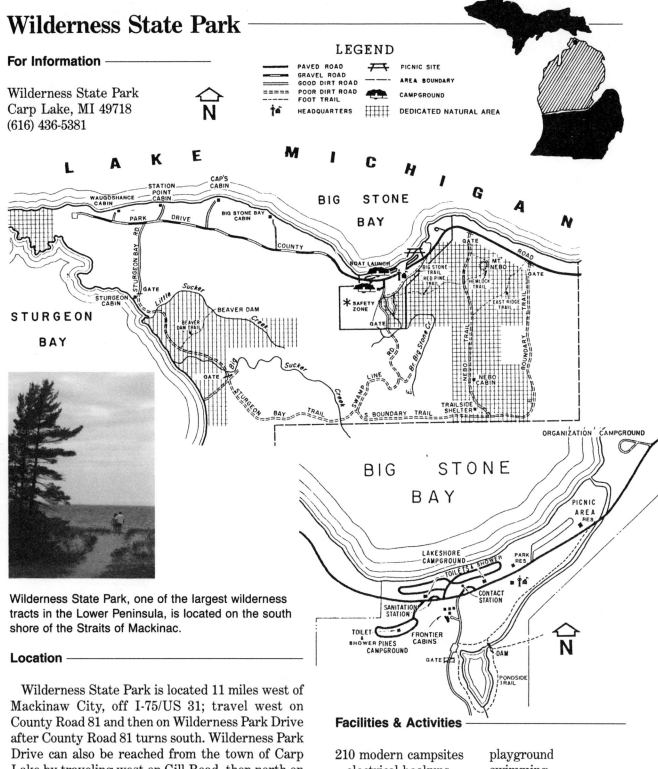

LEGEND

▬▬▬	PAVED ROAD	⛱	PICNIC SITE
▭▭▭	GRAVEL ROAD	– – –	AREA BOUNDARY
▭▭▭	GOOD DIRT ROAD		
=====	POOR DIRT ROAD	🏕	CAMPGROUND
- - - -	FOOT TRAIL		
🚶	HEADQUARTERS	▦	DEDICATED NATURAL AREA

Wilderness State Park, one of the largest wilderness tracts in the Lower Peninsula, is located on the south shore of the Straits of Mackinac.

Location

Wilderness State Park is located 11 miles west of Mackinaw City, off I-75/US 31; travel west on County Road 81 and then on Wilderness Park Drive after County Road 81 turns south. Wilderness Park Drive can also be reached from the town of Carp Lake by traveling west on Gill Road, then north on Cecil Bay Road (County Road 81). The 7,514-acre park, one of the largest wilderness tracts in the Lower Peninsula, is on the south shore of the Straits of Mackinac and contains more than 30 miles of shoreline. The park offers a wide abundance of flowers and a wealth of wildlife, so it is a perfect place for nature study.

Facilities & Activities

210 modern campsites	playground
electrical hookups	swimming
flush toilets	hunting
showers	fishing
sanitation station	boating
organization campground	boat launch
8 rustic cabins	network of hiking trails
(each sleeps 4 to 24)	snowmobiling
picnic area	cross-country skiing

REGION 2

Wilson State Park

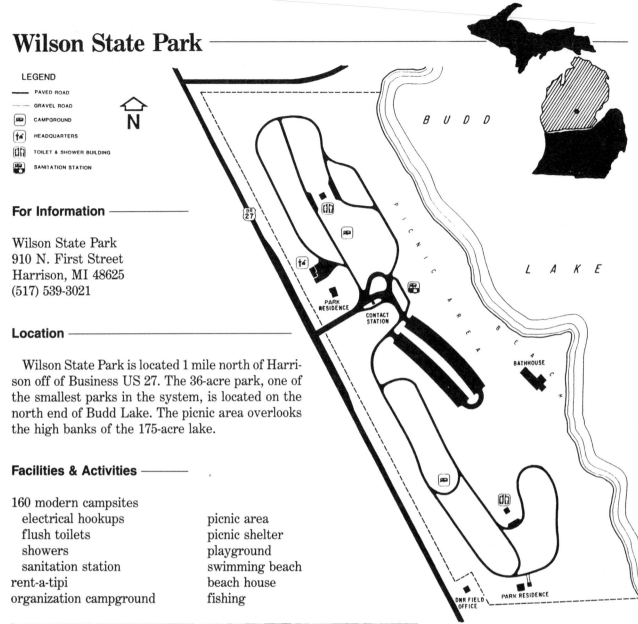

LEGEND

- — PAVED ROAD
- ⋯ GRAVEL ROAD
- 🚐 CAMPGROUND
- 🏠 HEADQUARTERS
- 🚻 TOILET & SHOWER BUILDING
- 🚽 SANITATION STATION

N

For Information

Wilson State Park
910 N. First Street
Harrison, MI 48625
(517) 539-3021

Location

Wilson State Park is located 1 mile north of Harrison off of Business US 27. The 36-acre park, one of the smallest parks in the system, is located on the north end of Budd Lake. The picnic area overlooks the high banks of the 175-acre lake.

Facilities & Activities

160 modern campsites
    electrical hookups
    flush toilets
    showers
    sanitation station
rent-a-tipi
organization campground

picnic area
picnic shelter
playground
swimming beach
beach house
fishing

A canopy can shelter the picnic table as well as lots of equipment if it happens to rain.

Young State Park

For Information

Young State Park
P.O. Box 3651
Boyne City, MI 49712
(616) 582-7523

LEGEND

▬▬▬	PAVED ROAD
- - - -	FOOT TRAIL
— — —	AREA BOUNDARY
═══════	GRAVEL ROAD

LAKE CHARLEVOIX

SPRUCE CAMPGROUND
(SITES 128-297)

TOILET & SHOWER BLDG.

PARK BEACH AREA

SANITATION STATION

PARK STORE

MIRROR LAKE

PICNIC

CONTACT STATION

PARKING

DEER FLATS

CAMPGROUND NATURE TRAIL

TOILET

PUMP HOUSE

TERRACE CAMPGROUND
(SITES 71-127)

TOILET

OAK CAMPGROUND
(SITES 1-70)

DEER FLATS NATURE TRAIL

WHITE BIRCH NATURE TRAIL

N

OFFICE, GARAGE & WORKSHOP

PARK RESIDENCE

PARKING

TOILETS

NATURE TRAIL

BOYNE CITY ROAD

Location

Young State Park is located 2 miles north of Boyne City on County Road 56 (Boyne City Road). From US 131, take M-75 into Boyne City and go north on County Road 56. The 563-acre park is at the east end of beautiful Lake Charlevoix and has 1½ miles of lakeshore.

The park store gets lots of customers from the bicycle crowd.

You get more exercise when you play shorthanded.

Facilities & Activities

293 modern campsites
  electrical hookups
  flush toilets
  showers
  sanitation station
organization campground
picnic area
playground
swimming beach
park store
fishing
boating
boat launch
network of nature trails
cross-country skiing

Region 3

Two lakes and a stretch of the Huron River are available for canoeing at Proud Lake Recreation Area. Canoe rentals are available off Garden Road.

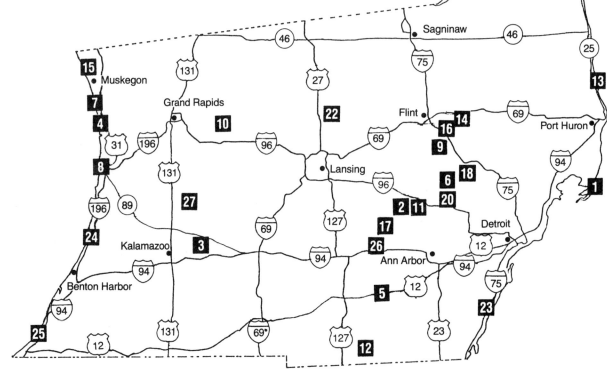

Algonac State Park

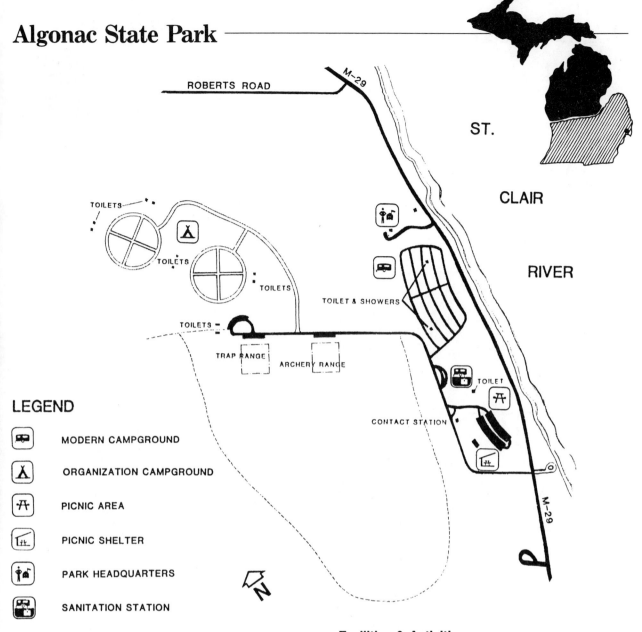

ROBERTS ROAD

M-29

ST.

CLAIR

RIVER

TOILETS

TOILETS

TOILETS

TOILET & SHOWERS

TOILETS

TRAP RANGE

ARCHERY RANGE

TOILET

CONTACT STATION

M-29

LEGEND

- MODERN CAMPGROUND
- ORGANIZATION CAMPGROUND
- PICNIC AREA
- PICNIC SHELTER
- PARK HEADQUARTERS
- SANITATION STATION

N

For Information

Algonac State Park
8730 N. River Road
Algonac, MI 48001
(313) 765-5605

Location

Algonac State Park is located 2 miles north of Algonac on M-29. The 1,307-acre park is on the St. Clair River; huge Great Lakes freighters on the international waterway between Lake St. Clair/Lake Erie and Lake Huron can be viewed from the park.

Facilities & Activities

298 modern campsites
  electrical hookups
  flush toilets
  showers
  sanitation station
organization campground
picnic area
picnic shelter
playground
trap and archery range
hunting
fishing
boating
boat launch
3 miles of hiking trails

Brighton Recreation Area

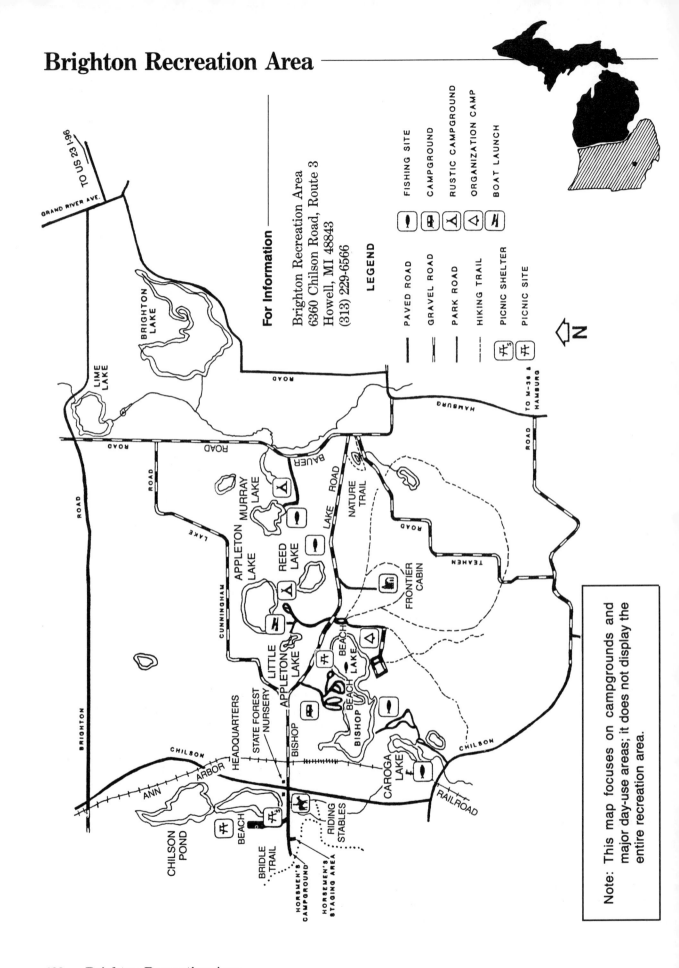

For Information

Brighton Recreation Area
6360 Chilson Road, Route 3
Howell, MI 48843
(313) 229-6566

LEGEND

———	PAVED ROAD
	GRAVEL ROAD
	PARK ROAD
– – –	HIKING TRAIL
⛺ₛ	PICNIC SHELTER
⛺	PICNIC SITE

🎣	FISHING SITE
⛺	CAMPGROUND
△	RUSTIC CAMPGROUND
◁	ORGANIZATION CAMP
⚓	BOAT LAUNCH

Note: This map focuses on campgrounds and major day-use areas; it does not display the entire recreation area.

Brighton Recreation Area (*continued*)

Brighton Recreation Area has excellent facilities for equestrians: a 25-site campground, 18 miles of bridle trails, a horsemen's staging area, and a concession-operated riding stable.

Location

Brighton Recreation Area is located southwest of Brighton; from I-96 just west of US 23, take exit 145 (Grand River Road) and travel south, then turn west on Brighton Road in downtown Brighton, go 3 miles, and turn south onto Chilson Road. This road is a main road into the 4,913-acre recreation area. Several internal park roads provide access to other areas. Anglers have access to 7 of the 10 lakes; boat regulations differ for the various lakes. Brighton has 1 modern campground, 2 rustic campgrounds, and an equestrian campground.

Facilities & Activities

150 modern campsites at Bishop Lake
  electrical hookups
  flush toilets
  showers
  sanitation station
50 rustic campsites (25 at Murray Lake; 25 at Appleton Lake)
  vault toilets
  hand pump
rent-a-tent
organization campground
25 horsemen's campsites
7 rustic cabins (sleep 8 to 20)
picnic area
picnic shelter
playground
swimming
beach house and concession
hunting
fishing
boating
boat launch
boat rental (rowboats, canoes, and paddleboats)
canoeing
horseback riding
riding stable
18 miles of bridle trails
7 miles of hiking trails
snowmobiling
cross-country skiing

Three swimming beaches are available at Brighton Recreation area: two are at Bishop Lake and a small one is at Chilson Pond. The beach on the east half of Bishop Lake is a large day-use area, and facilities include a bath house and a boat-rental concession. The other beach is adjacent to the Bishop Lake campground.

Fort Custer Recreation Area

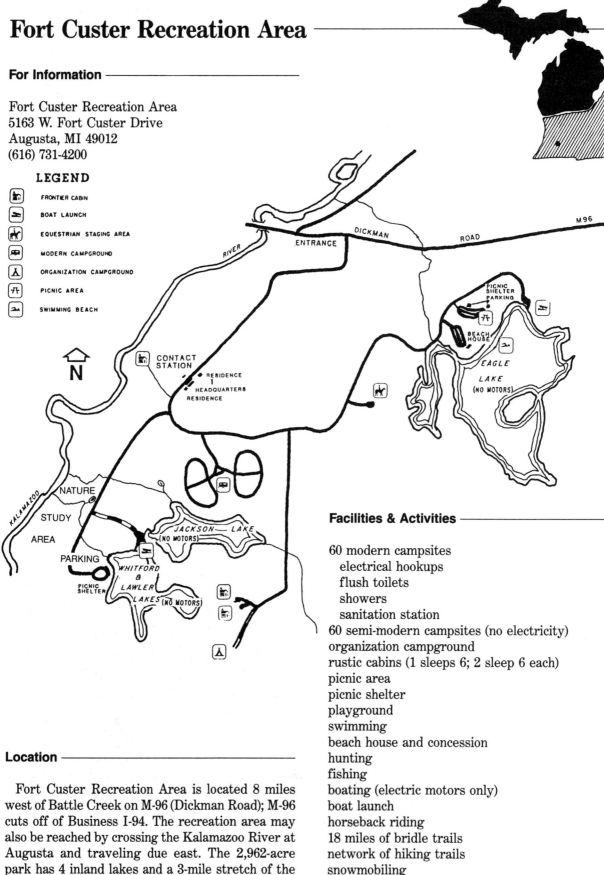

For Information

Fort Custer Recreation Area
5163 W. Fort Custer Drive
Augusta, MI 49012
(616) 731-4200

LEGEND

🏠	FRONTIER CABIN
⛵	BOAT LAUNCH
🐎	EQUESTRIAN STAGING AREA
🚐	MODERN CAMPGROUND
⛺	ORGANIZATION CAMPGROUND
🎋	PICNIC AREA
🏊	SWIMMING BEACH

Facilities & Activities

60 modern campsites
  electrical hookups
  flush toilets
  showers
  sanitation station
60 semi-modern campsites (no electricity)
organization campground
rustic cabins (1 sleeps 6; 2 sleep 6 each)
picnic area
picnic shelter
playground
swimming
beach house and concession
hunting
fishing
boating (electric motors only)
boat launch
horseback riding
18 miles of bridle trails
network of hiking trails
snowmobiling
cross-country skiing

Location

Fort Custer Recreation Area is located 8 miles west of Battle Creek on M-96 (Dickman Road); M-96 cuts off of Business I-94. The recreation area may also be reached by crossing the Kalamazoo River at Augusta and traveling due east. The 2,962-acre park has 4 inland lakes and a 3-mile stretch of the Kalamazoo River.

Grand Haven State Park

For Information

Grand Haven State Park
1001 Harbor Avenue
Grand Haven, MI 49417
(616) 842-6020

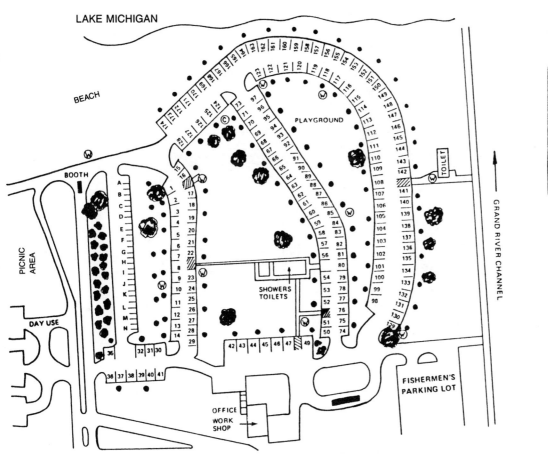

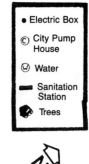

Location

Grand Haven State Park is located in Grand Haven along Harbor Drive; from US 31, travel southwest on one of the main streets (Jackson, Columbus, Washington, Franklin, or Howard), as these run into Harbor Drive. The 48-acre park, an urban park just 1 mile from the downtown area, is bordered on one side by Lake Michigan and on another by the channel of the Grand River. The picturesque Grand Haven lighthouse and pier is nearby and there is a bike path and boardwalk from the park to downtown along the Grand River.

Facilities & Activities

182 modern campsites
  electrical hookups
  flush toilets
  showers
  sanitation station
picnic area
picnic shelter
playground
swimming beach
beach house and concession
fishing
fishing pier (adjacent to park)
boating

REGION 3

Hayes State Park

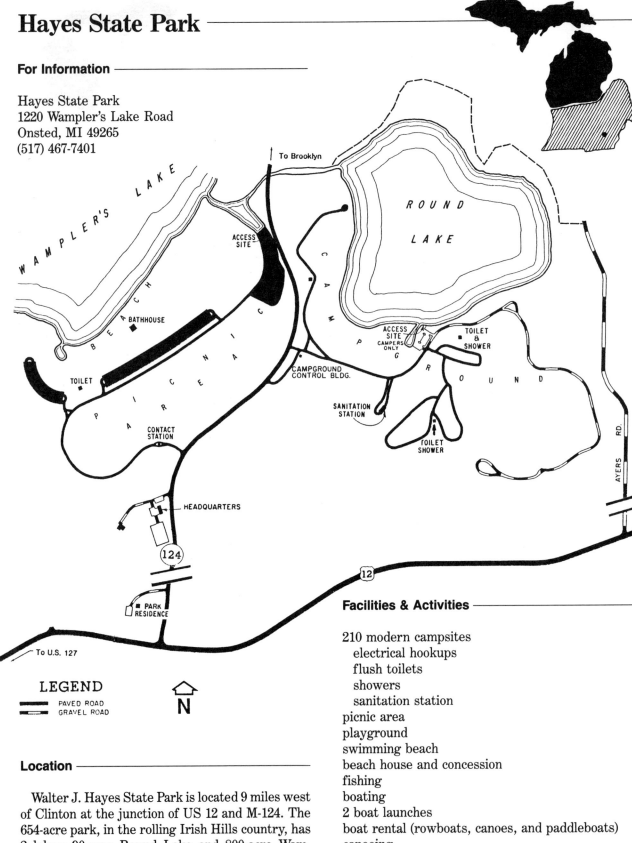

Hayes State Park
1220 Wampler's Lake Road
Onsted, MI 49265
(517) 467-7401

LEGEND

PAVED ROAD
GRAVEL ROAD

N

Location

Walter J. Hayes State Park is located 9 miles west of Clinton at the junction of US 12 and M-124. The 654-acre park, in the rolling Irish Hills country, has 2 lakes: 90-acre Round Lake and 800-acre Wampler's Lake. The day-use area is at Wampler's Lake, while the campground is located at Round Lake.

Facilities & Activities

210 modern campsites
  electrical hookups
  flush toilets
  showers
  sanitation station
picnic area
playground
swimming beach
beach house and concession
fishing
boating
2 boat launches
boat rental (rowboats, canoes, and paddleboats)
canoeing
2-mile hiking trail
2-mile cross-country ski trail

Highland Recreation Area

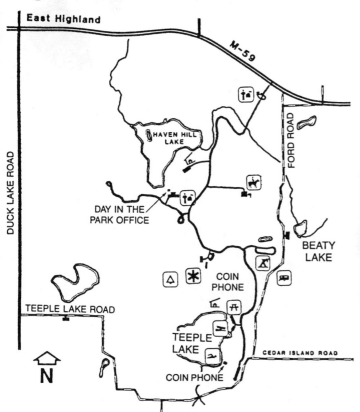

You have to come early on the weekends to get a choice picnic spot.

LEGEND

headquarters		winter sports area	
picnic area		beach	
shelter			
campground		boat launch	
organization camping		equestrian campground	

Note: This map focuses on campgrounds and major day-use areas; it does not display the entire recreation area.

Location

Highland Recreation Area is located 15 miles west of Pontiac and south of M-59. From Pontiac, the Haven Hill Lake/Teeple Lake area is reached via a park road immediately past Ford Road. The rustic campground, also utilized by horsemen, is located along the road to Teeple Lake. There is boat access to 10 of the lakes at this 5,900-acre recreation area. Many of these lakes are not shown on this map; they are west of Duck Lake Road and east of Milford Road.

Facilities & Activities

30 rustic campsites
  vault toilets
  hand pump
rent-a-tent/tipi
organization campground
1 rustic cabin (sleeps 5)
horsemen's campground
picnic area
picnic shelter
playground
swimming
beach house
hunting
fishing
boating
boat launch
horseback riding
riding stable
network of bridle trails
17 miles of hiking trails
Teeple Winter Sports Area
19.3 km of cross-country ski trails
cross-country ski rental
downhill ski run (with tow rope)
snowmobiling (west of Duck Lake Road)

Hoffmaster State Park

For Information

Hoffmaster State Park
6585 Lake Harbor Road
Muskegon, MI 49441
(616) 798-3711

LEGEND

━━━ PAVED ROAD

HEADQUARTERS

CAMPGROUND

PICNIC SITE

|||||| NATURAL AREA

In the eyes of a child, what could possibly be more fun than a day at the beach?

Location

P. J. Hoffmaster State Park is located north of Grand Haven and may be reached by traveling west for 3 miles on Pontaluna Road from US 31. Pontaluna Road runs east–west and intersects US 31 between Grand Haven and Muskegon. When traveling southeast on I-96 from Muskegon, take the Fruitport exit and turn right on Pontaluna Road shortly after making the exit. The 1,043-acre park is the site of the Gillette Nature Center, an interpretive center devoted to Michigan's sand dunes. A boardwalk stairway leads from the center to the dune overlook platform, where miles of Lake Michigan shoreline beach and endless dunes are visible.

Facilities & Activities

333 modern campsites
   electrical hookups
   flush toilets
   showers
   sanitation station
Sand Dunes Interpretive Center
picnic area
picnic shelter
playground
swimming beach
beach house and concession
fishing
3½ miles of bridle trails (staging area off Little
   Black Lake Road)
network of hiking trails
4.8 km cross-country ski trail

Holland State Park

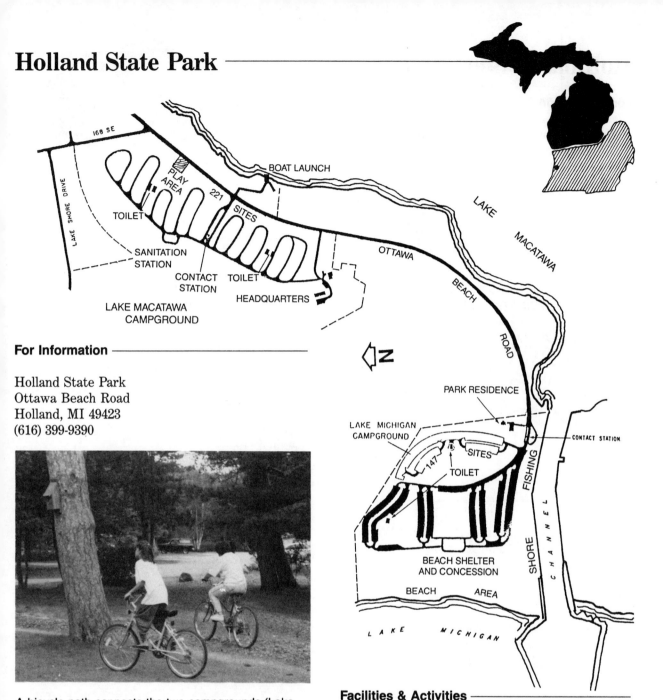

For Information

Holland State Park
Ottawa Beach Road
Holland, MI 49423
(616) 399-9390

A bicycle path connects the two campgrounds (Lake Michigan and Lake Macatawa) at Holland State Park.

Location

Holland State Park is located on the north side of Lake Macatawa, 7 miles west of Holland from US 31, via Lakewood Boulevard, Douglas Avenue, and, finally, Ottawa Beach Road. The 142-acre park has 2 separate units, one on Lake Michigan and one on Lake Macatawa. The Holland Harbor Lighthouse, located across the channel, and the wide sandy beach on Lake Michigan provide a beautiful setting for park visitors.

Facilities & Activities

368 modern campsites
  electrical hookups
  flush toilets
  showers
  sanitation station
picnic area
picnic shelter
playground
swimming beach
beach house and concession
fishing
boat launch
bicycle path

Holly Recreation Area

For Information

Holly Recreation Area
8100 Grange Hall Road
Holly, MI 48442
(313) 634-8811

LEGEND

MODERN CAMPING

SANITATION STA.

ORGANIZATION CAMPING

BEACH

PICNIC AREA

BOAT LAUNCH

HEADQUARTERS

N

Note: This map focuses on campgrounds and major day-use areas; it does not display the entire recreation area.

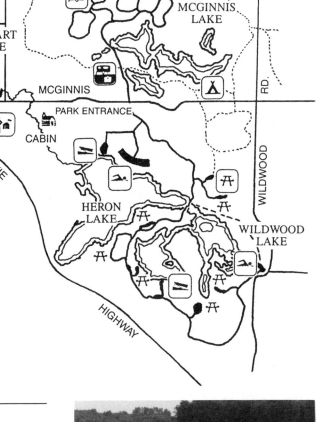

Location

Holly Recreation Area is located east of Holly and 12 miles northwest of Pontiac; from I-75, take exit 101 and travel east on Grange Hall Road. Just past Dixie Highway, when Grange Hall Road turns sharply to the left, continue straight; this is McGinnis Road, leading to the most developed area, which contains the campground and the day-use area. The 7,470-acre park, made up of 6 sections, has a diversity of terrains and numerous lakes.

Facilities & Activities

160 modern campsites
  electrical hookups
  flush toilets
  showers
  sanitation station
rent-a-tent/tipi
organization campground
1 rustic cabin (sleeps 6)
picnic area
picnic shelter
playground
swimming

beach house and concession
rifle, shotgun, and archery range
hunting
fishing
boating (electric motors only)
boat launch
boat and canoe rental
horseback riding
10 miles of bridle trails
25 miles of hiking trails
snowmobiling
cross-country skiing

What a lovely spot to place the swings . . . and they look roomy enough for adults.

Ionia Recreation Area

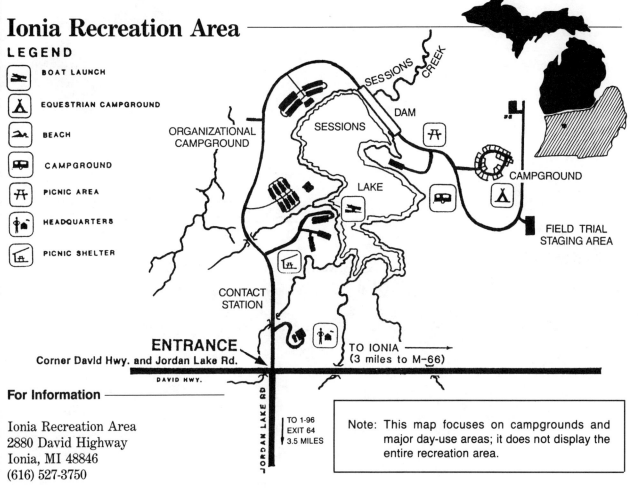

LEGEND

- ✈ BOAT LAUNCH
- 🏕 EQUESTRIAN CAMPGROUND
- 🏖 BEACH
- 🚐 CAMPGROUND
- 🎋 PICNIC AREA
- 👤🏠 HEADQUARTERS
- 🏠 PICNIC SHELTER

ORGANIZATIONAL CAMPGROUND

SESSIONS CREEK

DAM

SESSIONS LAKE

CAMPGROUND

FIELD TRIAL STAGING AREA

CONTACT STATION

ENTRANCE
Corner David Hwy. and Jordan Lake Rd.

DAVID HWY.

JORDAN LAKE RD

TO IONIA
(3 miles to M-66)

TO I-96
EXIT 64
3.5 MILES

Note: This map focuses on campgrounds and major day-use areas; it does not display the entire recreation area.

For Information

Ionia Recreation Area
2880 David Highway
Ionia, MI 48846
(616) 527-3750

Location

Ionia Recreation Area is southwest of Ionia; from the south, take exit 64 on I-96 and travel 3½ miles north on Jordan Lake Road to the park entrance. From Ionia, travel south for 4 miles on M-66, then 3 miles west on David Highway. The 4,108-acre park is the site of field-dog trials in the spring and early fall. A 50-site rustic horsemen's campground has been the only camping facility, but by 1992 the park will also have a 100-site modern campground.

Sessions Lake is stocked annually with several species of fish; the lake is probably best known for its largemouth bass.

Facilities & Activities

100 modern campsites
  electrical hookups
  flush toilets
  showers
  sanitation station
organization campground
50 rustic horsemen's campsites
  vault toilets
  hand pump
picnic area
picnic shelter
playground
swimming
beach house and concession
shotgun range
hunting
fishing
boating
boat launch
horseback riding
24 miles of bridle trails
9 miles of hiking trails
snowmobiling
9 miles of cross-country ski trails

Island Lake Recreation Area

For Information

Island Lake Recreation Area
12950 East Grand River
Brighton, MI 48116
(313) 229-7067

LEGEND

SPRING MILL POND

N

🏕 Picnic area	🏕 Rustic campground	🚐 Modern Campground
🏕 Picnic shelter	🏠 Frontier cabin	🏖 Beach
	🏛 Headquarters	🛶 Canoe access
		🛶 Canoe rental
		△ Organization campground
		🛶 Canoe campground

Note: This map focuses on campgrounds and major day-use areas; it does not display the entire recreation area.

Many people rent a canoe just to paddle around Kent Lake, but the best way to see Island Lake Recreation Area is to paddle the Huron River all the way to the Placeway Picnic Area.

Location

Island Lake Recreation Area is located 4 miles southeast of Brighton off of I-96; take exit 151 and travel south on Kensington Road to the park entrance. A scenic park drive winds 6½ miles along the south side of the Huron River beginning at Kent Lake and ending at Island Lake. Canoeing is popular at this 4,000-acre recreation area; the stretch from Kent Lake to Placeway Picnic Area is quite popular. There are two small campgrounds; a semimodern campground at Island Lake and a rustic campground to the west of the scenic drive between the Placeway Picnic Area and Island Lake.

Facilities & Activities

18 semimodern campsites	playground
flush toilets	swimming
25 rustic campsites	beach house and concession
vault toilets	hunting
hand pump	fishing
canoe campground	canoeing
organization campground	canoe rental
2 rustic cabins (each sleeps 20)	network of hiking trails
picnic area	snowmobiling
picnic shelter	

Lake Hudson Recreation Area

For Information

Lake Hudson Recreation Area
c/o W. J. Hayes State Park
1220 Wampler's Lake Road
Onsted, MI 49265
(517) 467-7401

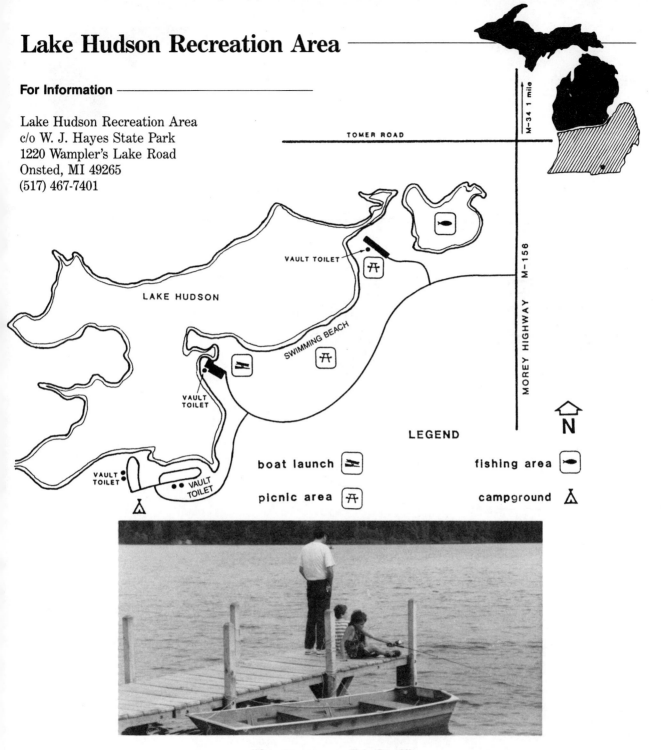

TOMER ROAD

M-34 1 mile

VAULT TOILET

LAKE HUDSON

MOREY HIGHWAY M-156

SWIMMING BEACH

VAULT TOILET

VAULT TOILET

VAULT TOILET

N

LEGEND

boat launch

fishing area

picnic area

campground

"Can you see any fish, Dad?"

Location

Lake Hudson Recreation Area is located southeast of Hudson; travel east on M-34 for 6 miles, then south on M-156 for 1½ miles to the park entrance. The 2,650-acre park is on a 500-acre man-made lake in an area that was originally farmland.

Facilities & Activities

50 semi-modern campsites
  electrical hookups
  vault toilets
  hand pump
picnic area

swimming
hunting
fishing
boating (no wake)
boat launch

REGION 3

Lakeport State Park

For Information

Lakeport State Park
7605 Lakeshore Road, Route 1
Port Huron, MI 48060
(313) 327-6765

LEGEND

⊟ MODERN CAMPGROUND

L A K E   H U R O N

B E A C H

PLAY AREA   PARK STORE

TOILET &
SHOWER

TOILET & SHOWER

SANITATION
STATION

ORGANIZATION
CAMPGROUND

TOILET &
SHOWER

ORGANIZATION
CAMPGROUND

CONTACT STA.

HEADQUARTERS

(25)

N

Village of Lakepo

CAMPGROUND

Once they get past the beach, these folks are in for some great sailing.

Location

Lakeport State Park is located 11 miles north of Port Huron on M-25. The 565-acre park consists of 2 separate units with the Village of Lakeport in between. The park is also split by M-25 so that in the day-use area, named the Franklin Delano Roosevelt Unit, cars park on the west side of M-25 and use a pedestrian overpass to reach the beach. Both units have beaches on Lake Huron.

Facilities & Activities

315 modern campsites
　electrical hookups
　flush toilets
　showers
　sanitation station
2 organization campgrounds
picnic area
picnic shelter
playground
swimming beach
beach house and concession
park store
fishing

Metamora-Hadley Recreation Area

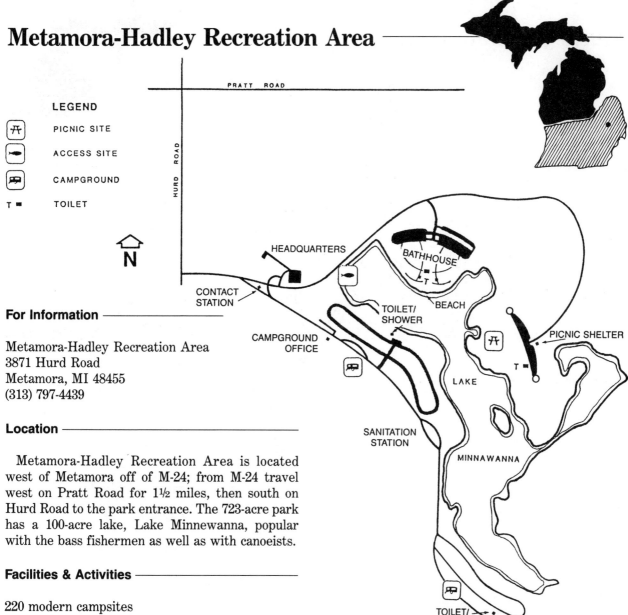

LEGEND

🎪 PICNIC SITE

⬇ ACCESS SITE

🚐 CAMPGROUND

T ■ TOILET

N

PRATT ROAD

HURD ROAD

HEADQUARTERS

BATHHOUSE

CONTACT STATION

TOILET/ SHOWER

BEACH

PICNIC SHELTER

CAMPGROUND OFFICE

LAKE

SANITATION STATION

MINNAWANNA

TOILET/ SHOWER

For Information

Metamora-Hadley Recreation Area
3871 Hurd Road
Metamora, MI 48455
(313) 797-4439

Location

Metamora-Hadley Recreation Area is located west of Metamora off of M-24; from M-24 travel west on Pratt Road for 1½ miles, then south on Hurd Road to the park entrance. The 723-acre park has a 100-acre lake, Lake Minnewanna, popular with the bass fishermen as well as with canoeists.

Facilities & Activities

220 modern campsites
  electrical hookups
  flush toilets
  showers
  sanitation station
picnic area
picnic shelter
playground
swimming
beach house and concession
hunting
fishing
boating
boat launch
boat rental (rowboats, canoes, and paddleboats)
canoeing
6½ miles of hiking trails
snowmobiling
cross-country skiing

Paddleboats are more easily kept on a straight path than canoes, but they definitely require greater leg strength.

Muskegon State Park

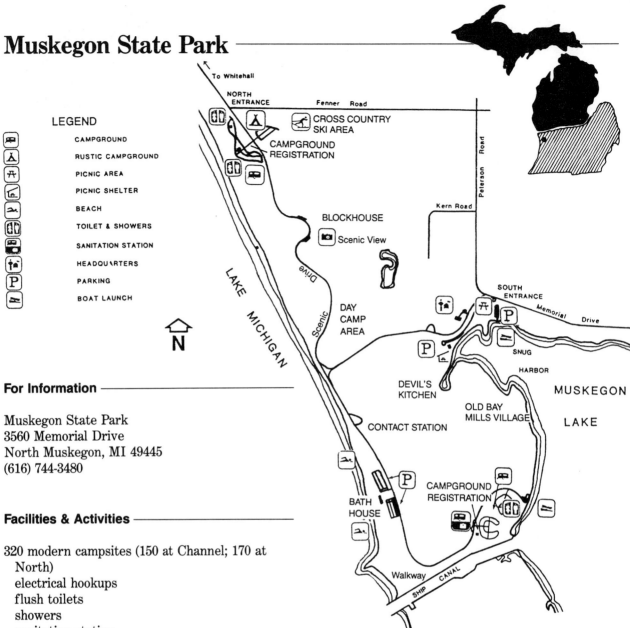

LEGEND

CAMPGROUND	
RUSTIC CAMPGROUND	
PICNIC AREA	
PICNIC SHELTER	
BEACH	
TOILET & SHOWERS	
SANITATION STATION	
HEADQUARTERS	
PARKING	
BOAT LAUNCH	

N

For Information

Muskegon State Park
3560 Memorial Drive
North Muskegon, MI 49445
(616) 744-3480

Facilities & Activities

320 modern campsites (150 at Channel; 170 at
 North)
  electrical hookups
  flush toilets
  showers
  sanitation station
30 rustic campsites at North Campground
  vault toilets
  hand pump
organization campground
picnic area
picnic shelter
playground
swimming beach
beach house and concession
fishing
fishing piers
boating
2 boat launches
network of hiking trails
Muskegon Winter Sports Center
8 km of cross-country ski trails
cross-country ski rental

Location

Muskegon State Park is located 4 miles west of
North Muskegon from US 31 via M-120, which becomes Memorial Drive. Follow Memorial Drive to
the park's south entrance; a day-use area is located
near this entrance. The North Campground can be
reached via Scenic Drive from the north or by traveling through the south entrance and turning right
on Scenic Drive. The Channel Campground and another day-use area are located at the south end of
the park. Much of the 1,357-acre park is a peninsula
surrounded by Lake Michigan to the west, Muskegon Lake to the east and a canal that connects the
two bodies of water. The Muskegon Winter Sports
Center is located in the state park near the rustic
campground at the north end of the park; the center
is not administered by the park.

Ortonville Recreation Area

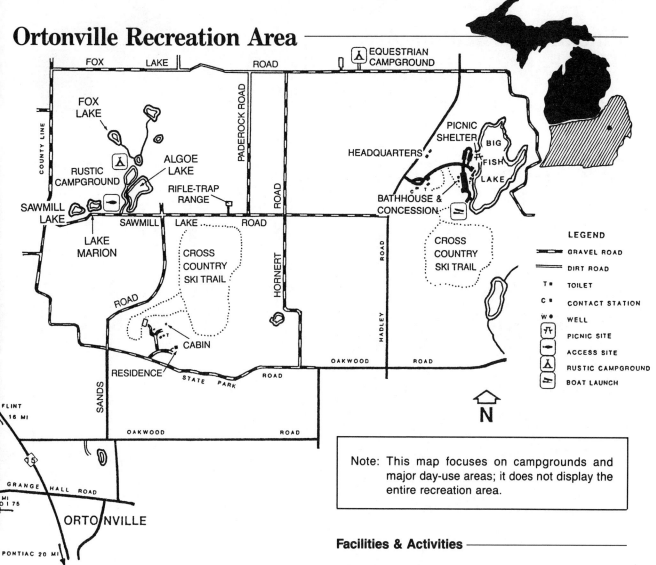

FOX LAKE ROAD

FOX LAKE

COUNTY LINE

ALGOE LAKE

RUSTIC CAMPGROUND

RIFLE-TRAP RANGE

SAWMILL LAKE

LAKE MARION

PADEROCK ROAD

SAWMILL LAKE ROAD

ROAD

HORNERT ROAD

CROSS COUNTRY SKI TRAIL

ROAD

CABIN

RESIDENCE

STATE PARK ROAD

SANDS ROAD

OAKWOOD ROAD

EQUESTRIAN CAMPGROUND

HEADQUARTERS

PICNIC SHELTER

BIG FISH LAKE

BATHHOUSE & CONCESSION

CROSS COUNTRY SKI TRAIL

HADLEY ROAD

OAKWOOD ROAD

FLINT 16 MI

GRANGE HALL ROAD
MI 0 1 75

ORTONVILLE

PONTIAC 20 MI

OAKWOOD ROAD

N

LEGEND

	GRAVEL ROAD
	DIRT ROAD
T ▪	TOILET
C ▪	CONTACT STATION
W ●	WELL
🛆	PICNIC SITE
→	ACCESS SITE
⚠	RUSTIC CAMPGROUND
	BOAT LAUNCH

Note: This map focuses on campgrounds and major day-use areas; it does not display the entire recreation area.

For Information

Ortonville Recreation Area
5779 Hadley Road, Route 2
Ortonville, MI 48462
(313) 627-3828

Location

Ortonville Recreation Area is located 4 miles northeast of Ortonville; travel north on M-15, east on Oakwood Road, then north on Hadley Road to reach Big Fish Lake, the popular day-use area. Several internal park roads provide access to other areas. The rustic campground is located on Sawmill Lake Road and the equestrian campground is on Fox Lake Road. There are some 19 lakes at this densely forrested 4,875-acre recreation area.

Facilities & Activities

32 rustic campsites
  vault toilets
  hand pump
organization campground
horsemen's campground
2 rustic cabins (sleeps 20 and 24)
picnic area
picnic shelter
playground
swimming
beach house
rifle and trap range
hunting
fishing
boating
boat launch
horseback riding
17 miles of bridle trails
17 miles of hiking trails
snowmobiling
cross-country ski trails

REGION 3

Pinckney Recreation Area

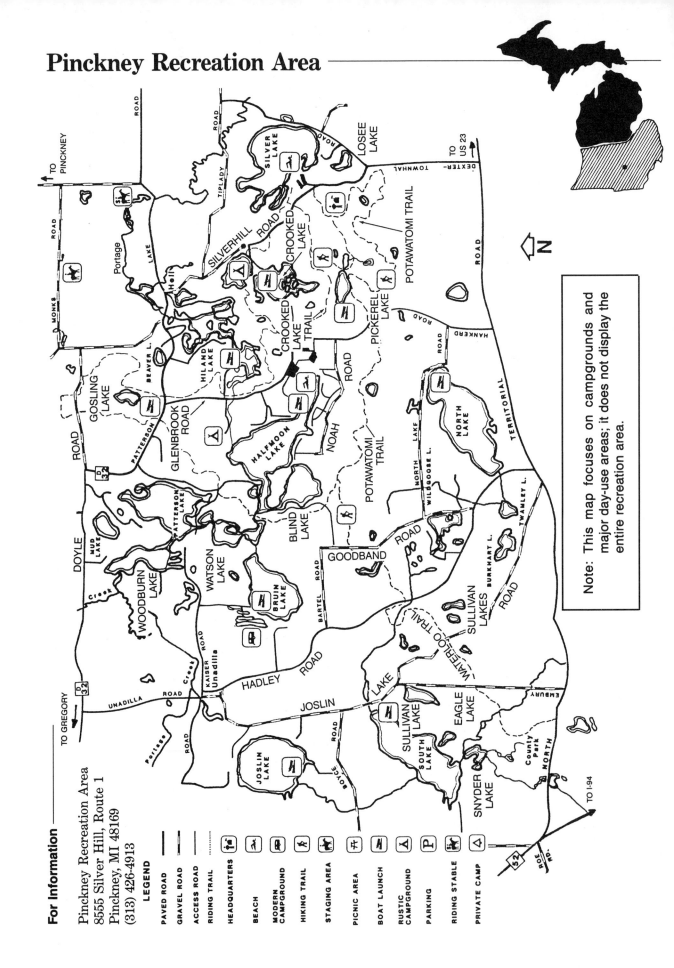

Pinckney Recreation Area (*continued*)

Location

Pinckney Recreation Area is located 4 miles southwest of Pinckney. The 10,842-acre recreation area is quite spread out and has a number of county roads and park roads passing through the area. The cluster of 7 lakes, which are connected by streams and short channels and which are often referred to as the chain-of-lakes, is the center of activity at Pinckney Recreation Area. Park visitors should first choose their activity and then study the detailed park map as well as the vicinity map to determine how to get to their destination. Notice that the 3 campgrounds and the 2 day-use areas are located along the 3 main roads that run north-south between Territorial Road and County Road D-32, which run east-west. From the north, County Road D-32 is accessible from both Pinckney and Gregory.

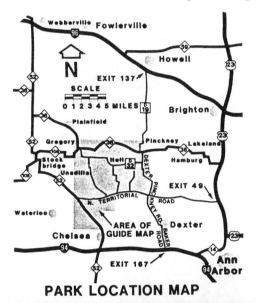

PARK LOCATION MAP

Rowboats, canoes, and paddleboats are all available for rental at Pinckney Recreation Area.

Pinckney Recreation Area has two day-use areas, each with a swimming beach: the west side of Silver Lake and the southeast side of Halfmoon Lake.

When approaching the recreation area from the south, Territorial Road is reached by taking exit 159 from I-94 and heading north on M-52 for 6 miles. Hadley Road is the first main road to the left; the modern campground at Bruin Lake is off this road on Kaiser Road. The second main road to the left is Hankerd Road; the day-use area at Halfmoon Lake is off this road. Continue on north to Glenbrook Road to the rustic campground that has 10 campsites. The third main road to the left from North Territorial Road is Dexter-Townhall Road; turn left at Silverhill Road to the day-use area at Silver Lake and continue on to the rustic campground which has 25 campsites.

Boats can conveniently be beached right at the picnic area.

Pinckney Recreation Area (continued)

Facilities & Activities

220 modern campsites at Bruin Lake
   electrical hookups
   flush toilets
   showers
   sanitation station
35 rustic campsites
   vault toilets
   hand pump
organization campground
picnic area
picnic shelter
playground
swimming
beach house and concession
hunting
fishing
boating
boat launch
boat rental (rowboats, canoes, and paddleboats)
canoeing
horseback riding
riding stable
5 miles of bridle trails
40 miles of hiking trails
backpacking trails with designated campsites
   northern portion of the 46-mile Waterloo-
   Pinckney Trail
   17-mile Potawatomi Trail
snowmobiling
9.7 km of cross-country ski trails

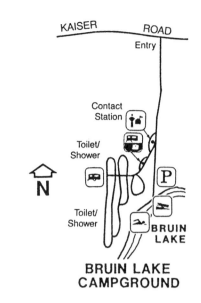

BRUIN LAKE
CAMPGROUND

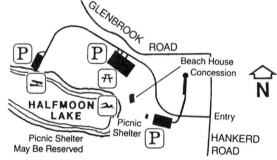

HALFMOON LAKE BEACH

Pinckney Recreation Area is often referred to as the chain-of-lakes. Although a wide variety of recreational activities are available, including backpacking and horseback riding, the cluster of seven lakes and connecting streams tend to be the center of activity.

Pontiac Lake Recreation Area

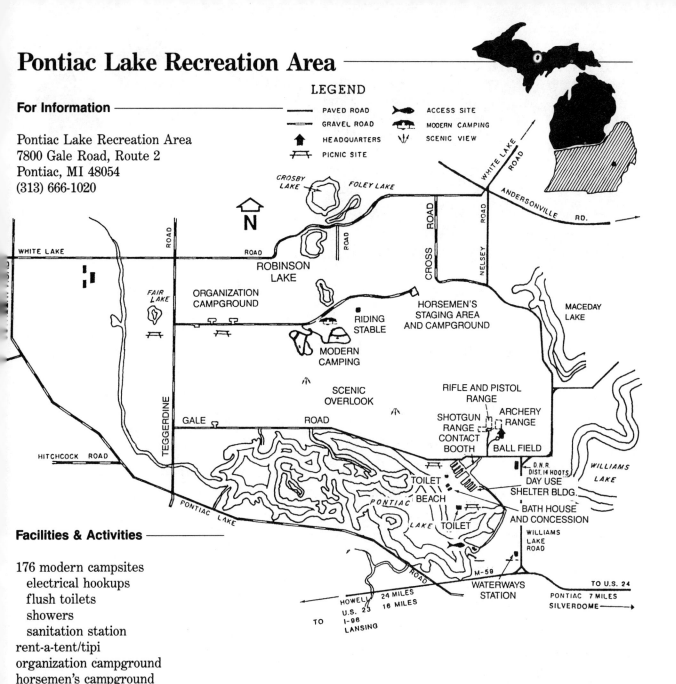

LEGEND

- —— PAVED ROAD
- ===== GRAVEL ROAD
- 🔺 HEADQUARTERS
- 🏕 PICNIC SITE
- 🐟 ACCESS SITE
- MODERN CAMPING
- 🎋 SCENIC VIEW

For Information

Pontiac Lake Recreation Area
7800 Gale Road, Route 2
Pontiac, MI 48054
(313) 666-1020

Facilities & Activities

176 modern campsites
  electrical hookups
  flush toilets
  showers
  sanitation station
rent-a-tent/tipi
organization campground
horsemen's campground
picnic area
picnic shelter
playground
swimming
beach house and concession
rifle, shotgun, and archery range
hunting
fishing
boating
boat launch
horseback riding
riding stable
17 miles of bridle trails
hiking trails
snowmobiling

Location

Pontiac Lake Recreation Area is located 9 miles northwest of Pontiac and accessible from either M-59 or US 24. From M-59, take the Williams Lake Road exit and travel north to reach the day-use area or take the Pontiac Lake Road and travel northwest, then right on Teggerdine and right on Maceday Road to reach the campground. From US 24, take either the White Lake Road exit or the Andersonville Road exit; then travel south on Nelsey Road to reach the recreation area. Pontiac Lake, the main attraction at this 3,700-acre recreation area, was created when the Huron River was dammed.

Port Crescent State Park

Sitting on the beach, reading a book and watching the waves—what could be more relaxing?

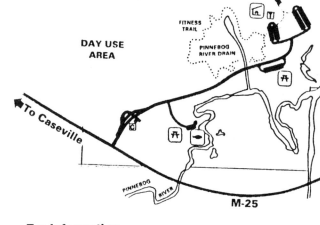

For Information

Port Crescent State Park
1775 Port Austin Road
Port Austin, MI 48467
(517) 738-8663

Location

Port Crescent State Park is located 5 miles southwest of Port Austin on M-25. The 565-acre park, near the tip of the Thumb, has about 4 miles of Lake Huron shoreline on Saginaw Bay with fine, almost pure-white beach sand. The day-use area provides access to the area known as "the dunes"; approximately 4 miles of the Pinnebog River gives opportunity for stream fishing and canoeing.

Facilities & Activities

181 modern campsites
  electrical hookups
  flush toilets
  showers
  sanitation station
organization campground
picnic area
picnic shelter
playground
swimming beach
beach house
hunting
fishing
boating
boat access to river (hand carried)
canoeing
fitness trail
network of hiking trails
4.3 km of cross-country ski trails

Proud Lake Recreation Area

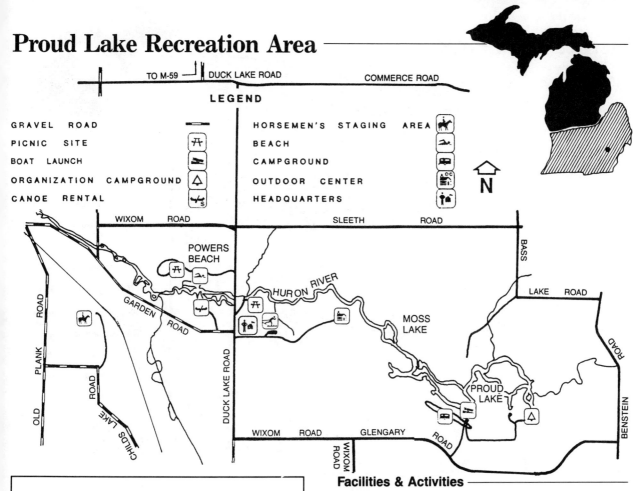

LEGEND

GRAVEL ROAD		HORSEMEN'S STAGING AREA	
PICNIC SITE		BEACH	
BOAT LAUNCH		CAMPGROUND	
ORGANIZATION CAMPGROUND		OUTDOOR CENTER	
CANOE RENTAL		HEADQUARTERS	

Note: This map focuses on campgrounds and major day-use areas; it does not display the entire recreation area.

For Information

Proud Lake Recreation Area
3500 Wixom Road, Route 3
Milford, MI 48042
(313) 685-2433

Location

Proud Lake Recreation Area is located 4 miles east of Milford and is accessible from either M-59 or I-96. From M-59, travel south on Milford Road, then east on Commerce Road, then south on Duck Lake Road to the day-use area. From I-96, take exit 159 and head north on Wixom Road; the campground is east from Wixom Road on Glengary Road. The 3,614-acre recreation area includes dense forests, two lakes, and a stretch of the Huron River.

Facilities & Activities

130 modern campsites
  electrical hookups
  flush toilets
  showers
  sanitation station
rent-a-tent
organization campground
Outdoor Center with cabins and dining hall (sleeps up to 128)
picnic area
picnic shelter
playground
swimming
beach house and concession
hunting
fishing
boating
boat launch
canoeing
canoe rental
horseback riding
10 miles of bridle trails
network of hiking trails
snowmobiling
12.9 km of cross-country ski trails
cross-country ski rental

Sleeper State Park

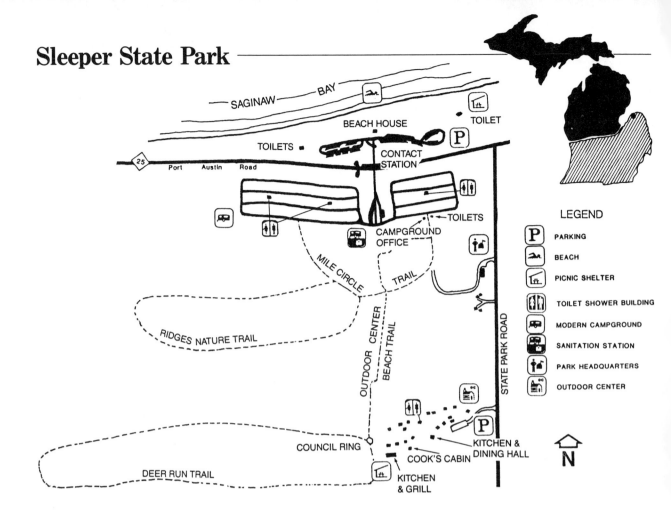

LEGEND

P	PARKING
	BEACH
	PICNIC SHELTER
	TOILET SHOWER BUILDING
	MODERN CAMPGROUND
	SANITATION STATION
	PARK HEADQUARTERS
	OUTDOOR CENTER

For Information

Sleeper State Park
6573 State Park Road
Caseville, MI 48725
(517) 856-4411

Sleeper State Park and Port Crescent State Park, its neighbor to the east, both have a network of hiking trails that become cross-country ski trails when there is sufficient snowfall.

Location

Albert E. Sleeper State Park is located 4 miles northeast of Caseville on M-25. The 1,003-acre park in on the shoreline of Lake Huron. The day-use area has ½ mile of sandy beach on Saginaw Bay, while the wooded campground area lies south of M-25. There is a pedestrian overpass connecting the two areas. An outdoor center is also located within the park. Designed for groups, it has sixteen cabins that sleep up to 120 persons. It also has a dining hall and kitchen. Phone (313) 755-5060 for information.

Facilities & Activities

280 modern campsites
  electrical hookups
  flush toilets
  showers
  sanitation station
Outdoor Center (sleeps 120)
picnic area
picnic shelter

playground
swimming beach
beach house
hunting
fishing
network of hiking trails
snowmobiling
8 km of cross-country ski trails

Sleepy Hollow State Park

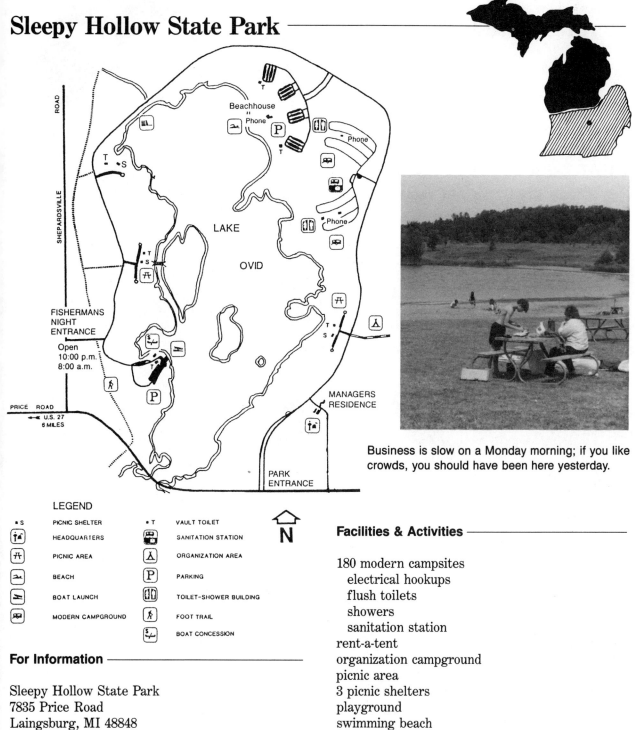

Business is slow on a Monday morning; if you like crowds, you should have been here yesterday.

LEGEND

▪S	PICNIC SHELTER	•T	VAULT TOILET
👥	HEADQUARTERS		SANITATION STATION
🌲	PICNIC AREA	🏕	ORGANIZATION AREA
🏖	BEACH	P	PARKING
🚤	BOAT LAUNCH	🚻	TOILET-SHOWER BUILDING
🚐	MODERN CAMPGROUND	🚶	FOOT TRAIL
			BOAT CONCESSION

For Information

Sleepy Hollow State Park
7835 Price Road
Laingsburg, MI 48848
(517) 651-6217

Location

Sleepy Hollow State Park is located 15 northeast of Lansing. From US 27 north of Lansing, travel east on Price Road for 7 miles to the park's main entrance. The facilities at this 2,678-acre park are centered around Lake Ovid, a 410-acre man-made lake. The surrounding area is reverted farmland.

Facilities & Activities

180 modern campsites
  electrical hookups
  flush toilets
  showers
  sanitation station
rent-a-tent
organization campground
picnic area
3 picnic shelters
playground
swimming beach
beach house and concession
hunting
fishing
boating (electric motors only)
boat launch
boat rentals (canoes, rowboats, and paddleboats)
biking
network of hiking trails
snowmobiling
8 km of cross-country ski trails

Sterling State Park

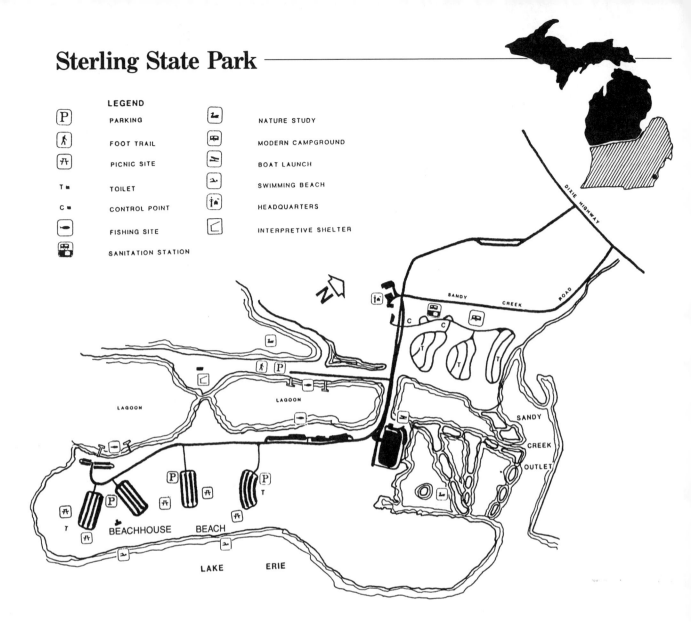

LEGEND

P	PARKING	☜	NATURE STUDY
人	FOOT TRAIL	🚐	MODERN CAMPGROUND
禾	PICNIC SITE	⊁	BOAT LAUNCH
T ▪	TOILET	☜	SWIMMING BEACH
C ▪	CONTROL POINT	👤	HEADQUARTERS
☜	FISHING SITE	⌐	INTERPRETIVE SHELTER
🚐	SANITATION STATION		

For Information

Sterling State Park
2800 State Park Road, Route 5
Monroe, MI 48161
(313) 289-2715

Location

Sterling State Park is located northeast of Monroe along the Lake Erie shoreline; exit I-75 on the Dixie Highway and travel east for 1 mile to the park entrance. The 1000-acre park offers excellent birding during the spring and fall migrations, since it includes 4 lagoons and the marshes that surround Sandy Creek Outlet. Sterling is the only Michigan park on Lake Erie, and it is best known for its mile-long sandy beach and good fishing.

Facilities & Activities

288 modern campsites
  electrical hookups
  flush toilets
  showers
  sanitation station
organization campground
picnic area
playground
swimming beach
beach house and concession
fishing
fishing piers
boating
boat launch
boat rental for lagoon area (rowboats, canoes, and paddleboats)
nature trail with observation tower

Van Buren State Park

An RV with a shade gives you a nice place to set up your picnic table.

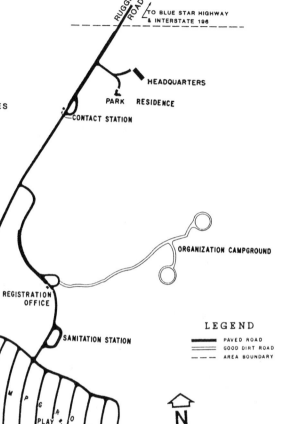

MICHIGAN BEACH

LAKE BEACH

ALCOHOLIC BEVERAGES PROHIBITED IN DAY USE AREA

BATHHOUSE & CONCESSION

PICNIC

TOILET

PICNIC

PICNIC SHELTER

RUGGLES ROAD

TO BLUE STAR HIGHWAY & INTERSTATE 196

HEADQUARTERS

PARK RESIDENCE

CONTACT STATION

ORGANIZATION CAMPGROUND

REGISTRATION OFFICE

SANITATION STATION

LEGEND
PAVED ROAD
GOOD DIRT ROAD
AREA BOUNDARY

CAMPGROUND
PLAY AREA
TOILET-SHOWER BLDGS.

N

For Information

Van Buren State Park
23960 Ruggles Road
South Haven, MI 49090
(616) 637-2788

Location

Van Buren State Park is located 4 miles south of South Haven on Ruggles Road, accessible from the Blue Star Memorial Highway. Take either exit 13 or exit 18 off I-196/US 31 and head west to the Blue Star Memorial Highway, then turn on Ruggles Road and proceed to the park entrance. The 326-acre park is on the shore of Lake Michigan and has more than ½ mile of sandy beach bordered with wooded dunes.

Facilities & Activities

220 modern campsites
  electrical hookups
  flush toilets
  showers
  sanitation station
organization campground
picnic area
picnic shelter
playground
swimming beach
beach house and concession
hunting

REGION 3

Warren Dunes State Park

For Information

Warren Dunes State Park
Red Arrow Highway
Sawyer, MI 49125
(616) 426-4013

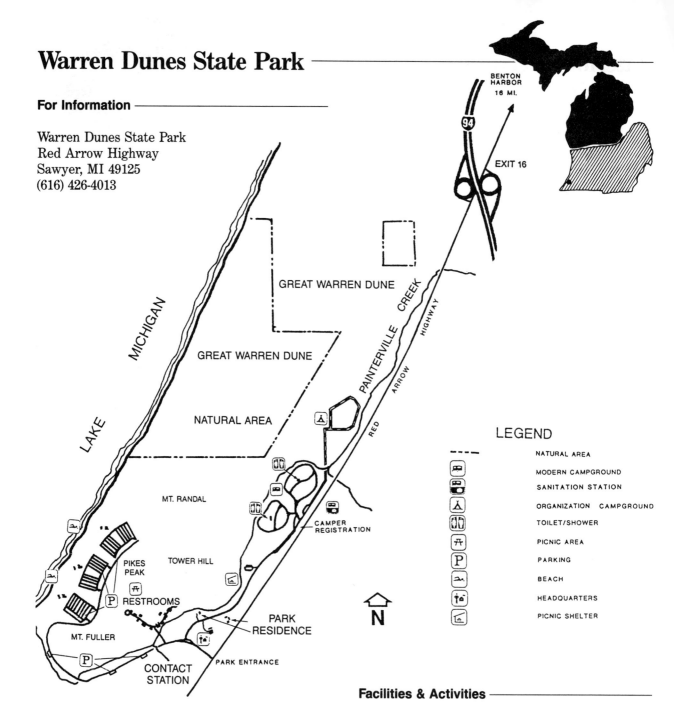

94

EXIT 16

GREAT WARREN DUNE

LAKE MICHIGAN

GREAT WARREN DUNE

NATURAL AREA

PAINTERVILLE CREEK

RED ARROW HIGHWAY

MT. RANDAL

CAMPER REGISTRATION

LEGEND

- – – – NATURAL AREA
- MODERN CAMPGROUND
- SANITATION STATION
- ORGANIZATION CAMPGROUND
- TOILET/SHOWER
- PICNIC AREA
- PARKING
- BEACH
- HEADQUARTERS
- PICNIC SHELTER

PIKES PEAK

TOWER HILL

RESTROOMS

PARK RESIDENCE

MT. FULLER

CONTACT STATION

PARK ENTRANCE

N

Location

Warren Dunes State Park is located 3 miles southwest of Bridgman off I-94; take exit 16 and follow the Red Arrow Highway southwest to the park entrance. When traveling from the south, the Sawyer Road exit can be taken to get on Red Arrow Highway. This 4,705-acre park is just 12 miles north of the Indiana/Michigan border and is the beginning of a string of parks on the sandy shoreline of Lake Michigan. The 2½-mile-long shoreline is bordered with sand dunes; several dunes are more than 200 feet high and have become a haven for hang gliders.

Facilities & Activities

197 modern campsites
  electrical hookups
  flush toilets
  showers
  sanitation station
organization campground
picnic area
playground
swimming beach
beach house and concession
hunting
network of nature trails
cross-country ski trail

Waterloo Recreation Area

LEGEND

- ══════ PAVED ROAD
- ┤┤┤┤┤ GRAVEL ROAD
- HEADQUARTERS
- PICNIC SITE
- ACCESS SITE
- CAMPGROUND
- RUSTIC CAMPGROUND
- RUSTIC CABINS
- BOAT LAUNCH
- CONTACT STATION
- BEACH
- SANITATION STATION

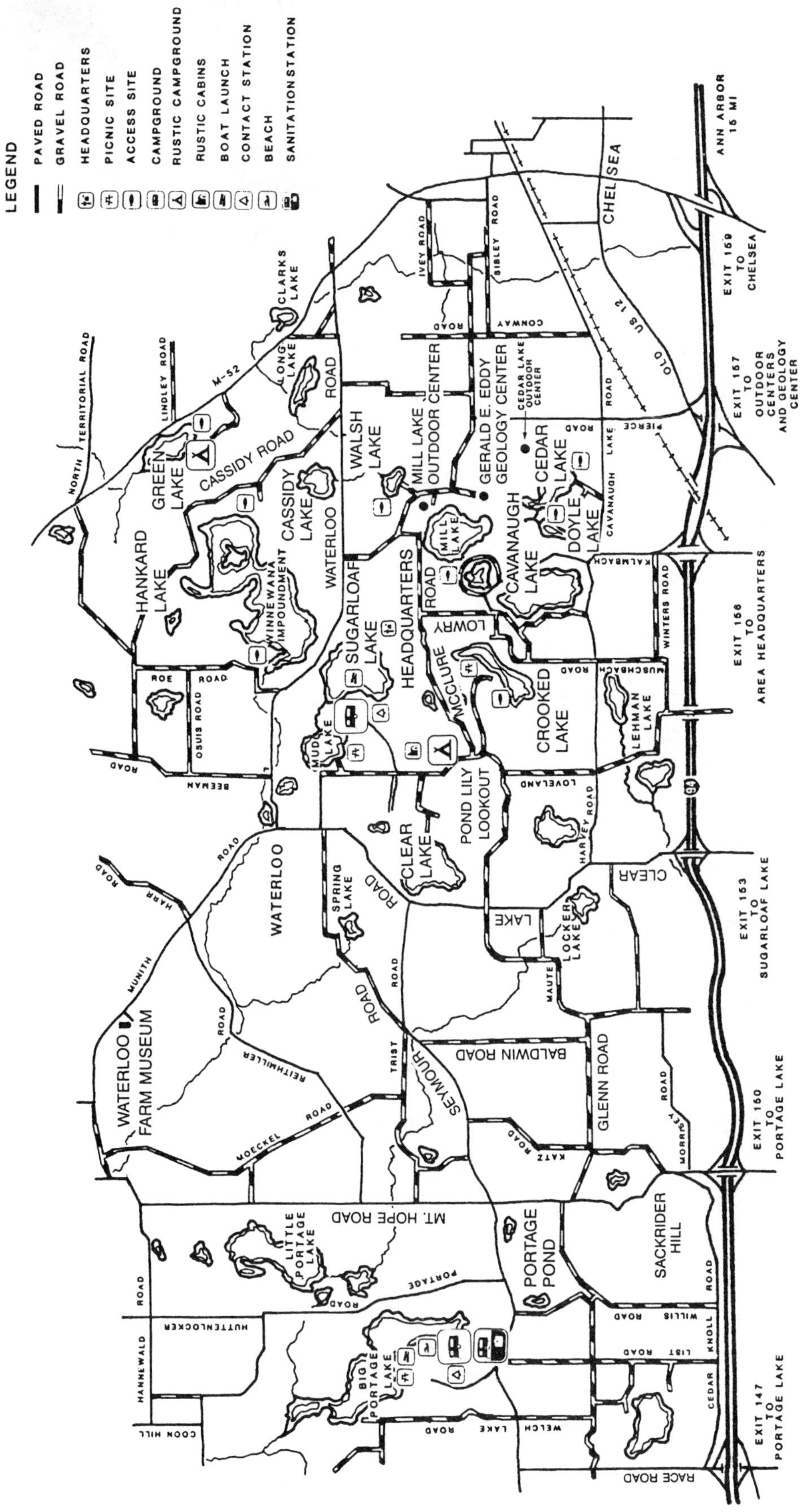

Note: This map focuses on campgrounds and major day-use areas; it does not display the entire recreation area.

For Information

Waterloo Recreation Area
16345 McClure Road, Route 1
Chelsea, MI 48118
(313) 475-8307

REGION 3

Waterloo Recreation Area (*continued*)

Location

Waterloo Recreation Area is located 7 miles west of Chelsea and accessible from I-94 and M-52. The terrain is hilly, with numerous small lakes; there is boat access to 16 of the lakes. The 19,750-acre recreation area is quite spread out and has a number of roads passing through the area. Park visitors should first choose their activity and then study the detailed park map to determine how to get to their destination.

There are 6 exits along I-94 between Ann Arbor and Jackson that lead north into the recreation area: exit 159 (M-52) to the rustic campground at Green Lake; exit 157 (Pierce Road) to the 2 outdoor centers and the geology center; exit 156 (Kalmbach Road) to the park headquarters; exit 153 (Clear Lake Road) to the modern campground at Sugarloaf Lake; and exits 150 (Mt. Hope Road) and 147 (Race Road) to the day-use area and the modern campground at Big Portage Lake.

There's plenty to do at Waterloo Recreation Area, but sometimes just taking a walk can be the most fun.

Facilities & Activities

374 modern campsites (194 at Big Portage Lake; 180 at Sugarloaf Lake)
   electrical hookups
   flush toilets
   showers
   sanitation station
25 rustic campsites at Green Lake
   vault toilets
   hand pump
organization campground
Cedar Lake Outdoor Center
   8 cabins (each sleeps 8 to 18)
Mill Lake Outdoor Center (sleeps 140)
3 other rustic cabins (2 sleep 20; 1 sleeps 8)
25 horsemen's campsites
Gerald E. Eddy Geology Center
picnic area
picnic shelter
playground
swimming
beach house and concession
hunting
fishing
fishing pier
boating
boat launch
horseback riding
25 miles of bridle trails
network of nature/hiking trails
backpacking trail—southern portion of the 46-mile Waterloo-Pinckney Trail
snowmobiling
cross-country ski trails

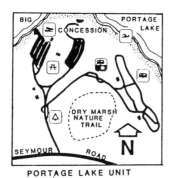

PORTAGE LAKE UNIT

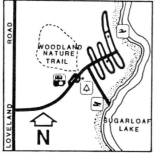

SUGARLOAF LAKE CAMPGROUND

Yankee Springs Recreation Area

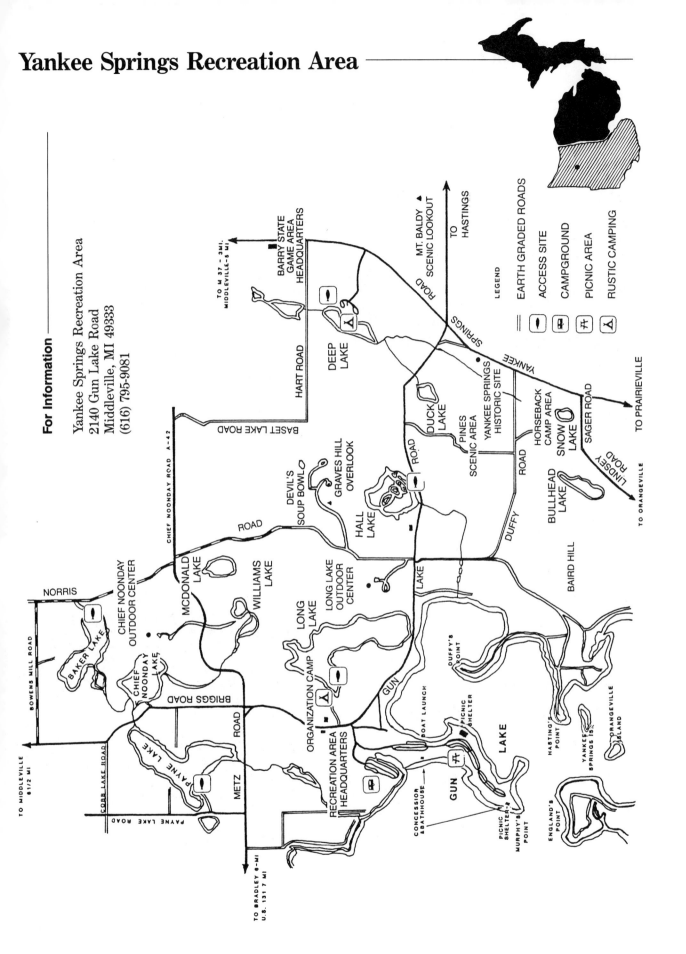

LEGEND

EARTH GRADED ROADS

ACCESS SITE

CAMPGROUND

PICNIC AREA

RUSTIC CAMPING

TO HASTINGS

MT. BALDY SCENIC LOOKOUT

TO M 37 - 3MI.
MIDDLEVILLE-5 MI.

BARRY STATE GAME AREA HEADQUARTERS

YANKEE SPRINGS ROAD

HART ROAD

DEEP LAKE

DUCK LAKE

PINES SCENIC AREA

YANKEE SPRINGS HISTORIC SITE

HORSEBACK CAMP AREA

SNOW LAKE

SAGER ROAD

TO PRAIRIEVILLE

LINDSEY ROAD

TO ORANGEVILLE

BULLHEAD LAKE

BAIRD HILL

DUFFY ROAD

BASET LAKE ROAD

CHIEF NOONDAY ROAD A-42

DEVIL'S SOUP BOWL

GRAVES HILL OVERLOOK

ROAD

HALL LAKE

MCDONALD LAKE

WILLIAMS LAKE

LONG LAKE

LONG LAKE OUTDOOR CENTER

GUN LAKE

ROAD

CHIEF NOONDAY OUTDOOR CENTER

NORRIS

BAKER LAKE

BOWENS MILL ROAD

CHIEF NOONDAY LAKE

BRIGGS ROAD

ORGANIZATION CAMP

RECREATION AREA HEADQUARTERS

PAYNE LAKE

COBB LAKE ROAD

METZ ROAD

PAYNE LAKE ROAD

TO MIDDLEVILLE
6 1/2 MI

TO BRADLEY 6-MI
U.S. 131 7 MI

DUFFY'S POINT

BOAT LAUNCH

PICNIC SHELTER

HASTING'S POINT

YANKEE SPRINGS IS.

ORANGEVILLE ISLAND

CONCESSION & BATHHOUSE

GUN LAKE

PICNIC SHELTER

MURPHY'S POINT

ENGLAND'S POINT

This is a familiar scene . . . it's nice to stay in touch, particularly when there are grandchildren back home.

Location

Yankee Springs Recreation Area is 9 miles west of Hastings and 5 miles south of Middleville and can be reached from either US 131 or M-37. From US 31 south of Grand Rapids, take the Bradley exit (exit 61) and travel east on County Road A-42 for 7 miles to its junction with Gun Lake Road; turn right. From M-37 south of Middleville, take Yankee Springs Road south to its junction with Gun Lake Road; turn right. A modern campground is located on the shores of Gun Lake, while rustic camping is available at Deep Lake. Nine lakes are located within this 5,014-acre recreation area, the largest being Gun Lake with a 2,680-acre body of water.

A network of bridle trails is located southwest of the horsemen's campground. A trail also leads east from the campground to join a network of trails in Barry State Game Area.

Facilities & Activities

220 modern campsites at Gun Lake
  electrical hookups
  flush toilets
  showers
  sanitation station
120 rustic campsites at Deep Lake
  vault toilets
  hand pump
organization campground
Chief Noonday Outdoor Center
  7 cabins (each sleeps 4–24)
Long Lake Outdoor Center
  20 cabins (each sleeps 4–24)
25 horsemen's campsites
picnic area
picnic shelter
playground
swimming
beach house and concession
hunting
fishing
boating
boat launch
horseback riding
network of bridle trails
15½ miles of hiking trails
snowmobile trails
14.5 km of cross-country ski trails

This roomy family tent is appropriate for use at either a modern or rustic campground.

Appendix

Camping Equipment Checklist

The following checklists are designed to guide you in planning your next camping trip. Your needs will vary according to the type, length, and destination of your trip, as well as personal preferences, number of persons included, season of the year, and budget limitations.

Obviously, all items on the checklists aren't needed on any one trip. Since using checklists helps you think more methodically in planning, these extensive lists should serve merely as a reminder of items you may need.

When using these checklists to plan a trip, the item may be checked (✔) if it needs to be taken. Upon returning, if the item was considered unnecessary, a slash could be used: ✖. If a needed item was forgotten, a zero could be used (0); if the item has been depleted and needs to be replenished, an encircling of the check could be used; ⓥ. This is of particular importance if you camp regularly and keep a camping box packed with staples that can be ready to go on a moment's notice.

Cooking equipment needs are quite dependent on the menu—whether you plan to cook and eat three balanced meals a day or whether you plan to eat non-cooked meals or snacks the entire

Typical Menu with Grocery and Equipment Needs

MEAL: Saturday breakfast		Number of Persons: 5
MENU	GROCERY LIST	EQUIPMENT
orange juice	Tang	camp stove
bacon	10 slices bacon	gasoline, funnel
eggs (scrambled)	8 eggs	folding oven
biscuits	1 can biscuits	frying pan
	peach jelly	baking pan
	honey	pitcher
	margarine	mixing bowl
	salt	cooking fork, spoon
	pepper	

trip. Many campers find it helpful to jot down the proposed menu for each meal on a 4″ × 6″ index card to help determine the grocery list as well as the equipment needed to prepare the meal. By planning this way, you'll avoid taking equipment you'll never use and you won't forget important items.

Shelter/Sleeping:

___ Air mattresses
___ Air mattress pump
___ Cots, folding
___ Cot pads
___ Ground cloth
___ Hammock
___ Mosquito netting
___ Sleeping bag or bed roll
___ Tarps (plastic & canvas)
___ Tent
___ Tent stakes, poles, guy ropes
___ Tent repair kit
___ Whisk broom

Extra Comfort:

___ Camp stool
___ Catalytic heater
___ Folding chairs
___ Folding table
___ Fuel for lantern & heater
___ Funnel
___ Lantern
___ Mantels for lantern
___ Toilet, portable
___ Toilet chemicals
___ Toilet bags
___ Wash basin

Clothing/Personal Gear:

___ Bathing suit
___ Boots, hiking & rain
___ Cap/hat
___ Facial tissues
___ Flashlight (small), batteries
___ Jacket/windbreaker
___ Jeans/trousers
___ Pajamas

___ Pocket knife
___ Poncho
___ Prescription drugs
___ Rain suit
___ Sheath knife
___ Shirts
___ Shoes
___ Shorts
___ Socks
___ Sweat shirt/sweater
___ Thongs (for showering)
___ Toilet articles (comb, soap, shaving equipment, toothbrush, toothpaste, mirror, etc.)
___ Toilet paper
___ Towels
___ Underwear
___ Washcloth

Safety/Health:

___ First-aid kit
___ First-aid manual
___ Fire extinguisher
___ Insect bite remedy
___ Insect repellant
___ Insect spray/bomb
___ Poison ivy lotion
___ Safety pins
___ Sewing repair kit
___ Scissors
___ Snake bite kit
___ Sunburn lotion
___ Suntan cream
___ Water purifier

Optional:

___ Binoculars
___ Camera, film, tripod, light meter

___ Canteen
___ Compass
___ Fishing tackle
___ Frisbee, horseshoes, washers, etc.
___ Games for car travel & rainy day
___ Hobby equipment
___ Identification books: birds, flowers, rocks, stars, trees, etc.
___ Knapsack/day pack for hikes
___ Magnifying glass
___ Map of area
___ Notebook & pencil
___ Sunglasses

Miscellaneous:

___ Bucket/pail
___ Candles
___ Clothesline
___ Clothespins
___ Electrical extension cord
___ Flashlight (large), batteries
___ Hammer
___ Hand axe/hatchet
___ Nails
___ Newspapers
___ Pliers
___ Rope
___ Saw, bow or folding
___ Sharpening stone/file
___ Shovel
___ Tape, masking or plastic
___ Twine/cord
___ Wire
___ Work gloves

Cooking Equipment Checklist

Food Preparation/
Serving/Storing:

___ Aluminum foil
___ Bags (large & small, plastic & paper)
___ Bottle/juice can opener
___ Bowls, nested with lids for mixing, serving & storing
___ Can opener
___ Colander
___ Fork, long-handled
___ Ice chest
___ Ice pick
___ Knife, large
___ Knife, paring
___ Ladle for soups & stews
___ Measuring cup
___ Measuring spoon
___ Pancake turner
___ Potato & carrot peeler
___ Recipes
___ Rotary beater
___ Spatula
___ Spoon, large
___ Tongs
___ Towels, paper
___ Water jug
___ Wax paper/plastic wrap

Cooking:

___ Baking pans
___ Charcoal
___ Charcoal grill (hibachi or small collapsible type)
___ Charcoal lighter
___ Coffee pot
___ Cook kit, nested/pots & pans with lids
___ Fuel for stove (gasoline/kerosene/liquid propane)
___ Griddle
___ Hot pads/asbestos gloves
___ Matches
Ovens for baking:
___ Cast iron dutch oven
___ Folding oven for fuel stoves
___ Reflector oven
___ Tote oven
___ Skewers
___ Skillet with cover
___ Stove, portable
___ Toaster (folding camp type)
___ Wire grill for open fire

Eating:

___ Bowls for cereal, salad, soup
___ Cups, paper
___ Forks
___ Glasses, plastic
___ Knives
___ Napkins, paper
___ Pitcher, plastic
___ Plates (plastic, aluminum, paper)
___ Spoons
___ Table cloth, plastic
___ _____
___ _____

Clean-Up:

___ Detergent (Bio-degradable soap)
___ Dish pan
___ Dish rag
___ Dish towels
___ Scouring pad
___ Scouring powder
___ Sponge

Hiking/Backpacking Checklist

This list is not meant to be all inclusive or necessary for each trip. It is a guide in choosing the proper gear. Although this list was prepared for the hiker/backpacker, it is quite appropriate for anyone using the backcountry, whether they are traveling by foot, canoe, bicycle, or horse. Parentheses indicate those optional items that you may not want to carry depending upon the length of the trip, weather conditions, personal preferences, or necessity.

Ten Essentials for Any Trip:

___ Map
___ Compass
___ First-aid kit
___ Pocket knife
___ Signaling device
___ Extra clothing
___ Extra food
___ Small flashlight/extra bulb & batteries
___ Fire starter/candle/ waterproof matches
___ Sunglasses

Day Trip (add to the above):

___ Comfortable boots or walking shoes
___ Rain parka or 60/40 parka

___ Day pack
___ Water bottle/canteen
___ Cup
___ Water purification tablets
___ Insect repellant
___ Sun lotion
___ Chapstick
___ Food
___ Brimmed hat
___ (Guide book)
___ Toilet paper & trowel
___ (Camera & film)
___ (Binoculars)
___ (Book)
___ Wallet & I.D.
___ Car key & coins for phone
___ Moleskin for blisters
___ Whistle

Overnight or Longer Trips
(add the following):

___ Backpack
___ Sleeping bag
___ Foam pad
___ (Tent)
___ (Bivouac cover)
___ (Ground cloth/poncho)
___ Stove
___ Extra fuel
___ Cooking pot(s)
___ Pot scrubber
___ Spoon (knife & fork)
___ (Extra cup/bowl)
___ Extra socks
___ Extra shirt(s)
___ Extra pants/shorts
___ Extra underwear
___ Wool shirt/sweater
___ (Camp shoes)

___ Bandana
___ (Gloves)
___ (Extra water container)
___ Nylon cord
___ Extra matches
___ Soap
___ Toothbrush/powder/floss
___ Mirror
___ Medicines
___ (Snake bite kit)
___ (Notebook & pencil)
___ Licenses & permits
___ (Playing cards)
___ (Zip-lock bags)
___ (Rip stop repair tape)
___ Repair kit—wire, rivets, pins, buttons, thread, needle, boot strings

MICHIGAN COASTAL DUNES

The Natural Heritage Program of the DNR Wildlife Division has produced a very attractive and informative 21″ × 32″ poster entitled "Michigan Coastal Dunes—a heritage worth saving." The poster not only displays and describes various types of dunes plants and animals, but it also describes coastal dunes in great depth. The following quote is particularly descriptive: "The windswept dunes gracing Michigan's Great Lakes shoreline represent the largest collection of freshwater dunes in the world. The diversity of environmental elements—wildlife, topographic relief, vegetation, habitats, and climatic conditions—occurring within these landforms represent a phenomenon unique to the State of Michigan. The dunes are not only one of the State's most spectacular natural features, they also are one of the most fragile."

Approximately 40 percent of the coastal dunes are in public ownership and managed by federal, state, or local units of government. For more information on sand dunes, visit the Gillette Nature Center—a sand dune interpretive center administered by the Michigan DNR. Located in P. J. Hoffmaster State Park, Muskegon, the center features multi-image presentations, and exhibit hall, hiking trails, and boardwalks into the surrounding dunes of the Park. Call (616) 798-3573 for information.

The accompanying map, used by permission from the DNR Wildlife Division, displays the general location of 21 Michigan sand dune viewing areas. Numbers on the map refer to sand dune viewing area list. Dark lines refer to coastal sand areas.

Remember that dune habitats are fragile and easily damaged by human activity. When visiting these areas, avoid damage to vegetation, and use boardwalks or designated trails when available.

1—Pictured Rocks National Lakeshore
2—Highway viewing, Hiawatha National Forest
3—Wilderness State Park
4—Petoskey State Park

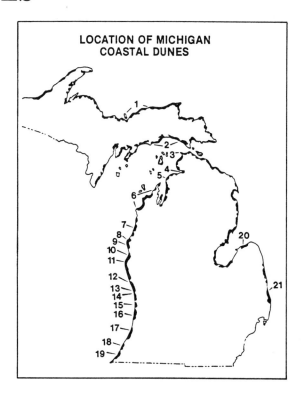

LOCATION OF MICHIGAN COASTAL DUNES

5—Fisherman's Island State Park
6—Sleeping Bear Dunes National Lakeshore
7—Orchard Beach State Park
8—Ludington State Park
9—Nordhouse Dunes, U.S. Forest Service
10—Mears State Park
11—Silver Lake State Park
12—Muskegon State Park
13—P. J. Hoffmaster State Park
14—Grand Haven State Park
15—Holland State Park
16—Saugatuck State Park
17—Van Buren State Park
18—Warren Dunes State Park
19—Gran Mere State Park
20—Albert E. Slepper State Park
21—Lakeport State Park

MICHIGAN LIGHTHOUSES

The numerous Michigan lighthouses are often a surprise to non-Michiganders. One must remember that in the past they served as an important part of the Michigan transportation system. The first lighthouses in Michigan were built between 1818 and 1822, and a number of them are still in existence. Although they are presently automated and some have been abandoned, they still hold a certain historic and majestic feeling of Michigan. Some lighthouses are located on private property; special permision may be necessary before entering.

The accompanying map, used by permission from the Michigan Department of Transportation, displays the general location of 104 Michigan lighthouses. Lighthouse numbers correspond with circled numbers on the map.

Michigan Lighthouses *(continued)*

1. Detroit River Light
2. Grosse Ile North Channel Front Range Light
3. Detroit Lighthouse Depot
4. William Livingstone Memorial Light
5. Windmill Point Light
6. Lake St. Clair Light
7. St. Clair Flats Old Channel Range Light
8. Peche Island Rear Range Light
9. Lightship Huron
10. Fort Gratiot Light
11. Port Sanilac Light
12. Harbor Beach (Sand Beach) Light
13. Pointe Aux Barques Light
14. Port Austin Reef Light
15. Charity Island Light
16. Gravelly Shoal Light
17. Saginaw River Rear Range Light
18. Tawas Point Light
19. Sturgeon Point Light
20. Alpena Light
21. Thunder Bay Island Light
22. Middle Island Light
23. Old Presque Isle Light
24. Forty Mile Point Light
25. Cheboygan River Range Front Light
26. Fourteen Foot Shoal Light
27. Poe Reef Light
28. Bois Blanc Island Light
29. Spectacle Reef Light
30. Round Island Light
31. Martin Reef Light
32. DeTour Point Light
33. Old Mackinac Point Light
34. McGulpin's Point Light
35. Waugoshance Light
36. Skillagalee (Ile Aux Galets) Light
37. White Shoal Light
38. Gray's Reef Light
39. St. Helena Island Light
40. Lansing Shoal Light
41. Seul Choix Point Light
42. Squaw Island Light
43. Beaver Island (Beaver Head)
44. Beaver Island Harbor (St. James) Light
45. South Fox Island Light
46. North Manitou Shoal Light
47. South Manitou Island Light
48. Little Traverse (Harbor Point) Light
49. Charlevoix South Pier Light
50. Mission Point (Old Mission Point) Light
51. Grand Traverse (Cat's Head Point) Light
52. Point Betsie Light
53. Frankfort North Breakwater Light
54. Manistee North Pierhead Light
55. Big Sable Point (Grand Pointe Au Sable) Light
56. Ludington North Pierhead Light
57. Little Sable Point (Petite Pointe Au Sable) Light
58. White River Light
59. Muskegon South Pier Light
60. Grand Haven South Pier Inner Light
61. Holland Harbor (Black Lake) Light
62. Saugatuck (Kalamazoo River) Light

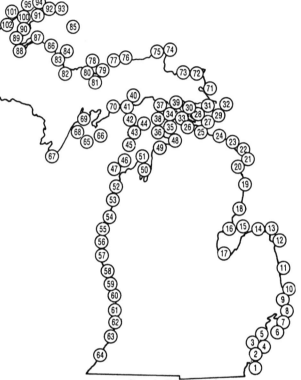

63. South Haven South Pier Light
64. St. Joseph North Pier Outer Light
65. St. Martin Island Light
66. Poverty Island Light
67. Menominee North Pier Light
68. Minneapolis Shoal Light
69. Peninsula Point Light
70. Manistique East Breakwater Light
71. Round Island Light
72. Cedar Point (Round Island Point) Rear Range Light
73. Point Iroquois Light
74. Whitefish Point Light
75. Crisp's Point Light
76. Grand Marais Harbor Range Light
77. Au Sable Point Light
78. Grand Island North Light
79. Grand Island East Channel Light
80. Grand Island West Channel Light
81. Munising Range Light
82. Marquette Harbor Light

83. Presque Isle Harbor Breakwater Light
84. Granite Island Light
85. Stannard Rock Light
86. Big Bay Point Light
87. Huron Island Light
88. Sand Point Light
89. Portage Lake Lower Entrance Light
90. Portage River (Jacobsville) Light
91. Mendota (Bete Grise) Light
92. Gull Rock Light
93. Manitou Island Light

94. Copper Harbor Light
95. Eagle Harbor Light
96. Rock of Ages Light
97. Isle Royale (Menagerie Island) Light
98. Rock Harbor Light
99. Passage Island Light
100. Eagle River Light
101. Sand Hills Light
102. Keweenaw Waterway Upper Entrance Light
103. Fourteen Mile Point Light
104. Ontonagon Light

MICHIGAN WATERFALLS

Waterfalls are found only in very special parts of the land; one of these is Michigan's Upper Peninsula. There are more than 150 waterfalls across the length and breadth of this rugged peninsula. Some are tall and stately like the Laughing Whitefish; some are broad and massive like the mighty Tahquamenon. All are spectacles of white splendor. They are great to behold in every season—even in winter, when they may conjure up strange ice formations, and especially in autumn when framed by maple crimson and aspen gold.

Some of the Upper Peninsula's waterfalls are located conveniently along well-traveled highways; some are located off the back roads of national forest or state forest land; and some are located on private property. If on private land, remember to secure permission from the land owner.

The accompanying map, used by permission from the Upper Peninsula Tourism and Recreation Association, Iron Mountain, cites the general location of waterfalls in Michagan's Upper Peninsula. Waterfall numbers correspond with numbers on the map.

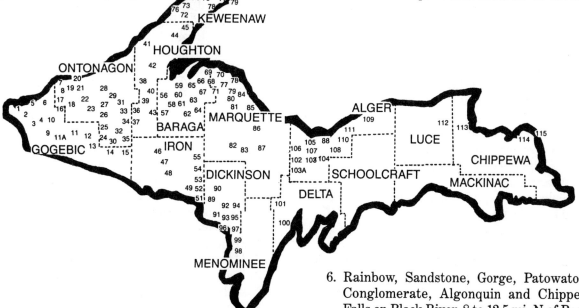

1. Superior Falls, Montreal River, 13.5 mi. NW of Ironwood.
2. Saxon Falls, Montreal River, 11 mi. NW of Ironwood.
3. Interstate Falls, Montreal River, 2 mi. NW of Ironwood.
4. Rocky Forty Falls, Siemens Creek, 3.5 mi. NW of Bessemer.
5. Manakik Falls, Maple Creek, 11 mi. NW of Bessemer.

6. Rainbow, Sandstone, Gorge, Patowatomi, Conglomerate, Algonquin and Chippewa Falls on Black River, 8 to 12.5 mi. N of Bessemer.
7. The Porcupine Mountains State Park has a large number of waterfalls, not all of which could be shown on this map. Ask park officials for directions.
8. Nokomis, Abinodju, Ogimakwe and Ogima Falls on Copper Creek, near Porcupine Mountain State Park.
9. Granite Rapids Falls, Black River, 2 mi. SW of Ramsay.

10. Gabro and Neepikon Falls on the Black River, 2 mi. N of Ramsay.
11. Yondota Falls, Presque Isle River, 3 mi. N of Marenisco.
11a. Nelson's Canyon Falls, Nelson Creek, 6.5 mi. NE of Marenisco.
12. Judson Falls, Slate River, 6.25 mi. E of Marenisco.
13. Kakabika Falls, Cisco Branch Ontonagon River, .5 mi. S of Jct. US 2 and County Road 527.
14. Ajibikoka Falls, Brush Lake, 5 mi. NW of Watersmeet.
15. Mex-i-min-e Falls, Middle Branch Ontonagon River, 7.5 mi. NE of Watersmeet.
16. Nimikon Falls, Presque Isle River, 13 mi. W of Bergland.
17. Deer Creek Falls, Deer Creek, 7 mi. NW of Bergland.
18. Rapid River Falls, Rapid River, 5 mi. NW of Bergland.
19. Nonesuch Falls, Iron River, 1.5 mi. W of White Pine.
20. Bonanza Falls, Big Iron River, 4 mi. N of White Pine.
21. Pewabeck Falls, Little Iron River, 3 mi. N of White Pine.
22. Little Trap Falls, Anderson Creek, 6.5 mi. N of Bergland.
23. Cascade Falls, W Branch of Ontonagon River, 7 mi. W of Bergland.
24. Wolverine Falls, Cisco Branch of Ontonagon River, 8 mi. W of Paulding.
25. 18 Mile Rapids Falls, South Branch of Ontonagon River, 5.5 mi. S of Ewen.
26. Flannigan Rapids Falls, South Branch of Ontonagon River, 5 mi. N of Ewen.
27. Sandstone Rapids Falls, Stranton Creek, 9 mi. N of Ewen.
28. Irish Rapids and Grand Rapids Falls on the Ontonagon River, 5 mi. NW of Rockland.
29. Victoria Dam, West Branch of Ontonagon River 4 mi. SW of Rockland.
30. Rock Bluff Falls, Bluff Creek, 1.5 mi. S of Paulding.
31. O Kun De Kun Falls, Baltimore River, 6 mi. SE of Rockland.
32. Bond Falls, Middle Branch of Ontonagon River, 3.5 mi. E of Paulding.
33. Three Rapids Falls, Middle Branch of Bluff Creek, 10 mi. NW of Agate.
34. Agate Falls, Middle Branch of Ontonagon River, 4 mi. W of Trout Creek.
35. Little Falls, Middle Branch of Ontonagon River, 4.5 mi. SW of Paulding.
36. Onion Falls, East Branch of Ontonagon River, 7 mi. NW of Kenton.
37. Sparrow Rapids Falls, East Branch of Ontonagon River, 3 mi. NW of Kenton.
38. Wyandotte Falls, Misery River, 1.5 mi. SW of Twin Lakes.
39. Vista Falls, North Branch of Sturgeon River, 6 mi. SW of Nisula.
40. West Sturgeon Falls, West Branch of Sturgeon River, 3 mi. S of Nisula.
41. Red Ridge Dam, Salmon Trout River, S of Redridge.
42. Ripley Falls, on Ripley Creek behind school at Ripley. Springtime flow only.
43. Sturgeon Falls, Sturgeon River, 9 mi. N of Sidnaw.
44. Hungarian Falls, Hungarian Creek, .5 mi. SW of Hubbell.
45. Douglass-Houghton Falls, Hammell Creek, 1 mi. NW of Lake Linden.
46. Snake Rapids and Chipmunk Falls, Net River 7 mi. W of Amasa.
47. Lower Hemlock Rapids and Hemlock Rapids on the Paint River, 3 mi. SW of Amasa.
48. Chicaugon, Chicaugon Creek, 6 mi. NW of Crystal Falls.
49. Horserace Rapids and Little Bull Dam on the Paint River, 6.5 mi. SE of Crystal Falls.
50. Brule Island Dam, Brule River, 11.5 mi. SE of Crystal Falls.
51. Michigamme Falls Dam, Michigamme River, 11 mi. SE of Crystal Falls.
52. Peavey Falls Dam, Michigamme River, 9 mi. SE of Crystal Falls.
53. Glidden Rapids, Michigamme River, 5 mi. SE of Crystal Falls.
54. Hemlock Falls Dam, Michigamme River, 6 mi. NE of Crystal Falls.
55. Margeson Falls, Margeson Creek, 9 mi. NE of Crystal Falls.
56. Prickett Dam, Sturgeon River, 10 mi. SW of L'Anse.
57. Tibbetts Falls, Sturgeon River, off M-28, 3.5 mi. NW of Covington.
58. Upper Falls, Sturgeon River, 1.5 mi. S of Alberta.
59. Upper Falls River, Falls River, and Lower Falls River on the Falls River, all within 1.5 mi. of L'Anse.
60. Daults Falls, Daults Creek, 3 mi. SE of L'Anse.
61. No Name Falls, Sturgeon River, 4 mi. S of Herman.
62. Tioga Falls, Tioga River, off M-28, 4 mi. NW of Nestoria.

63. Upper Silver Falls, Silver River, 2 mi. NE of Herman.

64. Upper Sturgeon Falls, Sturgeon River, 5 mi. SE of Herman.

65. Lower Silver Falls, Silver River, 6 mi. NE of L'Anse.

66. Slate Falls, Slate River, 3.5 mi. SW of Skanee.

67. Lower Leatherby Falls, East Branch of Huron River, 5 mi. SE of Skanee. Leatherby Falls, West Branch of Huron River, 7.5 mi. SE of Skanee. Upper Leatherby Falls, West Branch of Huron River, 8.5 mi. SE of Skanee.

68. West Branch Falls, West Branch of Huron River, 6.5 mi. SE of Skanee.

69. Lower Huron Falls, Huron River, 6 mi. E of Skanee.

70. East Branch Falls, East Branch of Huron River, 6.5 mi. SE of Skanee.

71. Big Falls, East Branch of Huron River, 7 mi. SE of Skanee.

72. Lower Falls, Gratiot River, 3.5 mi. NW of Ahmeek.

73. Upper Falls, Gratiot River, 3 mi. NW of Ahmeek.

74. Jacobs Falls, Jacobs Creek, 4 mi. SW of Eagle Harbor.

75. Copper Falls, on Owls Creek, between Eagle Harbor and US 41, approximately .5 mi. off road.

76. Eagle River Falls, Eagle River.

77. Manganese Gorge Falls, .5 mi. SE of Copper Harbor.

78. Haven Falls, at County Park, Lac LaBelle, on Haven Creek.

79. Lower Falls and Upper Falls, Montreal River, 5.25 to 5.5 mi. E of Bete Grise.

80. Wylie Dam Falls, Yellow Dog, 9 mi. SW of Big Bay.

81. Pinnacle Falls Dam, Yellow Dog, 8 mi. SW of Big Bay.

82. Black River Falls, Black River, 8 mi. SW of Ishpeming.

83. White City Falls, Middle Branch of Escanaba River, 7.5 mi. SW of Ishpeming.

84. Alder Falls, Alder Creek, 2.5 mi. SE of Big Bay.

85. Little Garlic Falls, Little Garlic River, 12 mi. NW of Marquette.

86. Morgan Falls, Morgan Creek, 3.5 mi. SW of Marquette.

87. Frohling Falls, West Branch of Chocolay River, 8 mi. NE of Gwinn.

88. Scott Falls, Scott Creek, 7 mi. NW of Munising.

89. Ford Falls, Menominee River, 2 mi. NE of Kingsford.

90. Twin Falls Dam, Menominee River, 4.5 mi. N of Iron Mountain.

91. Horse Race Rapids, Menominee River, 1 mi. S of East Kingsford.

92. Hydraulic Falls Dam, Menominee River, 1 mi. SE of East Kingsford.

93. Fumee Falls, on Fumee Creek off US 2, E of Quinnesec.

94. Piers Gorge on the Menominee River, SW of Norway.

95. Sturgeon Falls Dam, Menominee River, 3.5 mi. SW of Loretto.

96. Power Dam, Sturgeon River, 1.5 mi. NE of Loretto from US 2.

97. Quiver Falls, Menominee River, 3.5 mi. SW of Faithorn.

98. Pemene Falls, Menominee River, 10 mi. W of Carney.

99. Boney Falls Dam, Escanaba River, 8.7 mi. N of Cornell on County Road 523.

100. Chandler Falls, Small Stream, 3 mi. SW of Gladstone.

101. Rapid River Falls, Rapid River, 7 mi. N of Rapid River off US 41.

102. Laughing Whitefish Falls, Laughing Whitefish River, 19.5 mi. SW of Munising, 2 mi. N of Sundell.

103. Whitefish Falls, Whitefish River, 4 mi. NW of Trenary.

103a. Rock River Falls, 3 mi. S of Chatham on FR-2279, W three mi. on FR-2276 then S on FR-2293 one mi.; may have to walk entire distance on 2293. Half-mile steep walk down to falls.

104. AuTrain Falls, AuTrain River, .5 mi. from Forest Lake.

105. Horseshoe Falls, one block E, off M-28 in Munising. (Small admission fee.)

106. Alger Falls, Alger Creek, 1 mi. S of Munising.
107. Wagner Falls, Wagner Creek, 1 mi. from Munising on M-94.
108. Munising Falls, Munising Creek, 1.5 mi. NE of Munising.
109. Miners Falls, Miners River, 8 mi. NE of Munising in the Pictured Rocks area.
110. Chapel Falls, located off H-58 in the Pictured Rocks National Lakeshore between Miners and Sable.

111. Sable Falls, Sable River, 1 mi. W of Grand Marais.
112. Upper Tahquamenon Falls, Tahquamenon River, 24 mi. NE of Newberry, 14 mi. W of Paradise near M-123.
113. Lower Tahquamenon Falls, Tahquamenon River, 4 mi. from Upper Tahquamenon Falls.
114. Soo Rapids Falls, St. Mary's River, .5 mi. N of Sault Ste. Marie.
115. Black Pointe Rapids, 3 mi. E of Sault Ste. Marie.

MICHIGAN RESOURCES

Michigan Department of Natural Resources (DNR)
P.O. Box 30028
Lansing, MI 48909

DNR Information Services Center
(517) 373-1220
(general information on licenses, seasons; DNR programs, referral service)

Each DNR division is charged with specific responsibilities. The following list includes selected areas of only a few of the DNR divisions; specifically, those areas that may be of special interest to campers and others who recreate in the outdoors.

DNR Fisheries Division
(517) 373-1280
(information on fishing seasons and permits)

DNR Forest Management Division
(517) 373-1275
(information on state forest campgrounds and trails)

DNR Land and Water Management Division
(517) 373-1170
(information on natural rivers program)

DNR Parks Division
(517) 373-1270
(information on state park and recreation area campgrounds; state park trails; interpretive services; campsite reservations; wilderness areas)

DNR Recreation Division
(517) 373-9900
(information on boating public access sites)

DNR Wildlife Division
(517) 373-1263
(information on birds; other animals; endangered plant and animal species; hunting and trapping seasons and permits; public hunting access; nongame wildlife; sanctuaries; etc.)

Michigan Department of Transportation
Public Information Office
P.O. Box 30050
Lansing, MI 48909
(517) 373-2090

Michigan Travel Bureau
P.O. Box 30226
Lansing, MI 48909
1-800-5432-YES

National Park Service
Midwest Region
1709 Jackson Street
Omaha, NE 68102
(404) 221-3431

North Country Trail Association
P.O. Box 311
White Cloud, MI 49349

U.S. Forest Service
Eastern Region
310 West Wisconsin Avenue
Milwaukee, WI 53203
(414) 297-3693

Index